Shakespeare in Sable

Shakespeare in Sable
A History of Black Shakespearean Actors

Errol Hill

Foreword by John Houseman

The University of Massachusetts Press

Amherst, 1984

Copyright © 1984 by Errol Hill   All rights reserved
Printed in the United States of America
LC 83–18106   ISBN 0–87023–426–9
Library of Congress Cataloging in Publication Data
appear on the last page of this book.

The publisher gratefully acknowledges the support
of the National Endowment for the Humanities
toward the publication of this book.

An earlier version of chapter 4 appeared in *Women
in American Theatre*, ed. Helen Krich Chinoy
and Linda Walsh Jenkins (New York: Crown
Publishers, 1981), © 1981 by Helen Krich Chinoy
and Linda Walsh Jenkins. An earlier version of
portions of chapter 2 appeared as "S. Morgan Smith:
Successor to Ira Aldridge," *Black American
Literature Forum* 16, no. 4 (1982), © 1983 by
Errol Hill and Indiana State University.

Frontispiece, Ira Aldridge as Othello, Frankfurt,
1852. From a lithograph by S. Buhler, Mannheim.
The following note is appended to the picture:
"Represented by him at the Royal Opera House,
Berlin, before their Majesties the King and Queen
and Court of Prussia; at the Court Theatre,
Dresden, before the King, Queen and Court of
Saxony, and the imperial Court of Austria."

For Lah and Grace
who made it all possible

Contents

Illustrations

Acknowledgments

THE ORIGINAL IMPETUS for this study derived from a lecture on black Shakespearean actors which I delivered at the Pratt Institute of New York City on April 20, 1977, under the auspices of the Mellon Program of the Humanities. Since that time I have conducted periodic research on the topic in libraries and theater collections throughout the country. Most helpful as sources of information were the Schomburg Center for Research in Black Culture, situated in Harlem, the Performing Arts Research Center at Lincoln Center, the New York Public Library on Forty-second Street, and the Harvard University Theatre Collection.

A study of this scope cannot be completed without the generous cooperation of many people. I acknowledge with thanks assistance from several fellow researchers and from special collections such as the Hatch-Billops Oral History Collection in New York City and the Research Center for the Federal Theatre Project at George Mason University in Fairfax, Virginia. For information on Morgan Smith's career in Great Britain, I am indebted to Dr. Kathleen Barker, Honorary Secretary of the Society for Theatre Research, London. My deepest gratitude goes to the staffs of the Reference Department, the Interlibrary Loan Division, and the Theatre Collection of Baker Library at Dartmouth College. Their unstinting and prompt response to every inquiry enabled me to complete this work in the limited periods of time available to me.

The photographs reproduced in this book were drawn from many sources. Individual picture credit, where known, has been readily assigned. The pages of *Theatre World* were particularly helpful in identifying recent production photographs. Pierre Bastianelli, Chief Medical Photographer at the Dartmouth Medical School, kindly undertook to make reproductions as required.

Three of my professional colleagues read the manuscript and offered valuable criticisms. They are Henry B. Williams, emeritus professor of drama, and Charles Wood, Daniel Webster professor of history, both at Dartmouth College, and Thomas D. Pawley, dean, College of Arts and Science and professor of drama at Lincoln University, Jefferson City, Missouri. I acknowledge their generous assistance with gratitude. I must also thank Raymond McGill for his kind encouragement and helpful comments which were instrumental in bringing the project to fulfilment.

Finally, I am conscious of the debt I owe to my production editor Pam Campbell for her careful editing of the manuscript which has enhanced its accuracy, clarity, and consistency. I can only hope that the reception accorded the book will justify the enormous effort invested by so many people in its composition.

Foreword by
John Houseman

ERROL HILL IS PROFESSOR of drama at Dartmouth College, a scholar of black theater, and the editor of a collection of essays published under the title *The Theater of Black Americans*. In his introduction to that collection, Mr. Hill considers theater to be both art and industry, an expression of culture and a source of livelihood for artists and craftsmen, a medium of instruction and a purveyor of entertainment. He believes that "theatre as an institution can have a significant impact on the relentless struggle of a deprived racial minority for full equality and the need for spiritual well-being of a people divorced from their ancestral heritage through centuries of degrading slavery."

The present volume is concerned with a more specific subject—the historical record, over many years, of black actors as interpreters of the plays of William Shakespeare. Inevitably, it is a record of high potential, bright hopes, repeated frustrations, and tragic disappointments. Its only encouraging aspect is the realization that, as the years go by, the ratio of defeat seems to get smaller, the number of black performers knocking in vain at the doors of our playhouses grows less, and the number of black actors and actresses admired and sought for their unusual quality and power as interpreters becomes greater and more general—though it remains lamentably small.

When Mr. Hill, who is a native of Trinidad, was attending the Royal Academy of Dramatic Art in London, he won the admiration of the venerable head of that prestigious institution chiefly because, in Mr. Hill's words, "he could never get it straight that I came from the West Indies where I had spoken English all my life. He believed I was from darkest Africa and thought my cultivated English accent was a remarkable accomplishment."

This comic error symbolizes the general historical attitude of critics and public on both sides of the Atlantic toward black artists reckless enough to attempt the great classical roles and brave enough to defy the racial stereotypes of their time. Mr. Hill's documentation of their careers is of necessity generally limited to faded clippings from the black press, together with an occasional European review. We learn little about them as men or women or of their personal struggles, satisfactions, and defeats. Almost without exception, after their hard-earned moment of limelight, they return to the dark anonymity of the underprivileged world from which they briefly emerged.

The great public breakthrough occurred in London in 1930. It took the charismatic personality and the international reputation of Paul Robeson—added to the social security of a nation that, for all its chronic chauvinistic and horrible historical record, had no domestic color problem of its own at the time—to establish the undisputed right of a black man to perform a great Shakespearean role in the commercial theater purely on the basis of quality. One wonders if what made it possible was the fact that he was enacting the role of a Moor.

This change of attitude did not take place overnight; it occurred slowly, with frequent setbacks. For years Robeson's London triumph remained an isolated one. More than a dozen years would go by before he was seen in the part of Othello on an American stage. It took a major depression, a second world war, and twenty more years of reluctant integration to change our attitudes to the point where such fine artists as Frank Silvera and James Earl Jones would receive general acclaim—as actors rather than as black actors—for their successive and very different performances of *King Lear*. (It is significant that both these performances were given at Joseph Papp's Public Theatre rather than in a commercial situation.)

For my own part, I would emphasize the role played by the Federal Theatre of the New Deal's WPA (Works Progress Administration) in helping to break down some of the theater's worst racial barriers of the time. It has been argued that the famous "Voodoo" *Macbeth*, with which I was associated, was an exploitation of superstitious, primitive emotion rather than a classic performance of Shakespeare's flawed tragedy. Far more significant than the production's enormous public success was the formal decision of those directing the Negro Theatre Project to regard black actors (as black musicians had already come to be regarded) as artists whose emotional and physical equipment justified their employment, individually and collectively, as interpreters of the classical repertory. For instance, Jack Carter's next classical role, following Macbeth, was that of Mephistopheles opposite Orson Welles's Doctor Faustus in Marlow's tragedy. It is rarely mentioned in theatrical histories of the time, but it was a brilliant performance: he played the dark angel as a "cold, ascetic monk, his face and gleaming bald head moon-white and ageless against the surrounding night. . . . He had the beauty, the sadness and the pride of a fallen angel."* Another parallel production, planned at the time, was that of the superb black actress Rose McClendon in an integrated version of Euripides' Medea adapted by the black poet Countee Cullen. The project was abandoned at her sudden and tragic death.

The liquidation of the Federal Theatre and the outbreak of World War II marked a decline in the opportunities offered to black actors in the American theater. Progress did not resume until the mid-fifties and sixties and coincided with a general amelioration of the racial situation in this country and with a breakdown of the inhibitions facing black artists in our mass media.

All these elements are, of course, inseparable. Institutional theaters, on both sides of the Atlantic, long ago discovered that a great theater company cannot be maintained that devotes itself exclusively either to the classics or to contemporary plays. The two must be mingled and allowed to vitalize each other. In the same way, the future of black actors in the mass media and in the classics is closely connected with the future scope and energy of black theater in general.

"When will it end?" asks Mr. Hill regarding discrimination in the entertainment business. The answer, as he knows all too well, is a social, economic, and historical one. Artistically, as he has helped to record, the black theater worker's credentials were, long ago, solidly and irrevocably established.

---

*John Houseman, Run-Through, p. 236

Introduction:
A Personal Memoir

I MUST HAVE INHERITED my love of theater from my parents. Not that they were professional actors or avid playgoers. There was no professional theater in the West Indian island of Trinidad where I grew up and amateur productions were a rare commodity then. My mother was a chorister in the Methodist congregation in Port-of-Spain, and after she stepped down from the choir her voice could still ring the rafters from our pew in the front of the church. More than that, she was a veteran performer in religious plays. She had the gift of eloquent speech and it was unthinkable to present a sacred drama without asking Lydia Hill to read the principal part. She was well into her eighties when she played her last role, and I like to think that with her beautiful voice and clear diction she continues to enliven the regions of the departed.

My father was a bit of a histrion also. I didn't know him well. He went abroad on business when I was a child and stayed away. When finally he returned home to die I was already a man. He too was musical. He composed hymns for my mother to sing and would send them home to her from his voluntary exile. He also conducted his own church for a time and I am told that on Sunday mornings he would spellbind his small congregation with stirring exhortations.

My earliest recollection of performing was at morning prayers held by my mother on weekdays. Because we all went to church several times on Sunday we escaped the early morning ritual on that day— except on a feast day like Easter Sunday when mass was held at 5:00 A.M. and we had to rise earlier than usual. All the children would gather at my mother's bedside and would read one or two chapters from the Bible, sing a hymn, and say a prayer. We took turns at reading, and I recall how anxiously I awaited my turn and secretly practiced reading the chapter beforehand so that I would make a good impression on the family.

The Scriptures and Methodist hymns were the first literature I knew. Dramatic story and Shakespeare came later in the upper grades of elementary school. I was fortunate to have a gifted teacher, himself a novelist with a flair for language, who read poetry as if it had wings on which one could soar. From that time on I have never ceased to memorize pieces of beautiful prose and poetry so that I too might give them winged utterance. It seemed natural that growing up I should belong to the Boy Scout troop that had a reputation for singing and dramatics; that I should be ranked among the top debaters and reciters in the island; that I should start a drama group and write our own plays; and, finally, that I should be the first Trinidadian to win a British Council scholarship in drama for study at the Royal Academy of Dramatic Art, London.

The earliest play I recall being in was called *A Man in the Street*. It was a modern morality play staged at the Methodist school hall in Port-of-Spain. I had the lead; but on opening night I came down with roasting fever and ague and went to bed. They came to fetch me when the audience had assembled and it was time to start the play. I went on stage shivering from nerves and fever. It didn't matter. The young man, a Christ figure, was going to be martyred anyway before the play was over. Since that night, I have relived those nervous before-curtain spasms in every one of the scores of roles I've performed.

On entering the islandwide elocution contests, I first attempted to interpret Shakespeare. Later I prepared programs of Shakespearean readings, all memorized, that I would present at the least excuse. Our drama group was trained by two English retired professional actresses who had come to live in Trinidad. One was an exponent of the modern repertoire and the other, who had been a member of Sir Frank Benson's Shakespeare Company, insisted that the only way to learn acting was to start with Shakespeare. Before I took off for London and the Royal Academy of Dramatic Art, I had appeared in several plays, directed as many, and written a few. But I had never acted in a full-scale Shakespearean production. Apart from touring English professionals like the Glossop-Harris Company, only two groups in Port-of-Spain presented Shakespeare. One was the Roman Catholic secondary school for boys, which I did not attend. They always staged the Shakespeare play set for that year's school-leaving examination, and had the tradition of casting only white and light-skinned boys in the plays. The other drama group was adult and consisted of white residents and expatriates. I well remember the stir it created when the first brown-skinned Trinidadian, university-educated and a professional librarian, was allowed to read for a part in one of the company's productions. Those days of needless racial tension have passed.

Our amateur group didn't present Shakespeare, not because we lacked talent but because the production demands exceeded our resources. I like to think we had too much respect for Shakespeare to stage his work shabbily. Occasionally we did scenes from the plays as entr'acte pieces in our public productions. That was when we discovered we had a fine young Shakespearean actor in the group in the person of Errol John. He had been an athlete at school and moved with flawless grace. He also had a finely chiseled face and excellent diction. He became our leading actor.

At the Royal Academy of Dramatic Art I appeared in a succession of plays, including Shakespeare's, as part of my training. Being the only black student in the academy, I made up white for my roles. The professional make-up artist with whom we studied gave me special lessons in transforming myself with paint and wig to achieve verisimilitude with the all-white characters and cast. As students we would repair to the refectory for a meal between dress rehearsal and performance and there would be no time to remove makeup and reapply it. The sole satisfaction I derived from the laborious process of making-up white was sitting at table beside friends who could not recognize me under my disguise.

The only significant black role I ever had in an academy production was assigned to me when one of the directors sympathized with my situation and decided to produce a play with a leading black character. She chose *Deep Are the Roots*, an American play about racism in the South, and I got the lead part of Brett Charles. Now one of the white students had to make up in blackface to be my mammy! The production was so successful that the director took the play on tour to workers' union halls around London. This was most unusual for a Tory school.

When the time came for me to graduate, I selected a cutting from *Othello* as my classical test piece. Judging the performance were Vivien Leigh and Sir Lewis Casson. They awarded me distinction in acting, probably influenced by the school's principal, Sir Kenneth

Barnes, who could never get it straight that I came from the West Indies where I had spoken English all my life. He believed I was from darkest Africa and thought my cultivated English accent was a remarkable achievement. The academy sponsored a showcase for graduating students at one of the West End theaters which was attended by talent scouts for the London producers. Excerpts from a variety of plays were presented to display the most talented students, and on the basis of their performances coveted acting prizes were awarded, including the Bancroft Gold Medal for best actor. Although I had no wish to become a professional actor in England, I allowed myself to entertain great hopes for this showcase until I was cast as the Negro servant in Kaufman and Ferber's *Theatre Royal* (known in New York as *The Royal Family*). The role was a traditional darkie stereotype that effectively eliminated me from the competition.

The best part of my London years was going to the theater. I saw dozens, no, scores of productions of all types in London, at Stratford-on-Avon, and at the Edinburgh Festival. I went to regional repertory theaters and amateur productions, some of which were really rather bad. I tried never to miss a professional production of Shakespeare and saw some of the greatest English actors of the day in magnificent performances: Donald Wolfit, John Gielgud, Laurence Olivier, Alec Guinness, Michael Redgrave, the young Paul Scofield, and Richard Burton. Wolfit was all smouldering passion, Olivier the master technician, Gielgud the romantic, Guinness the clinician, Redgrave a daring adventurer. I watched these actors as if they were specimens under a microscope, studying every breath, word, move, pause, for meaning. In my three years of playgoing in Britain I never saw a black actor in Shakespeare.

When Errol John followed me to London I decided to do a showcase of my own with West Indian students at the Hans Crescent international students center in Knightsbridge. My first production was *Henri Christophe*, a verse play by Derek Walcott, the West Indian poet and playwright, with Errol John in the title role. He was brilliant. Henry Swanzy, BBC producer of West Indian programs, commended the production in the Jamaican paper *Public Opinion* of March 29, 1952: "The most important ingredient of any play's success is of course the acting. Here I do not think it excessive to say that the actor Errol John, another Trinidadian, put on a performance which was superlative in its authority and nervous energy. Although he is a small man, at all times he dominated the stage and his impact in the closing scenes was terrible in its intensity."

I followed this production with Sophocles' *Antigone*, staged in a West African tribal setting with the actors wearing authentic Ghanian kinti cloths borrowed from African fellow students at the center. Errol John played Haemon to my Creon. The production was another great success. In both of these efforts I had the strong support of Carlisle Chang, a Trinidadian painter and scenic designer, who was then a student at the Slade School of Art. Seeing Errol John perform in a different setting only confirmed my opinion that he was an actor of tremendous potential and I predicted a great career for him in the classical theater. That has not happened. He is black.

After I left the Royal Academy of Dramatic Art, I spent another year in professional theater, radio, and television in England learning the ropes. I became a regular reader on the weekly BBC Caribbean program and was placed on the roster of professional actors for radio drama. This was an opportunity to put my academy training immediately to work in the company of practiced professionals. I appeared in several distinguished radio plays on the BBC Home Service and was gratified to read flattering reviews in the English press. One particular review reminded me that the bedside Bible readings of my early years were still paying dividends. Writing in the *Star* of October 25, 1951, Maurice Gorham commented glowingly on a BBC dramatization based on the work of the Society for the Propagation of the Gospel: "I listened and was rewarded by hearing a stirring story of missionary adventure told with a minimum of radio tricks, and highlighted by the singing of Victor Mcunu and the acting of Errol Hill as a condemned slave. I don't think I have heard anything more moving on the air than the scenes in the condemned cell and Errol Hill's speaking of the Penitential Psalms."

The time had come for me to return home. I was offered a job in the extramural drama program of the new University of the West Indies in Jamaica. From this base I traveled frequently to other territories in the British Caribbean. I decided I would encourage the writing and production of indigenous plays to lay the groundwork for a West Indian national theater. That dream was aborted by political developments that brought about first the establishment, then the early dissolution of the West Indian Federation. The constituent government units of the erstwhile federation became so competitive that future collaboration in the arts was jeopardized. This period witnessed two ambitious interracial productions of Shakespeare when the English actor John Ainsworth, who had been a stand-in for Laurence Olivier during the filming of *Hamlet*, took up residence in Trinidad. Playing the lead roles himself, Ainsworth mounted productions of *Hamlet* and *Macbeth*, using the best local talent for his supporting cast, regardless of race. I undertook the part of Laertes in the *Hamlet* company that opened in Barbados, then played successfully in Trinidad and Guyana. The review of the opening night performance appeared in the *Barbados Advocate* of July 14, 1955, and was again laudatory:

> Errol Hill's Laertes is as good as anything I remember. His is the first Laertes I have seen who easily persuades me that so honest, frank and virtuous a young man could lend himself to the murderous conniving of the King. . . . Ranging, with no loss of his almost insolent masculinity, from the tender, protective affection for his sister and good-tempered, quizzical patience with the windy platitudes of his father, to a fiery passion of anger with the King and a scarcely controlled heartbroken grief at his sister's suicide, this is a truly memorable piece of sustained acting.

I continued to give readings from Shakespeare but less often than before, my energies being primarily devoted to promoting West Indian drama. This apparent dichotomy of interests led some of my detractors to accuse me of being a hypocrite. My feeling was that Shakespeare had reigned so long in the West Indies as the prerogative of the ruling class that he had to be psychologically dethroned by educated black leaders in order for a nationalist drama to emerge free from odious comparisons. I also believed that a new indigenous style of acting and production might be fashioned through working on materials based on the West Indian experience rather than on established Western dramas. We were never able to carry through that experiment.

In London, Errol John was having his problems too. His performances at Hans Crescent had led to a BBC engagement to read the part of King Lear on the Caribbean program but there his Shakespeare acting ended. Though he wrote the prize-winning play *Moon on a Rainbow Shawl* and made a number of television and film appearances, the lack of acting opportunities on the classical stage was irksome. In a letter home accusing me of choosing security, he vented his anguish in the pungent vernacular of the island:

You ever had to go for a part in a African film that you been counting the pennies on for a damn whole year and fer the casting director to look at you and say you ent black enough? And you almost as black as the ace of spades? Or when they call yer for a part . . . all yer playing is a big black nigger, or a fat greasy nigger, or a thin sooty nigger, or just any kind a nigger. How long you think you would of put up with that for the sake of your own future?

The sequel to this story is painfully ironic. Errol John was enjoying a writing fellowship in Trinidad when he received word from London. The Old Vic was preparing its last season of Shakespeare before being absorbed by the National Company that would be housed in the new theater complex on the south bank of the Thames. The season included *Othello* and the white actor cast as the Moor had suddenly died. Would Errol come and take over the role? This was 1962, some twelve years after Mr. John had arrived in England—twelve years of playing "just any kind of nigger." Now he was being called upon to assume one of the great poetic and tragic roles of Shakespeare, in a production designed for a different kind of actor in the final season of the historic Old Vic Company. The offer could not be despised, though it had caution written all over it in bold letters.

Errol John opened first in the company's production of *The Merchant of Venice* in which he gave a sympathetic portrayal in the small role of the Prince of Morocco. With *Othello* later in the season he was less fortunate. The London *Times* of January 31, 1963, found a basic fault in the casting of the two main figures with Iago, a man of twenty-eight, played by the veteran English actor Leo McKern, and Othello who is "declined into the vale of years" sustained by the West Indian in his thirties who, moreover, had had so little opportunity to play Shakespeare professionally in the dozen or more years since he settled in England. John's speaking of Shakespeare's verse, an area in which he excelled as an amateur, had obviously deteriorated, for some critics found it "maladroit." Yet Philip Hope Wallace in the *Guardian* of January 31, 1963, suggested what might have been possible when he wrote that although "Robeson, when young, had a finer ear than Mr. John, the essential force of the newcomer is not unlike Robeson's; it could make an audience quail."

At first the extramural drama program of the University of the West Indies seemed to be making good progress. Amateur groups were being formed, new plays were being written, the Jamaican campus supported an active theater movement. A new awareness of theater as an expression of a people's culture and heritage was evident. I went up to the Yale Drama School on a Rockefeller Foundation fellowship to complete graduate studies for a career in academic theater. It was my secret hope to build a West Indian national theater company from among the most talented graduates of the university who had studied under me. In 1965, a few years after my return home from Yale, I was sent as a teaching fellow to Nigeria to work in the School of Drama at the University of Ibadan, in preparation for leading a new cultural center on the Jamaican campus of our home university. Again politics intervened. Realizing that my university did not intend to place drama on its curriculum—there were always more pressing demands and insufficient funds—I left the West Indies and came to the United States.

On the strength of a recommendation from my Yale professor, the late John Gassner, I received and accepted an offer to teach at Dartmouth College. My first assignment was to play Malvolio in *Twelfth Night* and direct a major production in the Dartmouth College Repertory Company as part of the summer Congregation of the Arts. It was the first time in my career that I would play a Shakespeare part in its entirety and in a full-scale professional production. The next year I went one step further: I undertook the role of Othello with the company. Both productions were staged by Rod Alexander, artistic director of the repertory enterprise. This was one of the goals I had set myself as an actor decades earlier, little supposing it would come to pass in a remote New England town on the campus of a college I did not then know existed. Of my performance as Othello, Elliot Norton, writing in the *Boston Record American* of July 22, 1969, had this to say:

> In Errol Hill, a professional actor who is also a member of the Dartmouth faculty, they have a black Othello of uncommon dignity and marked eloquence who, in the ultimate scene, rises to something like true tragic greatness. . . . Mr. Hill is strikingly handsome in costumes that are presumably Moorish, which allow him to wear loose open cloaks, most of the time, and, in the scene where Iago finally breaks him down, an admiral's full-dress uniform, with a white jacket.
>
> His dignity and composure are, in the early moments, com-

pletely convincing. When he snaps out the great command: "Put up your bright swords, for the dew will rust them!" you accept him at once as the commander who has fought in many wars and is not only at home in the presence of danger, but completely in control of himself and those around him.

With Desdemona . . . he is as ardent as a bridegroom and as gentle as a man of breeding was once expected to be. His voice is beautifully modulated; he speaks all the great speeches eloquently. Eventually, in the scene that follows the killing of Desdemona, he is true to the text and the moment, and as he rages in self-accusation or runs wildly at Iago, or when he turns his dagger on himself, he is acting at the top of his bent.

The one flaw Norton and other reviewers found in the performance was a tendency to make Othello too intellectual in the early scenes. This resulted from a conscious effort on my part to avoid the conventional image of the noble savage. I saw Othello as a brilliant soldier and tactician, confident in his prowess, at ease in the Venetian court, a man not jealous but highly conscious of his reputation and with an idealistic view of the sanctity of honor. Once sullied, that honor could never be restored whole. Catastrophe must follow. For this reason I refused to believe Iago's slander of my wife until I had concrete proof and it was impossible to refute his allegations. When I dispatched Desdemona it was meant to be a ritual purgation of evil (the soliloquy "It is the cause" was spoken as a prayer on my knees) except that her struggles caused me to use force. At the end of the short run of the play I was just beginning to learn how I might refine the portrayal.

The story I have told here is repeated with variations many times over in this book. One is filled with admiration for those black Shakespeareans, men and women who, despite enormous problems beyond their own making, persevered in their desire to reach the highest realms of the actor's art. It is no fault of theirs that their stories are often incomplete, that their entrances and exits are frequently unmarked. They began to play Shakespeare at a time in America when most black people were enslaved, while those who were free were denied access to the legitimate stage. This ostracism continued for many decades after the end of slavery. As a result, to pursue the career of a black actor of Shakespeare became a much more precarious undertaking than the traditional uncertainties associated with the acting profession. For some, opportunities to practice their art professionally might lie in a foreign land, but those who remained at home were forced to take other paying jobs and act when they could. In this context, any serious attempt to present Shakespeare by black actors, be they amateur, semiprofessional, or fully professional, deserves our attention.

Another problem faced by black Shakespeareans was the absence of informed criticism. For the greater part of this study, the established white press ignored the work of black dramatic performers. When notices did appear in these columns, they were often couched in disparaging terms. The black press, on the other hand, took the opposite approach. It would applaud each new attempt to present a dramatic play, in whole or part, as evidence of racial progress that deserved encouragement rather than artistic evaluation. As late as 1939, Fannin S. Belcher, a black scholar of the drama, writing in the October issue of *Opportunity*, voiced this complaint: "In theory, we wish to be judged on merit alone; in practice, we cry for mercy because of racial limitations. . . . Placidly, ignoring the fact that the purpose of criticism is to inspire the best, few issues of the Negro press are free from an avalanche of superlatives describing the work of some actor, in a major or minor role of a first or second rate production." Being necessarily confined, as we are, to the black press for much of the information on early Shakespeareans, it is well to bear this comment in mind.

One cannot, however, ignore the fact that since theater holds a time-honored place in civilized life, the part that black Americans play in upholding the institution of theater reflects their status in the larger society. The history of blacks in America is one of upward striving to secure a place as full citizens entitled to equal rights in a free democracy. Until that status is assured, black achievement in any field bears a direct relationship to existing social and political conditions. When those conditions are inimical to black progress, as in the deplorable "Jim Crow era" that began toward the end of the last century, the absence of black effort in serious dramatic production is pronounced. When the reverse conditions obtain, as in the Federal Theatre period of the 1930s or during the more recent period of black activism in the 1960s and 1970s, the contribution of blacks to the national theatrical scene is of a high order.

A study of this scope cannot pretend to be exhaustive. I have tried to be as thorough as possible in recording nineteenth- and early twentieth-century material that is not easily available to readers. The information conveyed has been culled primarily from black newspapers, among the most useful being the *Globe*, the *Freeman*, and the *Age* from New York; the *Bee* from Washington, D.C.; the *Cleveland Gazette*; and the *Broad Axe* which was first published in Utah and later in Chicago. Few of the early West Coast black newspapers have survived except in scattered issues which yielded precious little information on black Shakespeareans. For particulars of performances in Britain in the nineteenth century, the columns of the *Era* were initially most helpful.

As the twentieth century progressed and opportunities for Afro-Americans to perform Shakespeare began to open up, I have tended to discuss major professional productions in which black actors have appeared in leading or otherwise substantial roles. Inevitably there are omissions; my intention has been not to present a complete record but rather to suggest trends and to note significant individual achievement. Nor have I tried to follow the lives of black actors in detail. My aim has been to show that consistently, for well over a century, black American actors have persisted in their efforts to interpret Shakespeare, regardless of the difficulties encountered in making these attempts. The record here presented should serve as a corrective to the commonly held image of black performers as minstrels and song-and-dance clowns from the end of slavery until well into the 1930s.

It may be hoped that the stories sketched in this book will now take their place on the shelves of history, the events they describe fraught with disappointment and despair to be repeated no more. Yet the struggle is not over. In an issue of the British magazine *Time Out* dated November 2–8, 1979, Alan Sinclair reported on black actors and actresses in England who are "mighty fed up with being cast as prostitutes, pimps and thieves." Sinclair noted that recent imports of black American productions such as *Bubbling Brown Sugar* and *For Colored Girls Who Have Considered Suicide When the Rainbow is Enuf*, despite British Equity's rules, had been granted work permits for American actors. This was detrimental to the chances of black actors in Britain being employed in the American shows. On the other hand, Sinclair observed, "Equity itself has been less than consistent. They prevented a black American actor, James Earl Jones, from playing in the BBC's *Othello*. However, they didn't raise an eyebrow at Donald Sinden 'blacking-up' for the role at Stratford and Scofield is about to do the same at the National." Here in America, after the notable advances of recent times, the situation is not much brighter. In a year when the motion-picture industry recorded some of its highest profits (1981–82), the National Association for the Advancement of Colored People (NAACP) threatened to mount a national boycott of films made by Hollywood studios that failed to provide representative employment for black actors and technicians. One is constrained to ask: When will it end?

Throughout this book, the terms "Negro," "Afro-American," "black American" and "colored American" are used synonymously to refer to Americans of African descent. The terms "Negro" and "colored American" have lately been considered derogatory and are used only where historically appropriate.

1
Shakespeare and the Black Actor

SHAKESPEARE HAS ALWAYS held a particular fascination for the serious dramatic actor. By tradition the highest homage of the profession is reserved for those actors who excel in portraying his chief characters. As a result, actors are eager to appear in Shakespearean roles as a test of their skill and as a way of establishing their standing in the profession. If these observations apply mainly to English actors, for whom the plays were originally written, they are equally pertinent to professionals in the English-language theater around the world. They are true also of black actors, and not only of those professionals who make their living on the stage.

The May 1975 issue of *Ebony* carried the story of John Nixon, a black dentist in Birmingham, Alabama, who from his student days had cherished a dream to play Othello. His chance came at last when the local Town and Gown Theater, affiliated with the University of Alabama and previously all white, became integrated. Nixon, who was noted for his outspoken defense of civil rights, received an invitation to join the theater group. In the interest of promoting racial accord, he agreed to do so and appeared in the play *J.B.* by Archibald MacLeish, taking the role of God. This was a "smashing success" and when he was asked what role he would next like to play, Nixon unhesitatingly replied "Othello." With the tacit approval of the hitherto segregationist governor of the state and with some concern about how their supporters among the social and academic elite of the community might react, the theater group produced Shakespeare's tragedy. That production, too, was a success, although some older folk were clearly distressed to see miscegenation featured so prominently on the Birmingham stage. Nevertheless, a thirty-three-year-old dream of a would-be black Shakespearean had finally been realized.

The enthusiasm of black actors for Shakespeare is genuine and perennial. Frequent disparagement from within and without the race has not chilled their ardor. The spectacle of black actors performing Shakespeare has often seemed incongruous to white critics and patrons who fail to note how irrational is the attitude that acclaims Shakespeare's plays for their universality and yet wishes to deny their interpretation by people of all races. Except in a few instances, the plots of these plays do not require racially identifiable characters. In the 1820s the first black American company to present Shakespeare was forced to desist when hostile white competitors persuaded the police to move against the black actors. Half a century later renewed attempts by Afro-Americans to establish a Shakespeare repertoire met with similar rejection. A comment in 1884 by the *Washington Post* reviewer of a performance at Ford's Opera House typifies the attitude then prevailing: "The idea of a troupe of Shakespearean actors of various shades of black is highly ludicrous and a Richard with a seal-brown skin and a typically African cast of countenance is calculated to excite the merriment of the most lugubrious."[1]

If whites, who comprise by far the largest part of the theater audience in America, felt this way about black actors, it is not surprising that black Shakespeare companies failed to win the public support necessary to their survival. Little wonder too that their efforts were usually ignored or belittled in accounts of Shakespearean production. The result is an incomplete record that has not only kept black people ignorant of what their race has achieved in Shakespearean staging, but has also denied students of Shakespeare the benefit of learning about possible new or different interpretations of the plays. White disdain has also meant that black actors, regardless of demonstrated skill and talent, have often been overlooked in casting roles for professional productions of Shakespeare, even when the play specifically called for a black character. While the situation has improved in recent years, old patterns of thought persist and make it difficult for aspiring black performers to be judged by objective standards.

In his book *Then Came Each Actor* published in 1965, Bernard Grebanier discusses recent productions of Shakespeare and tries to account for his irritation at seeing plays with interracial casts: "When Morris Carnovsky played Lear against Ruby Dee, when the Vivian

Beaumont Theater gives me a black Orsino and Maria, I am upset—
not out of racial prejudice but out of respect for Shakespeare's plays.
After all, a white man doing Othello blackens face, arm, legs and
hands. Is there any reason why a black actor should not whiten his
when doing a white role?"[2] The fallacy in his argument is obvious.
Othello requires a black (or blackened) actor in the part of the Moor,
but nothing in *King Lear* or *Twelfth Night* specifies that characters
should be of a certain skin color or racial type, nor does the plot hinge
upon ethnicity. Any oddity perceived in an interracial cast must surely be in the eye of the beholder, not intrinsically in the production.
Because four hundred years ago Shakespeare's company happened to
consist of white English actors is no reason to insist that his plays
must always be done by English actors or by white actors or by actors
disguised as white. He also wrote for an all-male company, but today
his plays are performed by both sexes. His physical theater, acting
style, speech patterns, and production techniques were all very different from those in use today, yet no one seriously advocates a return
to authentic Shakespearean staging methods except as an experiment. In a society that is as racially mixed as America, casting of
Shakespeare on the basis of merit and regardless of race should be the
rule rather than the exception.

Black Shakespeare actors have also had to contend with discour-
agement from members of their race. In the past, black writers have
been quick to commend the accomplished individual actor in Shakespeare, sometimes even to lavish praise beyond deserving. But some
critics were also concerned that black Shakespeare productions did
not have a strong appeal with audiences and might result in a profligate waste of talent that should be applied to more lucrative material.
As far back as 1891 the black journalist T. Thomas Fortune of the
New York Age, noted for his acerbic style, advised black actors to
stop flirting with Shakespeare and concentrate on becoming popular
comedians. Affirming that economic progress is the path to racial
progress, he argued: "The way to make money is to give people what
they want. . . . The Irishman and the African are naturally comedians. When they attempt to be tragedians they usually wind up show-
ing themselves to be clowns."[3] This sort of stereotyping from the pen
of a reputable black editor was reinforced some years later by a columnist in the *Colored American* who felt that since it would be
many years before the Negro actor could thrive as a professional
exponent of Shakespeare's plays, his most profitable field must be

vaudeville. The columnist then proceeded to place the fault for this state of affairs not on a system that deprived the black performer of opportunities for training and advancement in his chosen career, but on his lack of competence in the legitimate drama, as if that disability were inherent in his race.[4] Both of these writers conveniently ignored the spectacular achievements of the great black Shakespeare actor Ira Aldridge who had reached the pinnacle of acclaim in foreign countries where he was free to practice his craft as a respected professional.

It is nonetheless true that, in the late nineteenth and early twentieth centuries, talented black professionals were able to secure regular employment as minstrels, vaudevillians, and song-and-dance artists not only on the American stage, but in theaters in Europe, South Africa, and as far away as Australia. Weekly salaries ranged widely in the business. Average pay for a black vaudeville player in 1901 might be between $25 and $50 a week, but a star performer like Bob Cole or Ernest Hogan would receive $125, and a superstar like Bert Williams or George Walker could make up to $500 weekly.[5] No black Shakespearean in America at that time could be guaranteed either regular stage work or a decent wage. Solo reciters who included Shakespeare in their repertoires had to be constantly on the move, since they were seldom billed for more than a single performance at any one venue in a given season.

In the early decades of the twentieth century black critics began making new demands of the black actor. The song-and-dance image had been assiduously cultivated; it had kept many performers gainfully employed and had taken others to the summit of the profession. Now it began to pall. The idea that black performers were capable of little else besides providing low-brow entertainment for white folks became repugnant. In a 1907 article commenting on a new, well-crafted musical, *Shoo-Fly Regiment*, by the comedy team of Cole and Johnson, Emmett J. Scott of Tuskegee Institute wrote in the *New York Age* as follows:

> On the stage, as elsewhere, the Negro was discounted. He could not advance, he was and could remain only a knock-about comedian, a minstrel of the grosser kind, [these] were some of the discouraging and accepted beliefs. But here also success writ large has been achieved. It is comparative success only, to be sure, but a sure and steady advance from the old days when he

was tolerated only in minstrelsy, with his crude and suggestive humor and indifferent acting. His impersonations were worse than caricatures.[6]

The "steady advance" of which Scott writes was soon halted when Bob Cole, who had been forced into premature retirement in 1910 due to a nervous breakdown, committed suicide the following year. Cole was an artist of high intelligence and considerable talent. He was a vaudeville comedian as well as a playwright, songwriter, stage manager, and producer. He was enormously ambitious and constantly doing battle with white theater managers to secure improved working conditions and first-class houses for black productions. The stress of pursuing a stage career under such constant pressure eventually took its toll.

By the 1920s it was felt that the time had come to set about establishing black theaters in black communities. The black actor and dramatist were exhorted "to till the native soil of the race life and the race experience"[7] in order to produce "a national Negro theater where the Negro playwright, musician, actor, dancer and artist in concert shall fashion a drama that will merit the respect and admiration of America."[8] The vision is inspiring, but fifty years later it remains largely unrealized. Meanwhile, the serious actor, eschewing the siren call of the music hall and variety stage and ignoring the threat of financial insecurity, continued to look to Shakespeare as the supreme challenge and proving ground of his art.

A new formulation of the demand for a theater of black experience emerged as part of the black consciousness movement in the late 1960s and '70s. It condemned Shakespeare's dramas, and by association the black Shakespeare actor, as detrimental to the race. According to this view, the plays of Shakespeare, no less than those by other white playwrights, do not faithfully portray the black experience and may, in fact, be guilty of perpetuating insidious racial biases in their depiction of black characters. Once again the argument was heard, and this time more passionately, that the authentic black experience in all its manifestations will only be truly re-created in the theater when there is assembled a black company of dedicated and gifted artists working in an atmosphere of creative freedom and experimentation. From this point of view, the attraction to Shakespeare by leading theater practitioners of the race is diversionary and poses a constant threat to the establishment of a theater of black identity.[9]

Despite these arguments, the Shakespeare magic remains potent and cannot be dismissed simply as the consequence of white indoctrination. More credible reasons for his preeminence with actors are readily found. He has created some of the most demanding roles in stage history. The greatest actors of the past four hundred years have sought to master these roles and win renown. No actor worthy of the name can avoid the challenge posed by Shakespeare's heroes and heroines.

Then again, Shakespeare's characters are for the most part colorblind. Some of his popular heroes have even been acted by women.[10] There have been over a score of female Hamlets. Sarah Bernhardt was a notable Prince of Denmark at the end of the nineteenth century, and in living memory Judith Anderson, Eva Le Gallienne, and Siobhan McKenna played the role in New York. Also in New York at the time of writing, Joseph Papp has a virtually unknown young actress, Diane Venora, portraying Hamlet at the Public Theatre. Ellen Tree and Charlotte Cushman were both memorable Romeos. Women actors have attempted villainous characters such as Richard III, Iago, and others. Clearly an actor's sex, race, color, or national origin need not deter him or her from performing one of Shakespeare's major roles if the requisite talent exists.

Yet another reason for Shakespeare's popularity with both black and white actors is his gift for writing great dramatic poetry. Every actor born to the English tongue is in his debt and cannot help being seduced by his language. The passion to make that language and those thoughts one's own as a living character in the world of the play cannot be resisted, partly because they are capable of infinite gradations and also because they offer the individual actor a chance to stamp his own interpretation on the role he is playing.

Then there are the four black characters that Shakespeare wrote into his canon of plays. Now it is usually alleged that there is something unique about the black experience in the modern world. This belief is based on the peculiar circumstances surrounding the introduction of black Africans into the Americas. It is argued that the institution of plantation slavery with all its horrors, the years of struggle that followed the end of slavery, and the survival strategies devised by blacks to sustain life in the face of overwhelming odds have given black folk an unparalleled understanding of the vagaries of human existence. If that argument is valid, then black actors should rightfully expect to be chosen for roles that permit them to express the uniqueness of their race within the dominant white world of those four plays. Although Shakespeare's black characters were written to be performed by white actors in blackface, and despite the fact that the plays may reflect unwarranted racial attitudes current in Elizabethan England, black actors have earned the right to use the authentic racial experience in interpreting these roles for modern audiences. Most white actors, for instance, are apt to emphasize the supposed uncontrollable jealousy of Othello as the principal motive for his murder of Desdemona, but when Paul Robeson first played the part of the Moor in London, his approach was quite different. For him this was not a tragedy of personal vengeance; rather, as he said at the time of the production: "The problem [of *Othello*] is the problem of my own people. It is a tragedy of racial conflict, a tragedy of honor, rather than of jealousy."[11] For Robeson, Othello's main objective is to overcome the slurs on his race (explicit in the world of the play and implicit in the world of his audience) by his exemplary behavior under all conditions. That image of perfection he strives to maintain is shattered when Othello kills his wife, believing that she has betrayed him and tarnished his honor. His suicide follows inevitably.

The black experience, being a unique human experience, may well serve to produce new and insightful interpretations—not only of the four black but of all the heroes and heroines in Shakespeare's plays. The record shows that there has seldom been a time in the last one hundred and fifty years when there were not black actors of skill and intelligence to undertake these parts. Robeson had spoken of attempting Hamlet—"if I thought anyone would accept a black Hamlet"—and Macbeth.[12] Decades later, the questions that remain are: When will black actors be cast simply on the basis of talent in major Shakespearean roles? and Is it any longer true that audiences are unwilling to accept them in such roles?

Shakespeare's four black characters are Aaron the Moor, who appears in *Titus Andronicus* (c. 1592), the Prince of Morocco in *The Merchant of Venice* (c. 1597), Othello, in the play written at the height of Shakespeare's powers in 1604, and his only black female, Cleopatra, in *Antony and Cleopatra* (1606–1607). It may seem strange to include Cleopatra in this list, since she is seldom portrayed as a black woman even in contemporary productions, but there are two textual references to her color that leave no doubt. In the first speech of the play,

Philo refers to Cleopatra's face on which Antony is wont to turn his goodly eyes as "a tawny front," and soon after Cleopatra describes herself as one who is "with Phoebus' amorous pinches black." Phoebus, the Greek sun god, has colored her skin black.

As for the male characters, they are all Moors, that mixture of Berber and Arab people who live in northwest Africa. It would appear Shakespeare held the conviction that the Moors belonged to the black race. This belief was consonant with that of his queen, who in 1599 and 1601 had issued two edicts complaining of "the great numbers of Negars and Blackamoors which . . . are crept into this realm" and appointing a certain Caspar van Zenden to arrange for their speedy deportation.[13] In the only instance where Shakespeare actually uses the word "negro," in *The Merchant of Venice* (3.5.37–39), he employed it as a synonym for "Moor." Moreover, textual references to the blackness of these characters are quite specific. Aaron, for instance, is called "coal-black" and "raven-colour'd"; he wears a "fleece of woollen hair" and will have his soul "black like his face." The Prince of Morocco, much loved by women of his race, is in his own esteem a most eligible suitor to the Venetian heiress, Portia. He refers to his complexion as "the shadow'd livery of the burnish'd sun" even as she mocks his color by calling it "the complexion of the devil." As for Othello, the debate over his color has continued for one hundred and fifty years and deserves closer scrutiny.[14] At this point we would simply refer to Othello's own description of his coloring as conclusive proof of his blackness: "My name that was as fresh / As Dian's visage, is now begrim'd and black / As mine own face." A major part of the plot, in fact, hinges on the circumstance that he, a black man, chose to marry a young Venetian girl who is white. His nobility, valor, high office, and acknowledged services to the state count for little with those who would make mischief out of the accident of skin color.

But why the controversy over Othello's color when there is no such debate about Shakespeare's other two Moors? We learn that the established tradition until the late eighteenth century was to play Othello in blackface. The character was so presented by English professionals from the time of Thomas Betterton, a leading actor of the Restoration stage. Betterton apparently made a success of the role. Later star players were less fortunate. James Quin, a heavy, thick-set man, looked ridiculous in a large powdered wig topping his black face. The great David Garrick presented a similarly absurd figure in this role; his short stature swathed in flowing Eastern robes and plumed turban reminded audiences of those juvenile African butlers in gaudy attire who used to serve tea at private receptions according to the fashion of the times. Spranger Barry was also criticized for having too black a face that showed nothing except "a wide mouth and good eyes." Majestic John Philip Kemble looked incongruous in a blending of a British general's uniform with a Moorish jacket, contemporary trousers, and black face. Of this actor's performance in 1789 a critic first raised the question whether the Moor "should be as black as a native of Guiney [sic]." By the time Edmund Kean attempted the role in 1814, he preferred not to risk the ridicule of the age toward a black skin and decided to substitute a light brown tint.

About the same time, the English press and public were divided on the issue of the abolition of slavery then being debated in Parliament. Those who wished to retain slavery sought to denigrate black people as savages who would decline into barbarism if the guiding hand of their white masters was withdrawn. Coleridge, for instance, in his attempt to validate Kean's tawny-colored Moor, wrote that Shakespeare could not be "so utterly ignorant as to make a barbarous negro plead royal birth" and, further, that "it would be monstrous to conceive this beautiful Venetian girl falling in love with a veritable Negro."

Thus the controversy over Othello's color was double-edged. Having enslaved the black man, white Europeans sought to justify their actions by propagating an image of the African as a barbarous savage. When domiciled and admitted to civilized society, the African could become only an exotically costumed fetcher-and-carrier for his masters or a buffoon to entertain them. The problem was that white actors made up as blacks ran the risk of being identified with this image of ridicule. Moreover, Othello's noble qualities and regal bearing did not fit the black stereotype, hence the need to present him with a tawny skin. Curiously enough, no issue seems to have been made of the skin color of that other Moor, Aaron. Although *Titus Andronicus* has never been popular on stage and was seldom produced in the eighteenth and nineteenth centuries, this character is hardly ever discussed in many commentaries dealing with Othello's color, the general consensus being that Aaron is in fact black. He also happens to be one of the most brutal characters in all of Shakespeare's plays.

Shakespeare's company of players in Elizabethan England did not have black actors. The Moors in his plays were first acted by white men in blackface, a tradition that with rare exceptions has continued in England to this day. Only twice during the present century was a black man cast as Othello in a major London production of the play. The earliest mention of a black being considered for a Shakespeare role occurred in the mid-eighteenth century. His name was Ignatius Sancho and, while there is no evidence that he actually performed one of Shakespeare's characters, his story is of sufficient interest to warrant inclusion in this study.

Sancho was born in 1729 of slave parents en route from Africa to Spanish America. His mother died in childbirth, and his father, overcome with grief and rejecting the life of a slave, plunged overboard and drowned in the waters of the Caribbean. Taken to England at the age of two, the infant child was put in the care of three maiden sisters who believed that his obedience could be secured by keeping him ignorant. They called him Sancho after Don Quixote's steward. What reading and writing he learned were the result of his own diligent efforts. After reaching the age of twenty, Sancho found a patron in the duke of Montagu, who gave him books and in whose home he became a butler. Later he married a West Indian and set up shop as a respected middle-class London grocer. He wrote poetry and music; he was an accomplished art critic and a friend of the actor David Garrick (whom he much admired); and his portrait was painted by Gainsborough. He also wrote two pieces for the stage. His letters, published after his death, went through five editions between 1782 and 1803.

What little we know of Sancho's acting aspirations is briefly revealed in the following excerpt from a memoir of his life written by Joseph Jekyll, a member of the British Parliament. It appears that, prior to his marriage, Sancho had been somewhat profligate with his money and had fallen on hard times. Of this period in his life Jekyll writes: "Ignatius loved the theatre to such a point of enthusiasm that his last shilling went to Drury Lane, on Mr. Garrick's representation of Richard. He had been even induced to consider the stage as a resource in the hour of adversity, and his complexion suggested an offer to the manager of attempting Othello and Oroonoko; but a defective and incorrigible articulation rendered it abortive."[15] Of utmost significance in that brief report is the fact that in eighteenth-century England a black would-be actor could hope to be employed in an all-white company of professionals presenting Shakespeare's plays. No such option existed in America at that time, nor would it exist for almost another two hundred years. Sancho's speech impediment had deprived English audiences of seeing a black man perform Shakespeare on the public stage. It was a blessing in disguise, for he was no actor. England had no reservoir of black talent to draw upon and would have to wait for the arrival of a most gifted American actor in the next century to see the great Shakespearean heroes brilliantly delineated from a black perspective.

American productions of Shakespeare began in Philadelphia in 1749 with a company led by Walter Murray and Thomas Kean. Their repertoire included *Richard III*, which was destined to become the most favored play in the nineteenth century with both white and black actors. Little is known of the Murray and Kean company, which faded from the records in a few years. Its demise may have been hastened by the arrival of a full-blown English troupe of players, led by Lewis Hallam, which landed in Williamsburg, Virginia, in 1752. From that time on and for the next seventy and more years, imported English actors dominated the American stage. Among the most famous of these English professionals were George F. Cooke, the brothers James and Henry Wallack, Edmund Kean, Junius Booth, William Charles Macready, Mary Ann Duff, and Fanny Kemble. Not until Edwin Forrest scored a triumph with *Othello* in his New York debut in 1826 did a native-born actor challenge the preeminence of British players in Shakespeare on the American stage.

Forrest was a white man. Most blacks in America in his day were still chattel slaves, well over two million of them. North of the thirty-sixth parallel, free blacks faced a different problem. True, they were not held in bondage, but they were faced with limited opportunities for cultural advancement and with little or no chance to participate as equals in the recreational activities of the dominant white society. As a result, they formed small black enclaves within the larger towns and cities and began to create their own cultural amenities. From one of these enclaves in lower New York City there emerged in 1821 the first recorded black theater troupe in America, appropriately called the African Company.[16]

The manager of this enterprise, William Henry Brown, was a West Indian ex-seaman who started out in 1816–17 giving entertainments in a tea garden that he had fitted up in his backyard on Thomas Street. After some four years, Brown converted his upper apartments into a small theater and by September 1821 announced the opening performance by a group of black folk. This theater, seating three to four hundred people, was moved to two different locations on Mercer Street in succeeding years.[17] Dramas about black life were practically nonexistent at this time—as we shall see, Brown himself was induced to write a play for the company—while in the professional theater the plays of Shakespeare appeared with regularity. The African Company opened with *Richard III* and from its ranks came the first Afro-American Shakespeare actor. His name was James Hewlett.

Hewlett, a mulatto, was born in one of the West Indian islands or, by some accounts, in Rockaway, New York. He was probably among the earliest of that constant stream of enterprising West Indians who migrate to the land of opportunity, not always by lawful means, and who later find it prudent to claim American birth. He started out as a "very fine singer" in Brown's tea-garden entertainments but soon introduced dramatic exhibitions in which he would convincingly imitate the styles of professional actors whom he had observed on the stage of the prestigious Park Theatre in New York. It has been suggested that in these impersonations he may even have anticipated the celebrated English comic imitator Charles Mathews. When Brown established the Mercer Street theater, Hewlett became his leading actor and appeared in several of Shakespeare's plays, his favorite role being Richard III.

The African Company, despite a strong following among its black supporters, lasted only about three years. When white patrons became interested in viewing its productions, they were graciously accommodated in a specially partitioned section at the back of the auditorium. Of this development, George C. D. Odell, chronicler of the nineteenth-century New York theater, comments: "This partition, erected by a race so long segregated in the negro gallery of playhouses, strikes me as pathetic and ominous."[18] The ominous nature of white patronage for black productions of Shakespeare would shortly be demonstrated.

Mr. Brown, audacious manager of the black troupe, decided to challenge the great Park Theatre for a share of its audiences by moving his company into a hotel next door to the Park. This intrusion was not welcomed by the white theatrical establishment. According to a memoir of 1849, the influential and not-too-scrupulous manager of the Park Theatre, Stephen Price, "became actually jealous of the success of the 'real Ethiopian' and emissaries were employed to put them down. . . . Riots ensued, and destruction fell upon the little

James Hewlett as Richard III, 1821

theatre."[19] Another report describes how the police descended on the African Company during a performance, arrested the actors, and carried them off to jail, whereupon they were released by the magistrate only after they pledged never again to act Shakespeare.[20] As one black actress who had been cast as Juliet declared bitterly: "Nothing but envy [by the Park Theatre management] prevented the blacks from putting the whites completely out of countenance."[21] It is inconceivable that Brown's upstart little company from Mercer Street would actually have put the Park Theatre out of business or seriously diminished its receipts. Nevertheless, the determination of the white establishment theater at this early date to keep Afro-American performers out of the theatrical mainstream was prophetic of its attitude for generations to come.

The African Company folded, but not before it had given America its first drama by a black playwright. This was *King Shotaway*, a chronicle play about the insurrection of Caribs against the British on the island of St. Vincent. It was written by the irrepressible William Brown and had James Hewlett in the leading role of the Carib chieftain Shotaway.

When the troupe disbanded about 1824, Hewlett continued to perform his one-man imitations of famous actors in Shakespearean and other roles to piano accompaniment provided by his wife. He thought highly of his art, billed himself as "Vocalist and Shakespeare's proud representative," and was very distressed when Charles Mathews satirized the African Company in London at one of his comic presentations called "A Trip to America." Hewlett had befriended Mathews when the latter visited America and had even recited some of his favorite scenes at the request of the English comedian. He little thought that Mathews was studying the black performers in order to parody them in his comedy routines. Hewlett published an open letter to Mathews in which he chided the mimic for making fun of the blacks:

> You have, I perceive, by the programme of your performance, ridiculed our African Theatre in Mercer Street and burlesqued me with the rest of the Negro actors, as you are pleased to call us—mimicked our styles—imitated our dialects—laughed at our anomalies—and lampooned, shame, even our complexions. Was this well for a brother actor? . . . I was particularly chagrined

at your sneers about the Negro theatre. Why these reflections on our color, my good Mathews, so unworthy of your genius and humanity, your justice and generosity? . . . Shakespeare makes sweet Desdemona say, "I saw Othello's *visage* in his *mind.*" Now, when you were ridiculing the "chief black tragedian" and burlesquing the "real Negro melody," was it my "mind" or my "visage" which should have made an impression on you?[22]

Hewlett traveled to England in 1825 to fulfill an engagement at the Coburg Theatre in London, probably with the intention of upholding his reputation in answer to Mathews's burlesque, but there is no record of his appearance there. Instead he appeared in solo performances of *Richard III* and *Othello* in Albany, New York, in 1826, and the following year he was billed at the Court House in York, Pennsylvania, where in one of his appearances he imitated all the great actors of the time. That his art consisted of more than mere apish or comedic imitation of others can be seen in a contemporary report in the *Star* of December 22, 1825: "His songs were excellent, and his style, taste, voice and action such as would have done credit to any stage. His imitations of Kean, Mathews, and others were recognized as correct, and evinced a nice discrimination of tact . . . which ought to recommend him to every lover of pure acting. Hewlett is yet young enough to receive some of the advantages of education, and we should advise him to persevere in the way his genius seems to direct." This "celebrated tragedian," as the papers of the time dubbed him, was last heard of in 1831. Odell records his last known performance with a cryptic comment: "In July, Shakespeare's proud representative—Hewlett, to wit—gave imitations and took exhilarating gas. . . . Herein lurks a real tragedy of a Negro's thwarted ambition."[23] The sniffing of gas on stage was one of the low-comedy acts current at that time and Odell was probably bemoaning the fact that in the absence of a proper outlet for his talent, Hewlett was reduced to gimmickry. It is quite possible, however, that an unknown tragedy did cut short his career. Though still a young man, Hewlett vanished from the stage thereafter, and a later writer referred to him as "poor Jim Hewlett."

However he may have died, a contemporary admirer signing himself "A Friend to Merit" has provided us with a fitting eulogy when he called Hewlett "one of the most astonishing phenomena of the age, a young man who, notwithstanding the thousand obstacles which the circumstances of complexion must have thrown in the way of improvement, has, by the mere dint of natural genius and self-strengthened assiduity, risen to a successful competition with some of the first actors of the day."[24]

2
Involuntary Exiles

T
HE EXPERIENCE of Hewlett and the African Company made
it clear that America was not yet ready to accept black actors in
the legitimate drama. Those who were bent on a professional
career looked to other more hospitable lands. So it was that in the
middle of the nineteenth century three black Americans moved to
England, becoming involuntary exiles from home in order to pursue
their love affair with the Shakespearean stage. These actors were Ira
Aldridge, S. Morgan Smith, and Paul Molyneaux.

Ira Aldridge was the most accomplished American actor in nineteenth-century England and Europe and one of the finest Shakespearean interpreters of all time. He was born in New York in 1807.
His father Daniel Aldridge, himself a minister, expected Ira to follow
him in that profession. Young Aldridge was sent to the African Free
School, first established in New York in 1787 by the Manumission
Society, which provided free education to black children. At school
the young Aldridge was taught reading, writing, arithmetic, geogra-
phy, and English grammar. There he may have acquired his first love
of literature and the spoken word, for a visitor to the school in 1817,
impressed with the work being accomplished as with the behavior of
the students, wrote of a young lad about fourteen years old whom he
observed "reciting passages from the best authors, suiting the action
to the words."[1] Aldridge was early attracted to the stage. He frequent-
ed the professional theater and became a backstage attendant to the
English actor Henry Wallack.

Aldridge was associated with Mr. Brown's African Company and
had made his acting debut at the Mercer Street theater about 1821,

playing Rolla in Sheridan's drama *Pizarro*. He also performed Romeo there. In 1824, still only seventeen years old, he set out for England in the service of Henry Wallack, determined to become a professional actor himself in a country where, he had reason to hope, his skin color would not prove an insurmountable barrier to his advancement. His timing was impeccable. The British Parliament had abolished the slave trade in 1807 and was moving inexorably toward the liberation of all slaves in countries under British rule by 1833. Aldridge's appearance on the English stage, sustaining major roles of the most revered English dramatist, Shakespeare, was fortuitous. It provided substan-

*Ira Aldridge
as King Lear*

tial proof to the proponents of emancipation that, given the opportunity, the black man could rise from the degradation of slavery to the highest levels of artistic expression, equal to those of the white race.

The career of Ira Aldridge spanned four decades. In that time he performed over forty roles, including Othello, Aaron the Moor, Richard III, Shylock, Hamlet, Macbeth, and King Lear. He played in towns and cities throughout England, Scotland, Wales, and Ireland. He appeared in some thirty cities of Europe and Russia, among the most important being Vienna, Budapest, Prague, Munich, Stockholm, St. Petersburg, Moscow, Constantinople, Warsaw, and Paris. He performed in many towns that had never before seen Shakespeare on stage. He played the great tragic roles in bilingual productions, speaking English himself with foreign companies who spoke their native language.

Most theater historians will agree that the major thrust toward a naturalistic approach in speech and acting, an approach that now dominates the contemporary stage, occurred in the second half of the nineteenth century. Among those credited with promoting this innovative style are the Frenchman Charles Albert Fechter, whose Hamlet in London in 1861 is viewed as introducing realism to Shakespeare; the German Duke George II, producer of the Meiningen Players after his accession in 1866; André Antoine of the Théâtre Libre of Paris in the 1880s; and, of course, the Russian Stanislavsky of the Moscow Art Theatre in the decade of the 1890s. Overlooked in this catalogue of acting innovators is Ira Aldridge, whose performance in Shakespeare as early as 1857 had already begun to show a marked departure from the traditional histrionic grandeur associated with tragic acting. Playing Aaron the Moor that year in a production of *Titus Andronicus* in Hoxton, England, Aldridge received the following critique in the *Era*: "He rants less than almost any tragedian we know—he makes no vulgar appeal to the gallery. . . . He is thoroughly natural, easy and sensible, albeit he has abundance of physique at his command when the exercise of it is required. In a word, he obviously knows what he is at, and there is as little of the 'fustian' about him as there is in anybody on the stage."[2] Five years later, the leading Moscow critic S. Almazov elaborates on Aldridge's style and shows that the black tragedian is already well on the road toward psychological realism in acting:

Aldridge has nothing in common with those theatrical personalities from the West who visited us in recent times. His qualities consist not in picturesque poses and gestures, not in a melodic singing diction, not in an artificially (pseudomajestic) tragic gait. . . . He concentrates all your attention only on the inner meaning of his speech. He does not bother either about the majestic stride, but moves about completely naturally, not like a tragedian, but like a human being. No externality, no ballet-like grace and agility of movement, but a highly truthful understanding of art, a deep knowledge of the human heart, and an ability to feel the subtlest spiritual movements indicated by Shakespeare and to bring them to life before the public—that is what constitutes the essence of his acting.[3]

Surely it was fitting when in January 1858 the duke of Saxe-Meiningen commanded that Aldridge should be decorated with the Order of the Royal Saxon House. He was the only actor, native or foreign, to be so honored. The duke was one of several European heads of state to bestow highly prized accolades upon this exceptionally gifted actor.

Aldridge was ever conscious of his race and of the fact that his stage career made him vulnerable as an ambassador of African peoples. His blackness had a profound effect on the interpretation of many of his principal roles. Not only was the personal conflict of his stage character revealed in his performance but, wherever appropriate, the social implications of dramas involving racial differences were emphasized. His identification with the character of Othello was so complete that, after seeing him in the role, more than one critic felt that the part should never again be played by a white actor. He turned the comic role of Mungo, slave to a West Indian planter in Bickerstaffe's *The Padlock*, into a rebellion against slavery. His Shylock was so sympathetically portrayed at a performance in Russia that the Jewish community thanked him for his interpretation of a character that Jews have usually condemned as inimical to their race. He rewrote *Titus Andronicus*, considered at the time much too gruesome to be staged, to make it more palatable to audiences and to give himself yet another major black role. The blood-thirsty Aaron became a character of noble sentiment who was "gentle and impassioned by turns [and] fierce with rage as he reflects upon the wrongs which have been done him." One critic's verdict of these changes was that "a play not only presentable but actually attractive is the result."[4]

A particular anecdote quite at variance with Aldridge's concern to present ennobling images of his race has gained wide currency and

Ira Aldridge as Othello in England

deserves to be questioned. Its author is Dame Madge Kendal, an English actress roughly contemporary with Aldridge, who as Madge Robertson once played Desdemona to his Othello in 1865 toward the end of his career. In her memoirs Mrs. Kendal wrote of Aldridge's performance: "In the last act he used to take Desdemona out of the bed by her hair and drag her around the stage before he smothered her. I remember very distinctly this dragging Desdemona about by the hair was considered so brutal that he was loudly hissed."[5] This particular bit of stage violence was never reported in any published review of

Ira Aldridge as Aaron the Moor in Titus Andronicus, *1852.*

Aldridge's Othello, although he was not averse to incorporating original stage business in his performance. Not even those critics who were unsympathetic to the black actor because of his color and who wrote demeaning notices of his performances saw fit to mention this odious action that, according to Mrs. Kendal, even audiences condemned. There is, on the other hand, a report of an identical piece of stage business that was used by the English actor E. F. Saville, a brother of the renowned tragedienne Helen Faucit, in a popular dramatization of Dickens's *Oliver Twist*. This production opened in London in 1839 and Saville, who died in 1857, must have appeared in it at a time when Aldridge was beginning to make a name for himself on the London stage. Saville impersonated the villainous character Bill Sykes, whose murder of Nancy was a high point of the play:

Nancy was always dragged round the stage by her hair, and after this effort, Sykes always looked up defiantly at the gallery, as he was doubtless told to do in the marked prompt-book. He was always answered by one loud and fearful curse, yelled by the whole mass like a Handel Festival Chorus. The curse was answered by Sykes dragging Nancy twice around the stage, and then like Ajax, defying the lightning. The simultaneous yell then became louder and more blasphemous. Finally, when Sykes, working up to a well-rehearsed climax, smeared Nancy with red ochre, and taking her by the hair (a most powerful wig) seemed to dash her brains out on the stage, no explosion of dynamite invented by the modern anarchist, no language ever dreamed of in Bedlam, could equal the outburst. A thousand enraged voices which sounded like ten thousand, with the roar of a dozen escaped menageries, filled the theatre and deafened the audience, and when the smiling ruffian came forward and bowed, their voices in thorough plain English expressed a fierce determination to tear his sanguinary entrails from his sanguinary body.[6]

It is hard to believe that Aldridge would not be aware of this provocative scene that had been deliberately inserted in a popular melodrama to whip up audience outrage against the villain, according to the custom of the time. It is likewise improbable that, knowing its effect on the audience, Aldridge would have incorporated a similar scene in the most important Shakespearean play in his repertoire, one in which audience sympathy for the tragic hero was clearly desirable. In reporting the incident Mrs. Kendal does not say that she herself was subjected to such treatment when she played Desdemona to Aldridge's Othello. She wrote of him as having "gleams of intelligence" and being "quite *preux chevalier* in his manners to women." Yet the mischievous story continues to be widely reported.[7] Commenting on Mrs. Kendal's report, David Aldridge, nephew to the actor, wrote in 1890:

> I was with my uncle from 1842 to 1846, and traveled with him. It is most singular that I never witnessed his dragging Desdemona by the hair. I assisted him at most of the theatres in England and on the Continent and witnessed him in all of his parts, but I never saw him perform that act. He must have left that part out for my especial benefit. I well remember Mrs. Kendal in her great parts in tragedy and other actresses and actors.[8]

The career of Ira Aldridge has been called a curiosity; the great acclaim he received has been attributed to the novelty of his being the first black actor to assume major Shakespearean roles. It should be noted that Aldridge's talent did not emerge full-blown like Athena from the head of Zeus. It was painstakingly honed over eighteen years of arduous provincial touring in the British Isles before he was able to win acceptance in the principal cities of England and Europe. Even then there were metropolitan critics who could not see his talent because of his race.

At the start of his career, press reviews were far from complimentary. Even those observant writers who saw a spark of genius complained of his lack of polish in speech and movement. As he matured, however, his press notices grew increasingly more respectful. In his prime, the large majority of critics could not withhold abundant praise of his art. In Dublin, Aldridge's portrayals were called "the perfection of acting"; in Germany he was hailed as "the greatest of all actors"; in Danzig his Othello, Macbeth and Shylock were said to "leave him without a rival in the annals of the theatre"; in Poland his Othello was "as the poet's genius created him"; in France he presented "for the first time a hero of tragedy speaking and walking like a common mortal, void of exaggeration either in posture or exclamation." A critic in Russia compared him to "the greatest thing in nature," and in England, the hitherto persistently hostile critic of the *Athenaeum* who, in reviewing Aldridge's Othello, had earlier protested against a white actress being pawed about by Henry Wallack's black servant, finally capitulated and wrote:

We find that not only does the sable artist pronounce our language distinctly and correctly, but with elocutional emphasis and propriety, and that his general action is marked with elegance and ease. . . . Mr. Aldridge has formed a conception of Othello peculiarly his own and interprets many portions of the text in an original manner. . . . He is manifestly an intelligent man, has studied his art with earnestness and gained felicity in its exercise.[9]

The impression Aldridge made on seasoned theater critics cannot compare with the effect he produced on his audiences. One report must suffice to indicate the sort of impact he had on the theatergoing public. It is taken from a lengthy article written by the St. Petersburg correspondent of the French paper *Le Nord* which appeared on November 23, 1858:

From his first step on the stage the African artist captivated the entire audience by his harmonious and sonorous voice, by his simple, natural, and dignified declamation. We have now seen for the first time a hero of tragedy speaking and walking like a common mortal, void of exaggeration either in posture and exclamation. We soon forgot that we were at the theatre, and we began to follow the action of the drama as if it were real history.

The scene in the third act when the sentiment of jealousy is excited in the savage Moor, is the triumph of Aldridge; from the first moment of the cunning accusation against Desdemona, you see his eyes flash, you feel the tears in his voice when he questions Iago, followed by stifled sobs that almost choke him, and when at last he is convinced that his misfortune is beyond doubt, a cry of anger or rather the roaring of a wild beast escapes him, coming from the very bottom of his heart. That shriek still seems to sound in my ears; it sent a thrill of horror through all the spectators. Real tears roll down his cheek, he foams at the mouth, his eyes flash fire; never have I seen an artist so completely identify himself with the person he represents. An actor told me that he saw the great tragedian sob for several minutes after he came behind the scenes. The public did not fail to be deeply touched, all wept, both men and women.

Despite his success on foreign boards, Aldridge frequently thought of returning to America. In 1858, newspapers announced his impending return, but the trip did not materialize. Again in 1867 he received invitations from different parties and advertised his homecoming. With his thoughts turned homeward, Aldridge collapsed and died on engagement in Lodz, Poland, on August 7, 1867. He was sixty years old. The Civil War in America had ended slavery and, he probably hoped, had opened the way for the black actor to perform on the legitimate stage of his native land. Had he returned home, he would have

Ira Aldridge as Othello in Moscow

been sadly disappointed. In 1867 the only roles available to black performers were on the minstrel stage. Interracial casting was nonexistent, and there were no black companies with which he could work. A decade and more would pass before the first black actor appeared as the lowly Uncle Tom in the universally popular dramatization of Harriet Beecher Stowe's novel. Was there a chance that the celebrated tragedian, fresh from his triumphs in Europe, would break the color bar and be accepted as a legitimate Shakespearean actor, the peer of Edwin Booth, Edwin Forrest, Lawrence Barrett, and other native white Shakespeareans then acclaimed in America? One would like to think so, but the evidence does not corroborate this. Before the end of the century, two other Afro-Americans, shut out from the professional theater at home and inspired by Aldridge's success abroad, were to seek their fortunes in England.

Just one year prior to Aldridge's death, "the colored tragedian" Samuel Morgan Smith arrived in England. Aldridge had come at a time when the English press was aroused on the question of slave emancipation in British possessions. Morgan Smith's arrival coincided with the abolition of slavery in America. Both Aldridge and Smith began their careers at periods of heightened interest in the condition of black people, and both found a receptive public awaiting them in Britain.

Morgan Smith was born in Philadelphia, about 1833, evidently into a family of means, for he received a good education and at an early age became a devotee of Shakespeare. He used to attend the theater regularly and would study the work of actors on stage from the upper galleries, to which Afro-Americans were at that time relegated. Having resolved on a stage career, Smith went to Boston and New York to train under professional players. The Welsh actor William Henry Smith, who had migrated to America and had married a Philadelphian, was Morgan Smith's Boston coach. In addition to appearing in such popular melodramas as The Drunkard, W. H. Smith had played a season of Shakespeare in New York in support of Junius Brutus Booth, taking such roles as Edgar in King Lear, Laertes in Hamlet, and Mark Antony in Julius Caesar. He was an experienced and versatile actor, and the young Morgan Smith must have learned much from him.

Morgan Smith next sought to become more familiar with the work-

Morgan Smith

ings of the stage and applied for permission to visit backstage at several theaters, but his requests were uniformly denied. Concluding that there was no future for him in America, Smith set out for England with his wife and child, arriving there in May 1866. He had assiduously studied the plays of Shakespeare and other respected contemporary dramatists and felt thoroughly acquainted with their leading characters. Now he was ready to perform them.

What occurred within a few weeks after he reached England is so extraordinary that it is best reported in the words of a contemporary observer, Moncure D. Conway. Conway, a Harvard-trained Congregational minister and ardent abolitionist, had settled in London as pastor of a church in Finsbury. His report on Morgan Smith follows.

He arrived in England a little over a month ago; and within three days after his arrival he had made a contract for the management for one month of a little theatre at Gravesend, and had announced for its opening the play of *Othello*. The theatre is not an important one, but he took it in order to get a little practice. He went out, on the fourth evening of his arrival, having, as I said, never set his foot on a stage before, and took the part of Othello. . . . For about a month he played here successfully in the highest parts—Richard III, Macbeth, Hamlet, Shylock, Othello—twenty-one nights in all.

A friend of Conway's saw Smith perform the role of Richard III at the Gravesend theater. He reported that although the company was a very poor one and gave dreary performances, from the moment Smith entered as Richard, he, as a member of the audience, was "borne along on great waves of feeling and emotion, as he had rarely been in his life." Some time later, Conway was introduced to Smith at a reading given by the actor to a group of literary and stage personages in an English drawing room. He found Smith to be remarkably handsome, of a deep brown color, with singularly strong lines of face and an expression full of dignity, animation, and power. Smith's voice was perfectly modulated, clear, rich, and resonant, capable of uttering the widest range of emotions from tenderness and pathos to terror and rage. Conway concluded his article on a note of rebuke to his fellow Americans:

> There is but one opinion amongst those who have seen and heard Morgan Smith, on or off the stage, and that is that the provincial tour upon which he is now about to enter as a star actor will end with a position on the London stage as eminent as that of Ira Aldridge on the continental stage; and that America may ere long have more food for reflecting how well she is leading the van of Humanity, whilst some of her finest spirits can find a free arena for their development and movement only under the monarchies and aristocracies of the old world.[10]

A fuller account of Morgan Smith's one-month tenancy as actor-manager of the Theatre Royal in Gravesend can be gleaned from the pages of contemporary newspapers. The local press admitted that the company he recruited was the best to visit Gravesend for many years, yet the audiences remained scarce and the season, which ran from May 19 to June 16, was financially disastrous. This setback must have been worrisome for a black man with a family to support in England in the mid-nineteenth century. Yet Smith had attained one of his first objectives—namely, he had secured a professonal showplace for his talent. During the month, in addition to his managerial duties, he had appeared not only as the five Shakespeare heroes named in Conway's essay, but also in the principal roles of several non-Shakespearean dramas that were popular with audiences of the period. Among these plays were Bulwer-Lytton's *The Lady of Lyons* and *Richelieu*, Thomas Morton's *The Slave*, and stage versions of Mrs. Aphra Behn's seventeenth-century novelette *Oroonoko* (dramatized by Thomas Southerne) and of Sir Walter Scott's *Rob Roy*. That Morgan Smith was able to present such a wide range of characters within a month of his first public appearance on any stage testifies to the thoroughness and industry with which he prepared for his ambitious debut in the English theater.

It is noteworthy that, although Smith had carefully chosen to perform several black characters in established plays, like Aldridge before him, he did not restrict his appearances to such roles. This would have severely limited his repertoire, there being few leading black characters in the well-known dramas of his time. Critical reception of his performances in this his first season was generally favorable. His acting was considered to be studious and intelligent, his style effective and his elocution polished, while with each successive performance he seemed to gain greater authority over his craft. Shylock proved to be his most successful role. The Sunday *Times* of July 1, 1866, noted that

> his delineation of the part was highly impressive and wrought wonderfully upon the feelings of his audience. It was by far the highest impersonation with which this actor has yet presented us. It was very true to nature, quiet and artistic at the commencement, arriving by gradual stages to a point at which the ascendancy of strange and terrible passions, of baffled hate and powerless longing for revenge, became exceedingly impressive. The delivery of the line, "To cut the forfeit from that bankrupt there" electrified the audience.

His Gravesend season concluded, Morgan Smith began to seek engagements in the provincial theaters. He advertised his availability, citing flattering excerpts from newspaper notices and referring to himself as the "Coloured American Tragedian." His listed repertoire consisted of the five Shakespearean characters previously mentioned and seven non-Shakespearean parts. Only four of these roles were specifically nonwhite—Othello, Oroonoko, Gambia in *The Slave*, and Zanga in *The Revenge* by Edward Young. All twelve roles, along with Fabian the Creole in *The Black Doctor* (a play adapted from the French original by Ira Aldridge), would constitute Smith's principal acting assignments over the next eight years.

Most of his provincial engagements were for six nights, when Smith would play three, four, and sometimes five Shakespeare characters and fill in the remaining nights with plays by other authors. Occasionally a booking might be extended for a second week, and then he would have an opportunity to repeat a role with the same company. If he took a benefit night, Smith usually offered *Othello* on that occasion. He attempted only two additional roles in Shakespeare: Romeo and, infrequently, Iago, which he sometimes alternated with Othello when an aspiring actor-manager persuaded him to switch parts.

After Gravesend, Smith's next recorded appearance was at the Prince of Wales Theatre in Birmingham, then under the management of the celebrated tragedienne Mrs. Macready. He gave a round of impersonations for about a week, being particularly well received in the role of Richelieu. Then there came his initial London appearance at the Royal Olympic Theatre, where he opened as Othello on August 25, 1866. This London debut occurred at the end of the summer before the regular theatrical season had commenced. In this interregnum when playgoing was at a low ebb, many city theaters would present novelty items to attract audiences. Casting Othello with a new, authentically black actor must be seen in that light. Smith shared the bill with a child actor, one Master Percy Roselle, who sustained four characters in the afterpiece, *The Four Mowbrays*.

Notwithstanding the circumstances of his appearance, Smith's performance was obviously a success. In its advertisement in the *Times* of August 29, 1866, the Olympic Theatre hailed it as "the greatest legitimate triumph for years." The theater ran the show for a week and suspended its free list of tickets. The following week, however, the management announced another novelty: Miss Marriot was billed to appear in her celebrated impersonation of Hamlet for three nights only. Smith then returned to the theater on September 12 as Shylock, and he took a benefit night on September 19 as Hamlet. The

Playbill for Morgan Smith as Othello at Royal Olympic Theatre, London, 1866.

Era newspaper devoted generous space to reviewing *Othello* and *The Merchant of Venice* in its issues of September 2 and 16, 1866. Of Smith's performance as the Venetian Moor the critic wrote:

> He is a good actor, his attitudes being graceful and his movements free and natural. He acts with ease, intelligence and earnestness. His performance on this occasion was a highly creditable one, and was frequently applauded by the audience. His delineation of the Moor must be pronounced clever and, in some parts, very effective. The coolness and fortitude of Othello when standing unmoved before the enraged Brabantio were well assumed, as were also his surprise and disgust at the quarreling between Cassio and Montano in time of war. . . . His acting throughout the final act, though evincing the possession of great histrionic skill and indicative of careful study, did not, in our estimation, rise to the highest standard of personations of the impassioned Moor.

A similar reservation tinged the reception of Smith's Shylock. While conceding that Smith was "a skillful, careful workman" whose "delivery of the text was almost unexceptionably good; he spoke with distinctness, correctness, fluency and thoughtful discrimination," the *Era* reviewer felt that he lacked "deepseated and sustained feeling and power." It may be that Smith did not possess a powerful vocal instrument. If so, he made up for this deficiency by lucidity of utterance, placing the emphasis on Shakespeare's words rather than old-style histrionics. Thus, most of his later appearances in the provinces received high praise; he was invariably called before the curtain and was judged to play with singularity of conception and power; his Othello in particular was "entirely distinct and free from any of the old beaten track of many of his predecessors."

Following his London engagements, Morgan Smith embarked on a rigorous schedule of provincial appearances. The succeeding twelve months saw him appear in no less than twenty-nine different cities and towns in England, Scotland, Wales, and Ireland. Touring of country theaters throughout the British Isles from Cardiff to Dublin to Dundee to Lancaster and back to London, playing a different role every night of the week and changing companies almost every week, must have been exceedingly taxing on the young American, no less than on his wife, who presumably was left alone in a strange city to care for their child. Smith had been in England less than eighteen months when personal tragedy struck. On October 6, 1867, his wife, Mary Eliza Smith, died. She was twenty-seven. Two weeks later Smith was back on the road keeping engagements. On October 21 that year he appeared at the Theatre Royal, Barnstable, for six nights playing Othello, Hamlet, Richard III, Shylock, Macbeth, and Richelieu.

When Smith remarried, his new wife, Harriet, seems to have been a Caucasian and an actress. Beginning with a performance in Dundee on October 16, 1869, there are repeated occasions on which Smith presented *Othello* for his benefit night with the new Mrs. Morgan Smith playing opposite him as Desdemona. As time went on, Mrs. Smith assumed a number of other roles beside her husband, including Ophelia in *Hamlet*, Lady Macbeth, Juliet in *Romeo and Juliet*, and Queen Elizabeth in *Richard III*. She also took major female parts in a number of non-Shakespearean plays in her husband's repertoire, such as *Richelieu*, *Rob Roy*, *The Lady of Lyons*, and others. She may even have browned-up for the part of Zelinda, a quadroon slave in *The Slave*. By this arrangement, Smith made it possible for his second wife to be with him periodically on tour and to share the vicissitudes of life that confronted the peripatetic star actor.

After three years of touring in essentially the same roles, Morgan Smith began to seek new material suited to his particular talent and complexion. He arranged for a new and scenically spectacular version of *The Black Doctor* to be prepared under the title *The Rising of the Tide*, which opened at the Royal Alfred Theatre in London on July 11, 1869, to wild applause. The play was added to his repertoire and soon became a stock piece on the provincial circuit. Another play, *Child of the Sun, or, The Bondsmen Brothers*, a romantic drama first produced by Smith in February 1868, in which he played the role of the Chevalier St. George, was also later billed as written for Smith. In the months that followed, he had three new plays written expressly for him. These were *All But Love*, a drama set in Canada in 1757 in which he played Uncas, a Mohican chieftain who is loved by the daughter of a retired British officer; *The Fall of Magdala, or, The Death of King Theodore*, a historic drama of Ethiopia in which Smith took the part of the king; and *War*, a drama by Charles Daly set against the background of the Franco-Prussian war of 1870 that saw Smith in the role of a freed South American slave. All these plays were gradually included in the roster of pieces he offered to provincial managements.

After a decade of touring, Morgan Smith's repertoire had grown to some thirty-five different roles. Seven of these were principal characters from Shakespeare's tragedies, including Othello and Iago. Nine of his roles were black. His provincial engagements continued regularly during the theatrical season, mostly to the smaller towns across Britain, many of which looked forward to his return with enthusiasm. As summertime approached, Smith would often find an engagement in or near London. In May 1873 he was at the Surrey in London playing *Richard III*, *Othello* (with Mrs. Smith as Desdemona), *Dred*, and *The Slave*. Commenting on his appearances on this occasion, the *Era* of May 25, 1873, felt that *The Slave* was scarcely an adequate test of his numerous powers but went on to list his capital points as "good reading, unexaggerated action, a clear, powerful voice, a correct memory, and an intelligent apprehension of dramatic requirements. . . . His natural delivery and accompanying deportment secured him a reception which few coloured tragedians can boast of."[11]

By far the most popular melodrama of the century was *Uncle Tom's Cabin*, first dramatized and produced in New York and London in 1852. Aldridge never appeared in this play, and on the single instance when Morgan Smith found himself in the cast, he chose not to take the lead role of the long-suffering Uncle Tom, who was so loyal to his master that he chose not to escape to freedom. Instead, Smith appeared as George Harris, the proud black who detested slavery and ran away with his wife, Eliza, and their infant child. Smith comes across as one who was conscious of his race and who sought to keep his name and reputation unsullied. In this he continued the tradition of his predecessor, Ira Aldridge. The following incident will indicate an aspect of his character in dealing with a very trying situation.

In January 1872, while he was engaged to perform at the Macclesfield Theatre, a charge of theft was brought against Smith by the local tailor. It happened that Smith wished to purchase a new pair of trousers and asked the tailor to send him a few pairs to choose from. The parcel was sent, a pair selected and paid for, and the remaining pairs were returned. But the tailor and his assistant alleged that Smith had kept two pairs instead of one and demanded that he return the missing pair or pay for it. Although Smith strongly asserted his innocence, the police were sent for, and he was forced to accompany the officer to the station, followed by a large crowd of people. Stung at the indignity of his arrest, Smith demanded that a search be made at his lodging.

The search was carried out meticulously by the police, but no trousers were found and Smith was released from custody. That evening he performed his role in *Othello*.

The matter did not rest there, however. Smith instituted proceedings against the tailor, claiming damages to his professional reputation to the extent of £500. In his claim he argued that he was an accomplished member of an American university and an actor of good repute and that he had been subjected to a gross indignity by the defendant. In summing up the case, the judge (who, as it turned out, was the father of one of the defending attorneys) instructed the jury that the only question they had to decide was "whether there had been a felony committed and if there had, had it been committed by the plaintiff"! Despite this curious interpretation of the law by the learned judge, the jury found for the plaintiff and Smith was vindicated, though he was awarded only a paltry sum of £5 for damages.[12]

Smith was as jealous of his professonal as he was of his personal reputation. He looked on acting as a high art and chose his roles carefully to present those characters who were unfairly victimized or who suffered for a noble cause. As a result, few of his roles were comedic. Whereas Ira Aldridge excelled in both comedy and tragedy and had been a notable Mungo in Bickerstaffe's comic opera *The Padlock*, Smith never once assumed this role. It was some years after his second marriage to a white actress that he first appeared in a comedy, urged, one presumes, by a desire to provide his spouse with appropriate parts in his productions.

At the start of his career, the *English Leader* characterized Smith's approach to his art with these words: "Not the least of his merits is his high artistic ambition and his desire to prove that the race to which he belongs is capable of successful exertion in the arduous walks of the theatrical profession."[13] Eight years later, in its review of *The Slave*, which was one of Smith's staple productions, the *Era* of October 4, 1874, gives further evidence of how Smith used his acting to present positive images of his race:

> There is one scene in the play in which Mr. Morgan Smith is seen to wonderful advantage. We allude to that in which, reminding Zelinda, the Quadroon beauty, of the risk he has run and the dangers he has encountered for her sake, and in the rescue of her infant from a terrible death, he offers her his love, only to find that love rejected and a hated rival given the preference. All the worst

feelings of the Negro race seem for the moment to be concentrated in Gambia, and he thirsts for revenge. He seizes her child and would do it harm, but its pretty face and innocent prattle disarm his wrath, while later on with his rival in his power we see his better nature again gain the victory, and Gambia giving a blessing where he had threatened something worse than a curse. In these episodes of the play, and, indeed, throughout, Mr. Morgan Smith was more than equal to the task set before him and, as we have hinted, he was deservedly the recipient of the warmest of plaudits and of repeated calls before the curtain.

Romantic melodrama it might be, but acted with conviction and sensitivity, it could not fail to move audiences.

On March 22, 1882, at his home in Sheffield, England, Morgan Smith died of pneumonia, "deeply mourned by his dearly-beloved, sorrowing widow and son, and greatly regretted by a large circle of friends in both countries." He was only forty-nine years old and had been in retirement for some years. One wonders why he gave up the theater in the prime of life. He had suffered "a severe accident," the nature of which is unknown, in December 1875, but the next month he had sufficiently recovered to commence touring. Eighteen seventy-seven was a good year for engagements, but in 1878–79 there was a substantial decline in the number of his appearances as recorded in the press. Had his health become impaired?

As an interpreter of Shakespeare, Morgan Smith cannot be ranked with Ira Aldridge. He lacked that spark of greatness that is reserved for the privileged few whom the gods love. He did not have Aldridge's range and emotional power, his venturesome originality and the risk taking that accompanies it. Smith was more the master of pathos than of righteous anger. He was, nonetheless, a superior performer, a talented and painstaking actor of intelligence, a careful elocutionist devoid of rant and exaggeration, whose personal and artistic life was governed by a sure sense of taste, good judgment, and proper deportment. For some thirteen years he had maintained a rigorous touring schedule, playing in numerous towns, large and small, across Britain—in Aberdare, Aberystwith, Belfast, Birkenhead, Cardiff, Coxhoe, Dunfermline, Dewsbury, Dundee, and on through the alphabet to Wishaw, Wrexham, and Yarmouth. Often working with modest provincial companies that the name stars would spurn, he encouraged the staging of Shakespeare's plays by taking the leading roles himself.

Through his eloquent delivery of the text, coupled with a dignified bearing, he helped to spread a knowledge and love of Shakespeare in the byways of the dramatist's own country. Morgan Smith may not have been another "African Roscius," as Aldridge was once dubbed, but he was unquestionably a worthy successor to the great black tragedian.

Tracing the brief history of the third black Shakespeare actor who sought a professional career in England is a task tinged with sadness. What we know of him comes primarily from a feature article by James M. Trotter that was published in the *New York Globe* of April 28, 1883. Paul Molyneaux Hewlett, whose stage name was Paul Molyneaux, was born in Cambridge, Massachusetts, in 1856. He was the son of Aaron Molyneaux Hewlett, a mulatto who was the boxing coach and gymnasium director of Harvard College from 1859 to 1871. Prior to this period, Aaron Molineaux [sic] is listed in the Worcester, Massachusetts, directory for three successive years as a gymnasium instructor. He apparently owned the gymnasium, where his wife assisted him by teaching a class of physical fitness for ladies. In Cambridge, Coach Hewlett's children had the advantages of a good education. One son became a lawyer and the first black judge for the District of Columbia. A daughter married Frederick Douglass, Jr. Paul Molyneaux, although of athletic build and an heir to his father's pugilistic skill, turned his ambitions elsewhere. He became enamored of the stage and decided on an acting career, despite his father's expressed disapproval.

In deference to his father, young Hewlett suppressed his histrionic urge, but after his father died, Paul set about his plans methodically. He began serious training under Wyzeman Marshall of Boston, a retired tragedian of note who had become a teacher of elocution and acting.[14] After some time, Paul applied to Boston theater managers for a position in their companies, making it clear that he would start at the bottom and work his way up. But no one would have him because, as Mr. Trotter's article put it, "of the ill-favored accident of color." Disappointed but not discouraged, the prospective actor applied himself diligently to renewed study. He decided to test his histrionic skill by tackling a major dramatic role. The narrative continues:

So he gave himself, both night and day, hardly thinking of food and sleep, to the study of Shakespeare's famous valiant Moor, Othello, in the role of which, fortunately, being "off color" is rather an advantage than otherwise for the Negro impersonator. By one of those freaks of American color prejudice, Mr. Molyneaux found no difficulty in forming, outside of the theatres, a supporting company, all white and of good ability; the lady who was to enact Desdemona being talented and handsome.

The production took place in Boston before a friendly and discriminating audience of both races. It was 1880 and Molyneaux was twenty-four. The response to his performance was generous and confirmed his belief in his talent. Yet Molyneaux was keenly aware of his imperfections as an actor. He needed more training and stage experience but knew he would have to seek such opportunities outside America. He repeated the role of Othello a few times to ready himself for a career abroad. Then "without a friend in the wide world, he worked his way on a vessel to England, determined to there win unhandicapped by race prejudice a success which some day in the future should compel the respect and applause of his now unwilling and, as he thought, illiberal countrymen."

Within a few years of his arrival in England, Molyneaux played several times in the provincial theaters and occasionally in London, but details of his appearances have not been traced. The novelty of another authentic black like Aldridge or Morgan Smith was apparently wearing thin. With emancipation in England and America no longer issues to rally a following, Molyneaux found life very difficult indeed. Doggedly he persevered and had the satisfaction of reading reasonably good notices for his Othello in Britain. Two of these notices were carried without attribution in the *New York Globe* article:

Everyone has heard of the conscientious actor who blacked himself all over in order to do justice to the part of Othello. Mr. Paul Molyneaux has no need to resort to such a device. Nature endowed him with all the physical qualifications—a fine presence, a sonorous voice and last, but not least, a dark skin—requisite for depicting the famous Moor. Nor is he unable to appreciate or incompetent to realize the stormy passions that reigned in Othello's breast. His impersonation was at all times careful and conscientious; it was occasionally very impressive.

The second review in the *Globe* was more enthusiastic and must have greatly pleased the young actor:

> Mr. Paul Molyneaux gave one of the best, if not the best imper- sonation of the Moor we ever saw. The jealousy and anguish were depicted in a manner beyond praise. The whole heart and soul of the actor were thrown into the character and the result was per- fection. Mr. Molyneaux has the advantage of being half caste. The African Roscius (Aldridge) years since played the same char- acter, but we venture to say, not with that finished skill and deep pathos which characterize this gentleman.

The tribute is glowing, but without knowing its source and particu- lars of the production, one hesitates to give it due credit. A tantalizing entry in the *Cleveland Gazette* of November 28, 1885, only adds to the mystery: "Mr. Paul Molyneaux, the colored tragedian, plays Othello, Shylock, Richard III, and many other pieces, and is praised highly by the Eastern press." Again, it has not proved possible to iden- tify where and when these presumed performances took place.

Despite the upbeat tone of much of Mr. Trotter's article, it ended on a somber note, as if he had a presentiment of tragedy. He reported that Molyneaux had written and sent to Boston a small volume en- titled *The Curse of Prejudice; or, A Struggle for Fame*,[15] in which the author "pathetically describes his trials and privations both in America and England while contending for a position as an actor." Clearly, the knocks and rebuffs Molyneaux encountered had scarred his personality. It is therefore grievous but not altogether surprising to read an obituary in the Boston papers of June 1891: Paul Moly- neaux Hewlett, the colored actor, dead at the age of thirty-five from brain trouble. He had returned to America two years previously and was living with his brother in Washington, D.C., when he died.

Molyneaux's story suggests two further reasons why black actors are drawn inescapably to Othello. Success in that role alone, which has proved so difficult for some of the most seasoned actors to attain, seems necessary to legitimize the black performer's admission to the professional ranks of the Western dramatic stage. The role of Othello has stood as a formidable barrier that must be surmounted before the black actor can gain entry into the profession as a recognized artist of serious dramatic ability. Another reason for the fascination of Othel- lo can be deduced from Molyneaux's personal experience. The hatred Iago bears for Othello falls in the category of "motiveless malignity."

Although Iago tries to find reasons for his hatred, such as his belief that Othello has cuckolded him or that his general has promoted Cassio above him, these motives lack conviction and are soon discarded in the villain's single-minded pursuit of the Moor's destruction. Is it not possible that Iago's irrational malice typifies for blacks the senseless color prejudice they experience in their daily lives? And might not the production of *Othello* with a black actor as the Moor be seen as an opportunity vividly to convey to audiences the message that racism is the green-eyed monster that destroys not just its victim but also its perpetrator and innocent bystanders who fall in its clutches? Paul Robeson may have had such an interpretation in mind when he called the play "a tragedy of racial conflict."

Before we leave Paul Molyneaux Hewlett, a remarkable coincidence surrounding his name deserves passing reference. As is well known, the first American to rise to eminence in international boxing was Tom Molineaux, an ex-slave from Virginia who went to England in 1809 by way of New York. Within a year of his arrival in London, Molineaux secured a fight with the reigning champion, Tom Cribb, which he came within an ace of winning, confounding all predictions of his early defeat. The fight lasted thirty-three rounds, and, though he was beaten, it gained Molineaux a place in pugilistic history. Now, as we have seen, the first Afro-American actor of repute arrived on the New York scene around 1821 and was named James Hewlett. To find, later in the century, a young man named Paul Molyneaux Hewlett, who came of a boxing family and embarked on a stage career, seemed too coincidental to be the workings of mere chance. A search of available records in order to discover a link between the ancestors of Paul Molyneaux Hewlett and the two notable black achievers of the prize ring and the stage has failed to establish any logical connection. The following anecdote must therefore suffice to illustrate the courage, poise, and magnanimity of our would-be thespian. There is humor, too, in the incident, which will tend to mitigate the gloom of Hewlett's thwarted ambitions. The story comes from the *New York Age* of December 17, 1877:

> [Hewlett] was wont to wear an exceedingly broad-brimmed hat, which was not over-becoming to his small face. One day while walking along a street in Cambridge, Mass., a large and muscular young man remarked as he passed Mr. Hewlett: "Shoot the hat" or words to that effect. Mr. Hewlett was angered, and turning

abruptly around, walked up to the offending gentleman and said: "Look here, sir, I bought this hat and paid for it with my own money. It suits me first rate, and if you have anything to say about it, say it to me." The gentleman said not a word, but replied by doffing his coat, the import of which was plain to Mr. Hewlett. The latter gentleman also put himself in fighting trim and the encounter began in dead earnest. After some minutes, Mr. Hewlett got up off his man in the gutter, gave him his address, and invited him to call on him if he needed anything further. The gentleman in the gutter finally succeeded in getting himself together and wended his way home. The next day he called upon Mr. Hewlett at his home, informed him that he was heavy-weight champion at Harvard College, but was so pleased with Mr. Hewlett's style of fighting that he desired to be instructed by him. This is the same Mr. Hewlett who so successfully played Othello before a Boston audience (assuming the title role) with white support and who is now studying in Europe.

One is left with the uncomfortable feeling that had Paul Molyneaux followed in the steps of his father, he might have enjoyed a successful and lucrative career as a boxing coach. Instead, he came under the spell of Shakespeare and, given the conditions of his time, died prematurely of frustration.

3
No Place Like Home

IN AMERICA, THE DECADES immediately following the Civil War witnessed a flurry of activity in black theater. The scourge of slavery was gone and the period of Reconstruction, short-lived as it turned out to be, seemed to promise a redress of past wrongs and a steady movement of black folk toward full citizenship. Had not the influential Harriet Beecher Stowe predicted that "if slavery is destroyed, one generation of education and liberty will efface these stains"? Naive as that prediction was, black leaders were determined to prove her right. In every walk of life, the black press sought and found what their editors, journalists, and critics called "Negro progress." Thus, a writer in the *New York Globe* of January 26, 1884, could begin his review of a theatrical performance in the following manner:

> It is necessary for us in the establishment of a proper position in the American government to enter every field of activity and to show by our works aptitude, capacity, and ability equal to that shown by others. The higher the intellectual work we undertake the more conspicuous and honorable our success therein. Now it is acknowledged that proficiency and success in the dramatic art are the hardest possible of all accomplishments, requiring as they do a combination of all the natural and acquired forces of civilization.

On the established professional stage a new era of Shakespeare production was underway. Led by Edwin Booth, who in 1864 had assumed theatrical management in order "to bring out several of the

Shaksperian [sic] plays in a superior manner,"[1] a number of out-standingly competent white actors appeared regularly in cities and towns across the country. They set standards for acting and produc-tion that their black counterparts felt impelled to emulate to the extent that their talents and resources permitted. The only problem was, of course, that doors to the professional theater were closed to aspiring black actors. They could appear in minstrel shows in which they copied the caricature of black life portrayed by white actors in blackface, or as singers and dancers introduced to give a ring of au-thenticity to the ubiquitous Uncle Tom shows that toured the coun-tryside, but on the professional stage Shakespeare's Moors continued to be acted by whites in burnt cork.

Black actors who wanted to play Shakespeare in America had two roads open to them. They could become one-man or one-woman im-personators, as James Hewlett had done a half century earlier, or they could form their own black companies and establish a theater of their own as Mr. Brown had done with his Mercer Street enterprise. The former route is hardly satisfying to the actor who needs the full complement of a company and the interplay between characters in conflict within a physical environment in order to realize the full po-tential of a role. The latter route costs money, which few blacks of the time could provide, and in any case, its financial returns are problem-atical. Yet there were those who would not be discouraged.

Numerous black drama groups sprang up in cities across the na-tion. New York had at least ten such groups; Chicago had four; Phila-delphia, the District of Columbia, and San Francisco had three each; Providence, Baltimore and Louisville had two each, while at least a score of other cities contained black theater companies at some time in the last two decades of the century. Boston had a colored Shake-speare Club that met to read and discuss the plays, one of their mem-bers holding the office of "critic." New York also supported its first colored opera company, which was directed by the multitalented musician and tenor vocalist Theodore Drury.[2]

These groups, amateur or semiprofessional, presented dramatic plays as opposed to minstrel, vaudeville, and variety shows, which were the common fare of touring black professionals. Occasionally one would find a professional actor leading a company of eager ama-teurs. Some groups apparently were established for a single produc-tion, and consequently their names fade thereafter from the records;

others existed over several years. Four groups—in Brooklyn, New Haven, Philadelphia, and Washington, D.C.—named themselves after Ira Aldridge, thus testifying that his reputation was well recognized in black communities in America in the nineteenth century. About nine of these troupes presented Shakespeare, often in truncated versions, sometimes only as selected scenes. The plays most often produced were *Richard III* and *Othello*, with *Romeo and Juliet, Macbeth, The Merchant of Venice, Hamlet,* and *Julius Caesar* following in that order.

The most distinguished of all black troupes performing Shakespeare in this period was the Astor Place Company of Colored Tragedians in New York. This company, not yet named, first appeared in 1878 when Benjamin J. Ford, a waiter by profession, and his wife, Hattie E. Hill, presented *Richard III* with an all-colored cast at the Lyric Theatre on Sixth Avenue. There is no further mention of the troupe until 1884 when, under its new name, the company secured the Grand Central Theatre in Astor Place, near Broadway, for rehearsals and announced its intention to produce *Othello*, followed by *Macbeth* and *Romeo and Juliet. Othello* was presented on June 17, 1884, at the Brooklyn Atheneum before an audience of three hundred. Ford looked the part of the Moor, but his performance was disappointing; he lacked passion and his diction was faulty. Hattie Hill did not appear in this production. They must have quarreled and were still not reconciled in September of that year, at which time she denied in a press report that she was engaged to perform with Ford in John Banim's tragedy *Damon and Pythias* and in *Richard III*. The new leading lady was Alice Brooks, an octoroon who made a pretty and pleasing, if inexperienced, Desdemona. With the exception of newcomer J. A. Arneaux, who as Iago carried the show, the cast was undistinguished. Arneaux would later take control of the company as its principal tragedian and become the leading colored Shakespearean actor in America for the next several years.

Arneaux was born in Georgia in 1855.[3] His mother was a colored woman and his father, a white Parisian. He attended public school in the South before moving to New York, where he studied Latin, German, and other subjects. At the Berlitz School of Languages in Providence, Rhode Island, he mastered French, coming first in his class. He then went to Paris and took courses at the Academy of Belles-Lettres. Returning home, Arneaux appeared as a song-and-dance artist at

Tony Pastor's Metropolitan Theatre on Broadway and at the old
Globe Theatre. His first role on the legitimate stage was as a southern
planter in an original drama entitled *Under the Yoke, or, Bound and
Free* by the black playwright John S. Ladue, which was staged in 1876
at the Third Avenue Theatre, New York. In February 1884, Arneaux
announced the formation of a colored dramatic company under his
direction to prepare a new romantic play for presentation at the
Twenty-third Street Theatre. This project was abandoned, however,
and by April he had joined the Astor Place Company, playing Iago to
the Othello of Benjamin Ford.

Under Arneaux's management, the *Othello* production moved to
several theaters in the city, playing at the Eighth Street Theatre, at
Coney Island, and at the Cosmopolitan. In August the company was

J. A. Arneaux

racked by insolvency and internal discord and seemed on the point of disbanding. The *New York Globe* reported that "the supes, soldiers and other members of the company demand cash in advance. So how the 'businesslike manager without a dollar' can do this puzzles those who have tried."[4] Arneaux was not one to concede defeat readily. In October he appeared at the Lyric Hall supporting Miss Henrietta Vinton Davis, the leading elocutionist of the race, in selections from Shakespeare. His acting was generally applauded, although his voice was called "too effeminate." The following month, Arneaux revived the Astor Place Company and appeared with them at the Academy of Music in a hastily rehearsed production of *Damon and Pythias*, both he and Ford turning in weak performances in the title roles.

Conditions improved in the next two years. The company presented *Othello* and *Richard III*, their old standbys, at a number of venues in New York, including Steinway Hall, the Academy of Music, and the Lexington Avenue Opera House. Arneaux also performed in Providence, Rhode Island, and in Philadelphia, using local amateurs as his supporting players. By November 1885 his company had performed *Othello* sixteen times. As Richard of Gloucester, Arneaux attained his greatest triumph. Critics, black and white, were unanimous in their approbation. The *New York Freeman* of November 6, 1886, wrote of his Richard: "He has improved wonderfully, his voice more clear and his full force of expression and artistic skill surprised his most sanguine friends. The mantle of Aldridge has at last fallen upon worthy shoulders. His creation was excellent and had his support been as strong as he, they would need no other vocation than the profession for a livelihood." In playing Richard, Arneaux modeled himself on Edwin Booth, then the leading Shakespeare actor in America, but with an important difference which is explained in the following extract from a review in the *North American*:

> His walk, for instance, was something peculiarly his own, and if it apparently lacked the silent dragging of the foot of the generally translated, morose and cruel Gloster, its rather flippant step was in accordance with his well-sustained theory that Richard was a villain whose humors rapidly changed from wicked to jocose. It was in this spirit of merriment that Mr. Arneaux made Richard take the audience in his confidence by a lightness of phrasing after each of his gravest deeds that showed the insincerity of Richard's good professions. The idea is a novel one and

most effective. The evenness of Mr. Arneaux's performance, and his accurate recital of the lines, deserve great praise and showed earnest and careful study.[5]

In addition to Richard of Gloucester and Iago, other Shakespeare roles played by Arneaux were Romeo and Macbeth. In 1886 admiring colleagues and friends presented him with a testimonial reception and banquet in witness of his "persistent and successful efforts in placing the histrionic ability of our people upon a basis never before attained in our history."[6]

Arneaux was a journalist and newspaper editor as well as an actor-manager. He was a correspondent for the *New York World* and the *New York Sun*, both white papers, for which he wrote feature articles about black affairs and leading black personages. He was also on the staff of the *Literary Enterprise*, a black paper, of which he became proprietor, changing its name to the *New York Enterprise*. When in 1886 his office burned, he suspended publication of the paper. The next year he prepared and printed his own version of *Richard III* for amateurs and "to render it suitable for the drawing-room as well as the stage." He shortened the script by cutting speeches of subordinate characters like Tressel and the Earl of Derby and by reducing the length of some of Gloucester's soliloquies. Repetitive scenes such as those in Crosby Palace were collapsed into a single one. He introduced a break in the fifth act to give Richard time to change into full battle gear. For the battle itself, he used "several officers of the contending armies who systematically fence upon the stage to do away with the hideous hilarity of untrained supernumeraries who always excite laughter in the best regulated companies by their ridiculous parrying with battle axes."[7] The text of *Richard III* is seldom produced intact, and Arneaux was not the first nor the last to try to improve upon it. His effort surely did not deserve the hostile reception it got from the *New York Dramatic News*: "In his preface . . . he modestly classes himself with Cibber and the immortal bard, and then he states that he has simply smoothed the rough edges of Shakespeare. Ye gods! Imagine a colored gentleman hailing from the classic region of Sullivan Street 'smoothing the rough edges of Shakespeare'! By the way, I wonder if Mr. Arneaux used a razor on the text?"[8]

With his paper defunct, Arneaux was torn between continuing his profession as a newspaperman and pursuing his financially precarious avocation as an actor-manager of Shakespeare. He received offers of partnership from political associates who urged him to revive the paper, but he postponed doing so, since he was reluctant to give up the stage and knew that it was impossible to pursue both careers simultaneously. By January 1887 he had come to a decision; he announced that he would retire from the stage for a period of two years, during which time he would undertake intensive training for a full-time professional career. He planned to enter the Grand Conservatory of Music and Elocution in New York to study acting and stage diction. An 1887 biographical sketch of Arneaux reports that he did enter and graduate from the conservatory "where he gave diligent and ardent study for the purpose of completing his preparations for the stage," but he could not have stayed there for more than a year. In August 1888 he was in Montreal, Canada, seeking to recover from a condition of vertigo that had been troubling him for several months. Then in December he left for Paris, France, to complete his studies before, as the *New York Age* of January 18, 1890, put it, "entering upon continuous work in his chosen profession."[9] He was still in Paris ten years later, but whether or not he had a stage career while he was there could not be confirmed. His plans had called for him to return to America after training in Europe, but although his imminent arrival was announced in the press in 1891 with the additional intelligence that he planned to form a company to produce a play written for him in Paris, no further record of his appearances in this country has been traced.

As an actor of Shakespeare, Arneaux was on the stage for a period of under five years, yet his reputation was well on the way to becoming soundly established. He was obviously a highly literate man, possessed of a keen intelligence and a driving personality. By dint of arduous study and unflagging application, he quickly overcame the awkwardness to which the inexperienced actor is subject, especially in performing classic roles. By the time he left America, he had performed Shakespeare with all-black companies in New York, Brooklyn, Providence, Philadelphia, and Baltimore. He had encouraged and inspired other black actors by his example and by working with them in support of their productions. He had awakened the appreciation of black audiences for Shakespearean drama and he had demonstrated to a new generation of Americans that the time had come to admit the black actor to the legitimate dramatic stage.

Arneaux was but one of an impressive array of black actors and actresses who strode the boards in America during the closing decades of the last century. Chief among those who aspired to dramatic honors in Shakespeare, in addition to Arneaux, were Benjamin J. Ford, Charles Van Buren of Albany, Alice M. Franklin of Middletown, Connecticut, R. Henri Strange and B. Franklin Webb of Philadelphia, Hurle Bavardo of Baltimore, Charles Winter Wood of Chicago, Powhatan Beaty of Cincinnati, and Henrietta Vinton Davis, whose adopted city was Washington, D.C. Some of these were devoted amateurs who acted out of love for the legitimate drama while they pursued other salaried careers. Some were semiprofessional; they received a fee for performances but did not work frequently enough to make a living wage as actors and therefore had to supplement their earnings at other occupations. A few like Henrietta Vinton Davis were fully professional. Known as readers and elocutionists, they traveled constantly from city to city performing on weekends and on festive occasions at black churches, community halls, and public auditoriums, frequently as part of a musical and dramatic program organized by either a lyceum or a literary society or presented as a fund-raising activity for a church or charitable institution. They recited Shakespeare and other well-known dramatic and lyric pieces as solo artists, sometimes dressed in costumes appropriate to the roles they were impersonating. Occasionally some actors would come together to present selected scenes from Shakespeare in a regular theater, or they might be incorporated into a troupe of amateurs who were producing one of Shakespeare's plays and needed an experienced performer for the principal role. A brief survey of the activities of the leading black actors of this era will demonstrate the range of their performances.

Benjamin J. Ford first appeared in the 1878 production of *Richard III* at the Lyric Theatre in New York, when he played Gloucester to the Lady Anne of Hattie E. Hill. He performed regularly with the Astor Place Company, which he founded and managed before handing the leadership over to J. A. Arneaux. He took the part of Othello to Arneaux's Iago in several revivals by this company and also appeared as Richard III with it, eventually relinquishing the role to the more scintillating Arneaux, who made it his favorite part. After the Astor Place Company disbanded, Ford moved to Albany in 1888 and continued to perform with local amateurs in a number of popular nineteenth-century romantic melodramas such as *Ingomar* by Mrs. Maria Lovell and *Damon and Pythias*. Ford was felt to be the best Othello of his day, although he was often overshadowed on stage by the ever-popular Arneaux as Iago.

In Albany, Charles Van Buren was Pythias to Ford's Damon at the Academy of Music in 1888; he appeared in the romantic drama *Michael Erle, the Maniac Lover* in 1889 and in the 1890s played the title roles of Othello and Oroonoko. He was supported in these productions by groups of amateurs who, in the latter two plays, were white. His characterization of Othello, according to reports, far surpassed the expectations of the audience, some of whom were so surprised at the spectacle of a black actor playing the lead in an otherwise white company that they could not refrain from uttering nervous titters during the show. Van Buren also played Iago in scenes from *Othello* that were presented at the Albany A.M.E. Church in 1907.

The *Colored American Magazine* of January 1907 reveals that Professor Van Buren claimed to be distantly related to such disparate notables as Alexandre Dumas and Crispus Attucks. He was born in Washington County, New York, and at an early age evinced a skill in elocution. While at work in his father's barbershop he found time to cultivate his acting talent. He made Shakespeare his special study and was fortunate to have some of the best tutors in his histrionic efforts, among them Professor Charles Dennis of Oxford College, Father O'Reilly of the American College of Rome, and Herman Lind of Berlin. What combination of circumstances enabled Van Buren to receive instruction from these gentlemen is not known. In addition to his acting ability, Professor Van Buren was also musically accomplished. When he moved to Albany in 1881 he became a teacher of music and it was then that he was honored by the Albany Musical Association with the title of "Professor." His public stage appearances no doubt exceed those mentioned above, but no others are reported in available records.

Alice M. Franklin came from Middletown, Connecticut. Before she was twenty, her debut performance was announced at the Adelphi Hall in New York on September 24, 1885, "in Shakespeare and other dramatic and tragic recitals." She had trained in Miss Hunt's Dramatic School in New York, completing the course with distinction, and had spent the previous summer giving recitals at popular resorts to laudatory press notices. At Adelphi Hall her program consisted of a number of well-received humorous selections and two dramatic pieces, including a scene from *Romeo and Juliet* and the curse scene from *Leah, the Forsaken*, another nineteenth-century romantic melodrama which had been adapted from German by Augustin Daly. From the short account of her performance on this occasion, it appears that Miss Franklin was of pleasing appearance and possessed a strong rather than a flexible voice. She had a keen sense of the ridiculous and the art of infecting others with the same spirit. The reviewer felt that with more study and a greater attention to moderation she would soon rank among the foremost in her profession.[10] Further engagements followed in the weeks ahead, and Miss Franklin added more scenes from Shakespeare to her repertoire. Within a few months one critic wrote elatedly of her performance: "Miss Franklin throws her soul, as it were, into her work and trusts her fortunes to time, which will certainly place her within the much-coveted field of fame."[11]

Despite such commendation, Miss Franklin felt the need for more intensive professional training and decided in June 1886 to enter a theater school in Paris. At a farewell benefit performance in her honor at the Lyric Hall on Sixth Avenue, New York, she was assisted by J. A. Arneaux, who played Romeo to her Juliet in a scene from the play. Eighteen months later she returned to the United States, having completed her course of study. Again teaming up with Arneaux and with the actor Hurle Bavardo, she presented scenes from *Othello*, *Hamlet*, and *Macbeth* as well as the curse scene from *Leah, the Forsaken* at the Wilson Post Hall in Bavardo's home city of Baltimore on December 28, 1887. Her performance was well received, her reviewer affirming that "Miss Franklin has a better stage presence and knows more about stage business than any of her female contemporaries. . . . [She is] in the category of those who are destined to become fixed stars in the dramatic firmament."[12] A career of great promise seemed to beckon, but it never materialized. The Astor Place Company, the single professional troupe where she might have found a place, was about to close, and Miss Franklin seemed unprepared for the arduous peripatetic life of the solo elocutionist. In 1890 she made an abortive trip to Kingston, Jamaica, to join the Tennessee Jubilee Singers, who were then traveling through the West Indies, but she was back in America a short time later complaining of the unsuitability of the Kingston climate. A touring folk-singing troupe is hardly the most appropriate company for a neophyte Shakespearean. Reporting on her premature return, the *New York Age* commented: "Miss Franklin is one of the most accomplished of our dramatic artists, a woman of beautiful personal appearance and engaging manners, and if she ever once gets fairly started on the legitimate stage, I have no doubt will make a splendid reputation. The pioneers among us have so many obstacles to encounter and overcome that we often faint and fall by the wayside."[13] These words proved prophetic. A year had hardly passed before the same paper reported that Miss Franklin, after several years of study and training for the stage, had become so disgusted with the precarious nature of her work that she had decided to abandon the theater altogether.

Philadelphia, where American theater had flourished since the days of Murray and Kean, produced in the last century Morgan Smith and two other black Shakespeare actors: R. Henri Strange and B. Franklin Webb. Strange was a native of Virginia but was educated in Philadelphia and lived there. He graduated in 1880 as valedictorian of his class, displaying an aptitude for elocution. Although his parents held strict religious views, his love of theater was so great that he began a serious study for the profession under the tutorship of an old actor named Kelly. Then he entered the National School of Elocution in Philadelphia, graduating with honors. He had already appeared in a number of major roles before his performance as an "exceptionally good" Richmond in J. A. Arneaux's production of *Richard III* at the Philadelphia Academy of Music on January 28, 1887. In July that same year he played Othello to the Iago of B. Franklin Webb at Atlantic City, New Jersey, in a touring production by the Colored Tragedy Company of Philadelphia, which had been organized and managed by Alex G. Davis, the stage manager for Arneaux's Philadelphia debut performance. The overall quality of the performance was acclaimed, and one critic deemed Strange's Othello to be "a very fine piece of work in all its parts" that elicited well-merited applause from the audience. Strange became a favorite reader in annual appearances at summer resorts and in concert recitals on the East Coast. One report has him making his fourteenth annual tour of the Jersey coast.[14] His repertoire included selections of poetry, especially poems of the young black writer Paul Laurence Dunbar and Shakespeare's dramatic monologues. An example of the latter occurs in his program in April 1903 at St. Luke's Parish Hall in Washington, D.C., when he presented nine scenes from *Richard III*.

The colored journalist T. Thomas Fortune, notoriously critical of black actors who had the temerity to impersonate Shakespeare's tragic heroes, felt that Strange was essentially a humorous delineator who could provoke laughter by a wink or a contortion or a tone of voice. "What a man possessing such powers wants to bother with the uncertainties of stratagems and treasons, intrigue and murder, for, except to keep his hand in, I cannot understand," wrote Mr. Fortune. "Perhaps Mr. Strange does not understand it himself. In *Hamlet, Richard* or *Othello* I think Mr. Strange will always have trouble; in comedy he will always have smooth sailing."[15] This view was certainly not shared by other critics. In a tribute to Strange's work that appeared in the *Colored American Magazine* of September 1902, the following sentiments were expressed:

> He received his training . . . in Philadelphia, his home, where he has done more than any one man to develop that city's taste for the classic drama. He has a repertoire of plays that equals that of any star before the public today. He gave Shylock a few seasons ago, with full cast, in one of Philadelphia's leading theatres, and from time to time has given *Othello, The Bells, Hamlet,* and *Richard III.* On the concert stage, Mr. Strange stands without a rival. His reading from Poe, James Whitcomb Riley, Dunbar, and many others proves him the genius that he is.

The praise might be slightly overblown, but Strange's record as a Shakespeare performer is no less distinguished on that account. In 1911 he announced a season of three Shakespeare plays and *The Bells,* to be performed with a strong supporting company of twenty-one actors under the management of Leroy Wilkins of New York City. The Shakespeare dramas were the *Merchant of Venice, Hamlet,* and *Othello.* No further notice appears of this company. The next year Strange played opposite Henrietta Vinton Davis in a production of an original tragedy, *Christophe,* by the Afro-American playwright William Edgar Easton, at the Lenox Casino in New York. Along with the parts listed above, he was also seen as Macbeth and as Cassius in *Julius Caesar.*

Henri Strange was a professional. He had begun his career in 1887 and was still a featured player twenty-four years later when his Shakespeare season was announced. B. Franklin Webb was an experienced amateur of such caliber, judging from the single report of his performance preserved in the records, that he has earned a place among the notables. His performance as Iago in Strange's 1887 production of *Othello* is substantial proof that amateur status need not be synonymous with inferior histrionic ability. The *New York Freeman* of July 2, 1887, supplies the following:

The attention of the audience was rivetted in the remarkable and exceptionally brilliant Iago of Mr. Webb. This young man is an actor in the very broadest sense, and we have not seen the deep villainy imbedded in the character of Iago more thoroughly portrayed by any one. There were blemishes and crudities, as a matter of course; but taken all in all, the work was done with as much thoroughness and finish as if Mr. Webb had been a professional. . . . The audience was moved in an unusual degree by the splendid acting of Mr. Webb, and hated him thoroughly for the neatness with which he accomplished the destruction of the happiness of the confiding Othello. It is a pity that a young man with the dramatic ability possessed by Mr. Webb should be compelled to squander his time and talents in amateur work at odd times when he could easily make a fortune for himself and the enterprising manager who would give him a proper opportunity as a professional.

It can be presumed that neither the manager nor the opportunity appeared, for there is no record that Webb subsequently embarked on the glorious professional acting career befitting his demonstrated talent.

By contrast, Hurle Bavardo of Baltimore, Maryland, was one of the first professional black actors to receive significant notice in a New York trade paper. Costumed as Othello, his figure adorned the front page of the *New York Dramatic News and Society Journal* of May 8, 1883. The news item carried with this picture reported that Bavardo had made a study of Shakespeare and intended to give public readings and recitals. In fact, he had already made his acting debut two years earlier at a dramatic and operatic concert that took place at Chickering Hall in New York on May 31, 1881. On that occasion he had erroneously dubbed himself "the only colored, talented and cultivated Shakespearean in America," but unfortunately his later performances failed to sustain that grandiose title.

Bavardo was, to a large extent, self-educated and, though intelligent and entertaining as a conversationalist, he seemed to lack the rigorous discipline and finely tuned skills required of a truly professional actor. He also suffered from the most dreaded of all histrionic afflictions—a faulty memory. When he appeared with Alice Franklin in the balcony scene from *Romeo and Juliet* at the Academy of Music in Newark in 1885, he was "entirely unfamiliar with the part" as well

Hurle Bavardo
as Othello, 1883

as "unnatural and heavy."[16] Forming his own dramatic company for the occasion, Bavardo mounted a production of *Othello* in Baltimore in May 1887, but the most that the reviewer of that performance would commit himself to saying was that Bavardo was "up to the standard." When, however, he was back in Baltimore later that year in the company of J. A. Arneaux and Alice Franklin to present scenes from *Othello*, *Hamlet*, and *Macbeth*, he was quite outclassed and his Othello was ranked very poor. He forgot most of his lines, was not helped by having an inexperienced prompter, and his total performance was such a complete disaster that the critic feared it might cost him his reputation.[17] Subsequently, at the Zion A.M.E. Church in Boston in October 1890, Bavardo again embarrassed himself and disappointed his audience because he appeared out of costume and his pieces were not fully committed to memory. Mercifully, he dropped from the records after this performance, saving us the unpleasant duty of having to report further calamities.

Charles Winter Wood, on the other hand, was a quick study who was blessed with a retentive memory that served him in good stead in at least three crucial moments of his life. Known as the bootblack who became a college professor, Wood was something of a prodigy among Shakespeare actors. At the age of sixteen he already had his own company, had played Othello and Richard III, the latter with great success in Chicago and Detroit, and had been engaged to perform "throughout the West."[18] The circumstances that led to this accomplishment at such a youthful age are worth recounting.

The son of a Methodist minister, Wood was born in Nashville, Tennessee, in 1870. He came to Chicago when nine years old with his widowed mother, and, to earn money, he began to shine shoes, stationing himself at the old Unity Building on 79 Dearborn Street where many young lawyers had their offices. One of these was Jarvis Blume, an attorney who later became a judge. Learning that the young bootblack went to the theater and was fond of Shakespeare, Blume challenged him to learn and recite the ghost scene from *Hamlet* for a reward of one dollar. Blume had picked that scene so that he and his friends could laugh at the failure of the black lad to turn pale at the sight of the ghost. Blume was surprised at the short time that had elapsed for preparation of the scene when three days later the boy appeared with the announcement that he was ready for the test. An audience was assembled and "the tattered bootblack not only gave an excellent rendition of the long speech of Hamlet, but Mr. Blume insists to this day that the negro actually did pale under the strength of his emotions. . . . The delighted lawyers passed the hat and instead of being quizzed the black tragedian pocketed something like $5. That was in 1882, and the boy was about 12 years old."[19]

Mr. Blume arranged to have Wood recite before various small companies and introduced him to Professor Walter Lyman, a teacher of elocution who was so impressed that he engaged Wood as his office boy and agreed to give him daily lessons. By 1886 Wood had organized his own colored company and was producing the two Shakespeare plays aforementioned at the Madison Street Theatre and at Freiberg's Opera House in Chicago, with favorable press notices for his performances in the principal roles. He took a job as a store clerk in the city which allowed him time to pursue his theatrical interests in other towns. His usual partner on these outings was Miss Ada O. Brown, also of Chicago, with whom he appeared periodically in Cleveland and Detroit, but he also performed scenes from *Hamlet* with Henrietta Vinton Davis. Occasionally, too, he would be invited to act the lead in scenes from *Richard III* with a company of white actors. In the frenzy of activity that occurred during 1886 and 1887, Wood could hardly have foreseen the further opportunities that would arise from his recital of Hamlet's ghost speech before the amazed attorneys.

In December 1887, Frank S. Hanson, a wealthy Chicago businessman at whose home Wood had given a reading, offered to send him to college in Beloit, Wisconsin, with tuition and pocket expenses paid. Associated with Hanson in this proposal was Charles L. Hutchinson, who later became president of the Corn and Exchange Bank of Chicago. There was, however, a condition attached to the offer. Hanson, a prominent church member, did not approve of theater as a profession and urged Wood to discontinue his aspirations in that direction and instead prepare himself for a career in the ministry. Eventually it was agreed that Wood would choose between the pulpit and the stage after graduating from college. He embarked for Beloit in January 1888.[20]

Because he was academically unprepared to enter college directly, Wood was first enrolled at Beloit Academy, a preparatory school, where he stayed for almost four years. He was admitted to Beloit College in 1891 and graduated in 1895 with a B.A. in Greek. He distinguished himself in drama and oratory, winning the home and state oratorical contests in 1895 and placing second in the interstate finals, one point behind the winner. About the time of his arrival in Beloit, the college had begun its noteworthy program of annual productions of Greek plays in English under Professor Joseph Emerson, who was succeeded by Professor Theodore Wright. The college's claim that over a period of forty years from 1885 it had sponsored a larger number of presentatons of Greek drama in English than anywhere else in America is probably correct. In 1893 Wood appeared as Heracles in *The Alcestis* and in 1895, his senior year, he was in Sophocles' *Oedipus Rex*, which was "the first play given at the Opera House with tickets at public sale. All the seats were sold in one hour. The drama was given two nights in Beloit and later in Central Music Hall, Chicago, on the present site of the Marshall Field store. Charles

Wood's ('95) rendering of this most difficult role of Oedipus was greeted with tears as well as with bursts of applause."[21] Three years after he left Beloit, Wood was suddenly recalled from Chicago to take over the role of Alcestis when a student who was cast in that part fell ill just before the opening date. Once again Wood's quick-study aptitude saved the day.

On his return home from Beloit and in deference to his patron's wishes, Wood entered the Chicago Theological Seminary, from which he graduated in three years with the doctorate in divinity. It seemed as if the classical actor had indeed opted for the ministry, but his passion for the theater would not be denied. After only a few months at a pastorate in Warren, Illinois, Wood accepted a position at Booker T. Washington's Tuskegee Institute, where he taught English, drama, public speaking, and became director of the Tuskegee Players. If he were not to make his living on the professional stage, at least he could practice his craft within the respectable walls of academe and convey his love of Shakespeare and the classics to the young black students whom he instructed. (He was also Tuskegee's first football coach, having played the game at Beloit as an undergraduate.)

Wood remained at Tuskegee for almost four decades, during which time he delivered public speeches and gave recitals in his travels on behalf of the institute. In his appearances he began to incorporate folktales from the South along with his standard repertory from Shakespeare and other well-known writers. He billed himself as "the celebrated impersonator, humorist, orator and scholar." At least twice his tenure at Tuskegee was interrupted. He went to Columbia University on scholarship and took a master's degree and, on another occasion, he took leave to join the cast of the only Broadway play that seemed to combine in a single production his devotion to teaching, his love of theater, and his own deep religious conviction. He had once shared the stage in Chicago many years previously with Richard B. Harrison in a production of *Damon and Pythias*. When that actor was chosen, in 1930, to play the principal role of De Lawd in Marc Connelly's *The Green Pastures*, Wood was invited to become his understudy. For five years Wood stood in the wings waiting, without having the opportunity to perform any of the major roles for which he was a standby. Then on the fateful afternoon of March 2, 1935, as an expectant audience was filing into the Forty-fourth Street Theatre in New York City, Harrison collapsed in his dressing room. He was not

Charles Winter Wood

to recover. For the third time in his life Wood was called upon to perform at short notice and was equal to the task. The play ran for an additional six weeks with Wood as the star, and he was finally able to secure the critical acclaim for his mature acting talent that he richly deserved.

Following Richard B. Harrison in this part was no simple matter. Writing in the *New York Times* of Charles Wood's performance, Brooks Atkinson made this point and went on to say:

He is playing the role like a man who respects the destiny that has descended on him. He is of slighter build than his noble predecessor; his movements about the stage are a little nervous. But the lower tones of his voice, which he is learning to use, have the calm resonance of a shepherd of believers. Although he has not yet had time to fill the vast measurements of the part and does not sustain in every scene the grave deliberation of a great, lonely, sympathetic figure, his playing is firm with sincerity. Particularly in the most compassionate scenes when the play gives him its best support—like the march into the Promised Land—Mr. Wood has the character "The Green Pastures" requires of its people.[22]

When this production closed, Wood returned to teaching at Tuskegee, at Bennett College in North Carolina, and at Florida Agricultural and Mechanical College. In his later years he devoted his energies to organizing and developing dramatic clubs in southern black colleges in conjunction with Professor Randolph Edmonds and others. He retired in 1949 after a professonal teaching and acting career of over half a century and died at his home in Queens, New York, four years later. In 1946 Beloit College established in his name a full tuition scholarship to be held by a worthy student of his race, while Florida A. & M. University named a theater after him. "Charles Winter Wood, Negro tragedian," wrote the *Afro-American Ledger* of Baltimore, "possesses the true dramatic gift and if he were white he would be the star of some fine tragedy."[23] Wood never became the fine interpreter of Shakespeare that his early stage career had promised. Destiny led him in another direction. Yet his passion for great dramatic literature and his dedication to teaching doubtless had an influence on his students that was equal to or surpassed that of any professional actor of his time. And he enjoyed a brief moment of glory on his beloved stage, not in Shakespeare, it is true, but in one of the most exalting roles of the modern drama, one that had tremendous appeal to audiences of all races.

With Powhatan Beaty of Cincinnati we confront a man with an extraordinary background for a Shakespeare actor. Under the caption "The Western Garrick," his story was published in the *New York Globe* of May 3, 1884. Beaty was born in Richmond, Virginia, and was taken to Cincinnati in 1849. He attended school there and made his first public appearance at a school concert. Later he was apprenticed to a colored cabinetmaker who had an extensive furniture business. Because of his known interest and talent, Beaty continued to receive instruction from several teachers, including James E. Murdock, a white professional actor from Philadelphia who had retired to his farm in Ohio after a distinguished stage career. Murdock became known as a fine acting coach and had written a book on vocal culture.

When the Civil War broke out, Beaty was one of the first blacks to report to Ohio Governor Todd for duty, despite the Cincinnati may-

or's cutting rejection of colored volunteers with the words, "This is a white man's war and no niggers need apply." Beaty was appointed First Sergeant of Company G, 5th U.S. Colored Troops. The *New York Globe* story sums up his military exploits.

At New Market Heights, Company G entered the field with 83 men and 8 commissioned officers. It came out with 15 men and Sergeant Beaty in command. The rest were ready to come home on their shields. Once more they were ordered into the fight and when Sergeant Beaty emerged with his remnant of twelve men and himself, a noble thirteen, General Butler complimented him on the field and awarded him one of the five medals given for distinguished bravery. Again, at Fair Oaks, Beaty acquitted himself so grandly that he was complimented in general orders to the Army of the Potomac. Congress subsequently voted him a medal to be struck at the Philadelphia mint. Twice he was recommended by Col. Shurtlief for a commission but it never came. He passed through thirteen battles and many more skirmishes without receiving a scratch, though the bullet holes in his clothes testify to many narrow escapes. He was mustered out as brevet lieutenant.

Beaty came home to his trade and continued to study privately for the stage. Of a generous nature, he was always ready to put his talent at the service of others and he began to give public readings for charitable causes. In 1876 the citizens of the town gave him a complimentary testimonial at which he performed with the best local talent, but no details survive of that exhibition. He wrote a play entitled *Delmar, or Scenes in Southland* which was privately produced in 1881 with him in the lead role of a rich southern planter. Although the play was favorably received, it did not move into the public theater and Beaty was too modest to promote it himself.

By 1884 Beaty had become assistant engineer of the Cincinnati waterworks. He continued to perform at every opportunity. When, in January 1884, Henrietta Vinton Davis was booked to appear in Cincinnati, Beaty joined her in a grand dramatic and musical festival which was a huge success. As a result of this collaboration, he was invited to participate with Miss Davis in a Shakespearean production in Washington, D.C., which will be treated more fully later. For the present, two excerpts from reviews of Beaty's performance in Cincinnati appeared in the *New York Globe* article and are reprinted here. The first comes from the Cincinnati *Commercial*:

> The finest part of the entertainment was reserved for the last—the selections from Macbeth. The scenes rendered include the murder of Duncan, and were well calculated to test the dramatic power of the actor. Miss H. V. Davis made a magnificent Lady Macbeth and Mr. Powhatan Beaty as Macbeth threw himself into his part with masterly energy and power.

The second review, though not of a Shakespeare play, is even more revealing of Beaty's histrionic powers. He had performed the part of the Roman slave Spartacus in *The Gladiator*, a blank-verse melodrama by Robert Montgomery Bird that was one of the most popular plays of the early nineteenth century. The review appeared in the *Colored Patriot*:

> Mr. Powhatan Beaty's rendering of Spartacus was a gracious surprise. It has been some time since we heard that gentleman, but we were not prepared for the evidence of study and cultivation he manifested. All the emotions of the piece were depicted in his countenance and when he actually changed color and his face blanched with pallor, we could scarce realize it. Powerfully built, rugged and strong in his general appearance, he looked every inch a Roman gladiator. The audience leaned forward and eagerly listened to catch every word of his impassioned delivery, and when he finished they fell back into their seats with a sigh of relief that plainly expressed how they had been affected. Mr. Beaty is indeed a grand artist and has wisely selected the tragic muse for the shrine of his artistic devotion.

Beaty will next be heard of at Ford's Opera House in Washington, D.C., then in Philadelphia. On both occasions he was supporting Miss Davis, who had arranged these performances. Among Afro-Americans, she was the premier elocutionist and interpreter of Shakespeare's heroines, the one artist who devoted herself totally to the stage over a considerably longer period than any of her contemporaries.

4
From Artist to Activist

NONE OF THE PREVIOUSLY mentioned figures working in America compiled a stage record as prolonged and consistently meritorious as Henrietta Vinton Davis. Her career encompasses all of the promise, high expectations, and frustration experienced by black actors of her generation. She had prepared herself thoroughly for an acting career and devoted most of her adult life to the profession. She served her apprenticeship as a solo elocutionist and as a dramatic performer in scenes with other actors. She directed plays in which she took the principal role, and she traveled extensively from one end of the country to the other, winning national recognition for her skills as an interpreter of classical roles. When all of these efforts failed to gain her a place in a recognized professional company, Miss Davis joined the Marcus Garvey movement and dedicated the rest of her working life to the uplift of her race.

Henrietta Vinton Davis was born in Baltimore, Maryland, in 1860. Her father, Mansfield Vinton Davis, was a talented musician who died shortly after his daughter's birth. At the age of fifteen she graduated from school in Washington, D.C., having already displayed an aptitude for elocution. Then, after passing the required examination, she became a teacher in one of the Maryland public schools, moving from there to a higher teaching position in Louisiana, where she remained for some years. When her mother became very ill, Miss Davis returned to Washington to be near her and took a job as copyist in the office of the Recorder of Deeds. It was during the time she held this position, from 1878 to 1884, that she made a decision to pursue a career on the dramatic stage and began to prepare seriously for the profession.

Miss Davis became a student of Marguerite E. Saxton, a white woman and an esteemed elocutionist of Washington who, upon discharging her trainee at the conclusion of her studies, wrote the following inspiring letter: "My dearest Pupil: I shall watch with the keenest interest your future career. You have studied diligently, faithfully; you have talent, youth and beauty; in fact, all the qualifications essential to success, and I have, I think, a right to feel proud of you."[1] Later Miss Davis continued her training with Edwin Lawrence of New York City and Rachel Noah of Boston, where she also attended the Boston School of Oratory. Her professional debut as a public reciter took place at Marini's Hall in Washington, D.C., on April 25, 1883. On hand to introduce her was the man under whom she then served in the Recorder's Office, Frederick Douglass, the leading black statesman of the age. It could not be a more auspicious start to what seemed a long and brilliant career on the concert platform and the legitimate stage.

Miss Davis had been advertised as "the first lady of her race to publicly essay a debut in Shakespeare and other legitimate characters." Her recital program included speeches of two of Shakespeare's heroines—Juliet and Portia. Clearly elated with this new evidence of racial progress and proud to support a local resident, the *Washington Bee* rhapsodized:

> She came forward and from the time she said her first line to the close of the last sentence, she wrapped the whole audience so close to her that she became a queen of the stage in their eyes. One moment all was serene and quiet, deep pathos, —the next, all was laughter. . . . She is our first American lady reader, she will in due season become our star on the stage of tragedy and the drama.[2]

Miss Davis opened in Boston on July 17, 1883, appearing at the Young Men's Christian Hall on Boylston Street. Supporting her on the program were two Boston artists, the soprano Adelaide G. Smith and Samuel W. Jamieson, a pianist. She had acquired professional managers, James M. Trotter and William H. Dupree, who announced a touring schedule immediately after her Boston engagement. It covered a number of towns and cities in the eastern states. The Boston correspondent of the *New York Globe*, writing of her performance there, recognized Miss Davis's potential as an actress but was less enthusiastic about her impersonations. He thought she would make a stronger impression in scene work with other actors than in solo recitations. A few weeks later at the Bethel A.M.E. Church in New York, Miss Davis scored a resounding success, her commanding presence and deep sonorous voice reminding one reviewer of Charlotte Cushman, first lady of the American stage. As Juliet, in the potion scene from *Romeo and Juliet*, she was "so true to the concept of a truly great artist as well as to nature, that the audience, electrified by the beautiful acting and the elocution of Miss Davis, applauded her to the very echo."[3]

By the end of her first season of performances, Miss Davis had achieved a marked improvement in her readings. She had added speeches of Rosalind in *As You Like It* and Cleopatra in *Antony and Cleopatra* to her repertoire, and expressed her desire to appear next season in a regular stage production supported by a full company of

Henrietta Vinton Davis

actors. This ambition seemed close to fulfillment with the announcement that Miss Davis had been engaged by Thomas T. Symmons, manager of the recently formed Bohemia Dramatic Club, to appear at Whitey's Opera House, Detroit, on April 14.[4] The club had quickly acquired an enviable local reputation, and Mr. Symmons, a baritone soloist who subsequently took over Miss Davis's management and became her husband, planned to put his company on the road in a new drama with her as leading lady. There is no evidence that this project ever materialized. Miss Davis continued to build her reputation in frequent appearances around the country. One year after her Washington debut the *New York Globe* commented on her development as an actress:

> Miss H. Vinton Davis has shown undoubted talent as a delineator of Shakespearian characters. Her conceptions are rich and original, while her stage presence is graceful, easy and natural. In humorous delineations she shows to good advantage, but her strongest forte is in characters like Lady Macbeth and Juliet. This artist is yet in her youth and has plenty of room in which to rise to an honorable position.[5]

On an earlier visit to Cincinnati in 1884, Miss Davis had teamed up with Powhatan Beaty in scenes from *Macbeth* and *Ingomar, the Barbarian*. The occasion was a testimonial dramatic and musical concert in honor of Miss Davis, and the affair, presented to a crowded audience in Melodeon Hall, was a huge success. The local newspapers, black and white, had been lavish in their praise for both principals: Miss Davis was a colored lady of considerable talent who made a magnificent Lady Macbeth while Beaty, as Macbeth, "threw himself into his part with masterly energy and power." When, in their other selection, he entered as Ingomar, arrayed in a wolf-skin lap robe, "and cast himself at the feet of Parthenia and in heavy tones implored her to tell him what love was like, there wasn't a dry eye in the house."[6]

This collaboration worked so well that Beaty was invited to participate in an ambitious production at Ford's Opera House in Washington, D.C., on May 7, 1884. The program consisted of three scenes from *Macbeth*, *Richard III*, "which was performed almost entirely," and a scene from *Ingomar*. Miss Davis played Lady Macbeth, Lady Anne, and Parthenia; Beaty was Macbeth, King Henry VI, and Ingomar. Completing the company that was specially assembled for the performance were a number of local amateurs, among them W. R.

Davis as Gloucester (afterwards King Richard), William H. H. Hart as the Earl of Richmond, and selected students from Howard University. Citizens and soldiers were supplied by the Washington Cadet Corps. Directing the production was Marguerite Saxton, the elocution teacher who had coached Miss Davis. The Opera House, seating more than 1,100, was filled to capacity with an audience of both races. Frederick Douglass and his family occupied a private box.

As may be expected, the black press were generally ecstatic in their reviews of this noteworthy production taking place in one of the principal dramatic houses of the capital, the very theater, in fact, where Lincoln, the Great Emancipator, had been fatally shot. There seemed to be something historic in the event beyond the mere performance of a group of Afro-Americans made up of one professional actress, some experienced amateurs, and raw students in scenes from Shakespeare in the nation's capital, less than twenty years after the declaration of freedom. The *New York Globe* of May 17, 1884, commenced by saying that the three principals covered themselves with glory. It went on to discuss the performances of the leading actors:

As Lady Macbeth, Miss Davis displayed wonderful powers of conception. While we failed to discover in her acting the dull, heavy, declamatory style complained of by some critics, to me it was plainly apparent that Miss Davis has great reserve dramatic powers, which have not been drawn upon because of the influence that always somehow represses the spontaneous outflow of genius in beginners. . . . Mr. Beaty would compare very favorably with many white actors I have seen. He possesses the art of losing sight of self, and the impression he would make, and seems to be entirely absorbed in the part he takes, as though it were real and not theatrical. The perfect adaptation of Miss Davis to her chosen profession is undisputed. She has earned the plaudits of professional critics, and her success has opened the dramatic door to many. Thus leap by leap the colored man and woman encroach upon the ground so long held sacred by their white brother and sister.

Some voices in the black press noted the disparity in quality between the seasoned players and the beginners. The performance of W. R. Davis, for instance, who was making his first stage appearance, was justly criticized: "He recited Gloster's [sic] soliloquy in a manner which would be discreditable to a schoolboy ten years old."[7] However, as the scene progressed, he gained in confidence and strength. Referring to notices in the white press about the production, one reviewer comforted the players with the argument that they should all feel highly flattered because they were not being criticized as colored people nor as beginners. Instead, they should regard such criticism as a compliment, since every paper had discovered among a few faults great merit in the budding actors and actresses.[8]

Another area of weakness was the fencing scene between Richard and Richmond. It provoked such tumultuous jocularity that it almost ruined the whole evening. It is perhaps only fair to point out that the heckling in this scene and at other parts of the evening's performance came primarily from a section of the white audience. The reputable *Washington Post* gives an illuminating description of the atmosphere in the Opera House during the show:

> There were many white people in the house who seemed disposed to turn to comedy the tragic efforts of the actors. In this they were not wholly successful, for the earnestness and intelligence of several of the leading performers were such as to command the respect of those most disposed to find cause for laughter in everything that was said or done. . . . The scene from *Macbeth* went creditably, all things considered, Miss Davis and Mr. Beaty showing a knowledge of the requirements of the parts which they essayed which, it is safe to say, surprised those in the audience competent to judge. The most enjoyable thing of the evening was *Richard III*. Here the "guying" disposition of the audience found ample opportunity to vent itself, although the title role was not badly filled by Mr. W. R. Davis, while Mr. W. H. H. Hart's Richmond was a most creditable performance for an amateur. . . . The combat between Richard and Richmond waked the most derisive plaudits from the auditors, and "Time" was repeatedly called by particularly irreverent individuals.[9]

More than sixty years had elapsed since the African Company in lower New York was harassed by white spectators and forced to give up playing Shakespeare. The reception accorded these black Shakespeareans in Ford's Opera House showed how little had changed in the mental attitude of a certain class of white theatergoers, who refused to accept black performers in serious dramatic roles. W. R. Davis did not allow the hostile reception of his debut performance to dissuade him from the theater. He formed a company of amateurs and in a few years was presenting scenes from *Othello, Richard III,* and *Julius Caesar* at Richmond, Virginia.

A word should also be said about the future career of William H. H. Hart, the amateur who played Richmond. He was at the time a student at Howard University, although he was older than most undergraduates, for his age is given as twenty-eight. From his notices, he comes across as an intelligent, personable, and ambitious man slated for a professional career: "an excellent personage. He acted with ease, grace, and elegance. . . . His elocution was rich and showed a broad culture. If he would devote his attention to the drama he will press closely on some of the leading white tragedians of the hour." Hart chose not the stage but the study of law, a close parallel in terms of elocutionary demands. He applied for admission to some of the best law schools in the Washington area but was uniformly rejected. In his anguished humiliation, he addressed a letter to Dr. J. C. Welling, president of Columbian College (now George Washington University), which reads, in part:

> Desiring to study the science of the law, I find that on account of my color the National University Law School will not admit me. The Georgetown University Law School excludes Negroes and women, and the Columbian University Law School closes its doors in my face. The authorities of the Columbian University have done me a great wrong, and the law ought to furnish me a relief from it. But your friends have the ears of justice, they have wealth, intelligence, power, position and everything upon their side except reason, except the divine teachings of Christ, except benevolence, except blind, exact and severe justice, and except that jewel of the Anglo-Saxon heart—fair play.[10]

Hart returned to Howard University, where he took several more degrees. He earned the Bachelor of Laws, Master of Laws, and Master of Arts. He became a professor of criminal law at Howard, an assistant librarian of the Library of Congress and dean of Howard's department of agriculture. In 1897 he founded the Hart Farm School for dependent children.

Hart decided against the theater, but Miss Davis persevered. Over the next ten years she continued to give concert performances in an ever-widening circuit of cities, touring the South and West in addition to eastern states. A committee of twenty representing the citizens of Chicago presented her with a gold star in recognition of their esteem and admiration at a musical and literary entertainment given for her benefit.[11] Appearing before a mostly white audience in Evanston, Illinois, she held them "spellbound by the intensity of dramatic truthfulness she displayed" and was called "the most talented artist on the American stage."[12] In North Carolina, the Goldsboro *Argus* hailed her as "the greatest living genius of her race. . . . Her prodigious memory, her graceful control of every thought, word and action, her powerful delineations and her compass and modulation of voice are truly wonderful."[13] There were renewed calls for her to be accepted into a regular company presenting Shakespeare and other dramatic classics. The *New York Freeman* found it singular that none of the brilliant musical and elocutionary exponents of the race had so far obtained a footing on the legitimate stage and cited lack of money as the principal drawback. It urged some public-spirited individual of means to take an interest in Miss Davis's career.[14] All that was necessary to the fullest development of her dramatic powers, wrote the Boston correspondent of the *New York Freeman*, was an opportunity to be heard by the great devotees of the drama through free access to the competitive arena.[15] T. Thomas Fortune, writing in the *New York Age*, included Miss Davis among a few colored women actors who could achieve fame and fortune on the regular stage if only she could find a sponsor.[16]

All appeals were in vain. Henrietta Vinton Davis, despite her manifest excellence as an actress, was unable to gain admission into the ranks of legitimate theater companies, then exclusively under white management, because of her color. This racial boycott not only denied her professional fulfillment but deprived the theater itself of a superbly talented actress whose art might have enriched the lives of countless playgoers. The irony of the color bar as it applied to this actress is that Miss Davis was herself light complexioned and not noticeably different from dozens of other actresses on the professional stage of inferior ability but without the stigma of African ancestry. A description of her physical appearance occurs in the Buffalo *Sunday Truth*:

> Miss Davis is a singularly beautiful woman, little more than a brunette, certainly no darker than a Spanish or Italian lady in hue, with illustriously expressive eyes and a mouth moulded upon Adelaide Neilson's. She has a rich, flexible and effective voice which she well knows how to manage, and her use of the

English language is not only excellent but exemplary. She is not only an elocutionist but an actress of very decided force, as she demonstrated in selections from *Romeo and Juliet*, particularly in the potion scene, a piece of work we have rarely seen excelled. We could not help thinking what a magnificent Cleopatra she would make to a competent Antony. She has made the part a study, we have been informed since seeing her in Association Hall, and hope to view her in it some day. Her reading of *Mary, Queen of Scots* was also very fine and elicited much applause.[17]

Miss Davis appeared only once with J. A. Arneaux's Astor Place Company, in its rather hurried and indifferent production of *Damon and Pythias*. That was in 1884, the year after her debut. The next year she was billed to play Desdemona to Beaty's Othello in a colored dramatic company being organized in Cincinnati, but there is no mention of the production in available records, and it is doubtful whether it ever occurred. Then in 1893, after ten years of continuous concert recitals, she was again seen in a full-scale production of a dramatic play. Her marriage to Symmons had apparently come apart (he was once arrested for wife-beating while drunk), and she had gone to live in Chicago where, in addition to her concert appearances, she began to offer classes in elocution. She became acquainted with an original drama about the Haitian revolution written by William Edgar Easton. Titled *Dessalines*, the play is an old-fashioned romantic melodrama of lofty sentiment that deals with the struggle between the mulattoes and the recently freed blacks for control of Haiti. Dessalines saves Clarisse, sister of one of the mulatto leaders, from death; his ferocity is tamed by her innocence, and, as the blacks celebrate their victory in battle, the couple realize they are in love with each other. Miss Davis recruited a company and produced the play, taking the role of Clarisse herself. It was presented in Chicago and may have toured to other cities. In 1898 she again appeared in a full production of an original play, this time one that she helped to write. This was a five-act drama of the South entitled *Our Old Kentucky Home*, written in conjunction with the black journalist, John E. Bruce. In it Miss Davis had the part of a Creole slave, Clothilde, whose courageous attack on a fort helped to bring about the end of the Civil War and reunite her with her lover, one of the freed slaves who had enlisted in the Union army. The show played in eastern cities with marked success.

When, two years later, it was announced that Miss Davis had signed for *The Country Coon*, a musical farce comedy written by Ernest Hogan with Allan Dunn, one could sense that her situation was becoming desperate. Hogan was one of the leading minstrel and vaudeville comedians, famed for his song "All Coons Look Alike to Me." He was billed as "the unbleached American" and had recently returned from a successful trip to Australia with Curtis's Afro-American Minstrels. Now he was about to start a new company playing musical farce-comedy. It was the last place one would look for an artist of the caliber of Henrietta Vinton Davis. She had done everything that could possibly be expected of a dedicated actress to maintain the integrity of her art, which was devoted to the interpretation of dramatic masterpieces; now in utter frustration she was reduced to playing in the popular music hall. She had presented a range of Shakespearean characters—Juliet, Lady Macbeth, Cleopatra, Ophelia, Portia, Desdemona, Lady Anne, and Queen Elizabeth—as well as other tragic heroines from the nineteenth-century drama—Calanthe, Mary Stuart, Leah, and Parthenia. The privilege of presenting these roles in their entirety had been denied her, but the dramatic monologues and selected scenes she was permitted to perform were done to universal acclamation. Now she would play what? It is reassuring to report that the production didn't come off, the comic business doubtless finding a place in Hogan's spirited vaudeville repertoire where it belonged. The experience of performing in a coon show could well have been soul-destroying for her. Instead, she journeyed to Indianapolis in May to appear in a spectacular pageant of "The Negro" which was staged by Charles S. Sager for charitable purposes. There were scenes from the South at the time of the freedom proclamation and at the royal court of Dahomey where the queen (Miss Davis, one presumes) receives the ambassador of the United States and presents an entertainment in his honor. Then Miss Davis was back on the concert circuit, extending her itinerary to the Northwest and West Coast, where she stayed for some three years before returning to her adopted home city of Washington, D.C.

In 1903 she revived *Our Old Kentucky Home* in Denver and again played Clothilde, recited at the Palm Garden in New York in 1908, and staged a new production of Easton's *Dessalines* at the Trinity Congregational Church, Pittsburgh, in 1909, when she doubled in the roles of the flower girl Zingarella and the comic Dominique. The final major production in which she appeared, according to available rec-

Henrietta Vinton Davis as Pere L'Avenge in William Edgar Easton's **Christophe,** *1912.*

ords, was a second original drama by Easton, who returned to the subject of the Haitian revolution in *Christophe: A Tragedy*, focusing on another of the black generals who led the successful slave uprising. Miss Davis produced this play at the Lenox Casino in New York City, opening on March 21, 1912. She played the dual role of Valerie and Pere L'Avenge, appearing opposite the Shakespearean actor R. Henri Strange, who took the title role. She had been acting continuously for nearly thirty years.

Having grown up under the influence of Frederick Douglass, who had been a neighbor and family friend as well as her employer in the office of Records and Deeds, Miss Davis was well aware of the current political issues as they affected the condition of black folk in America.[18] In 1892 she had expressed her support for the Populist party in a letter to one of its leaders, Ignatius Donnelly, and had volunteered to lecture on its behalf. In 1912–13 she traveled to Jamaica (West Indies), Panama, and Costa Rica, accompanied by the contralto soloist Nonie Bailey Hardy, to give a series of performances, and she became involved in benevolent social work with the local populations. The Jamaican Marcus Garvey founded his Universal Negro Improvement Association (UNIA) in New York in 1917 and Miss Davis must have watched the growth of this mass movement with considerable interest. The exact date when she joined is unknown, but by June 1919 she held the important offices of national and international organizer and later that year she became a director and vice president of the ill-fated Black Star Line, one of the cornerstones in Garvey's program for uniting all peoples of African descent. Miss Davis remained among the movement's top leadership for several years, traveling to Jamaica and Liberia in its behalf. She did not altogether abandon the theater, for in December 1927 she staged a pageant entitled *Ethiopia At The Bar Of Justice* for the UNIA at the Ward Theatre in Kingston, Jamaica. The pageant must have been well received, for it was revived in April and November of the following year. All told, Miss Davis's work with Garvey's movement spanned twelve years and represents the longest tenure of any prominent UNIA officer except for Garvey himself. She died in 1941 in Washington, D.C., at the age of eighty-one.

The *Colored American* of February 22, 1902, provides a fitting summation to the theatrical career of this artist:

Miss Davis is a remarkable woman, and had she not been handicapped by unfavorable racial origin, she would today by virtue of her acknowledged talents take rank with dramatic artists of the Leslie Carter, Maude Adams, Julia Marlowe and Henrietta Crosman school. This thought strikes us, since Washington is so honeycombed with prejudice against the Negro to the point that in few theaters can we secure a decent seat and colored traveling companies cannot secure dates—why could not an enterprising manager organize here a stock company on the order of Lafayette Square and produce plays of current human interest, adapted to the refined tastes of our best people who now refrain from attending the existing theaters because of the unjust treatment they are compelled to endure? The natural head of such an organization would be Miss Davis. With such a versatile artiste, capable of assuming roles from tragedy to light comedy, and a few other actors as a nucleus, a stock company of undoubted drawing qualities could be built up in a season. An adequate theater could be constructed or a suitable hall could be remodeled to serve the purpose at a moderate expense. Now why not a theater for our people as a solution of the embarrassments that now confront us?

The question remained unanswered. Decades would pass before a company of Afro-American actors, capable of playing Shakespeare and the classical drama, would inhabit a theater of its own. When that time came, black actors and producers would feel impelled to focus on an all-black repertory, as if Shakespeare had become irrelevant to the urgency of the times. At the height of her powers as a dramatic actress and Shakespeare interpreter, Henrietta Vinton Davis turned from the stage to politics. In so doing, she hoped to gain for black Americans the equality of opportunity that had been denied her in the profession for which she was so well equipped. Though the Garvey movement failed in its stated objectives, it left a legacy of black self-worth that has continued to fuel demands for a just society. By her dedication to her craft, her achievement as an artist, and her commitment to the improvement of her race, Miss Davis's contribution stands preeminent.

Before turning from the nineteenth century to the new challenges of the twentieth, one may attempt to summarize the experiences of black Shakespeare actors. First, it is noteworthy that these artists approached their craft with total seriousness. Whatever their backgrounds, most actors appreciated the need for professional instruction and often at great sacrifice underwent periods of training to improve their skills before embarking on their careers. Some even returned to acting school for additional training after they had been performing professionally. Next, it is clear that in the last century the professional American theater considered no black actor or actress eligible to play a name character in any of the regular productions of Shakespeare with white companies. That there were qualified black performers is unquestionable; thus the reason for their exclusion was simply their color. Shut out from the legitimate stage, black actors could either become solo elocutionists or team up and present cuttings from Shakespeare, which is how most of them survived, but neither of these options is wholly satisfying to the dramatic artist. Or the black actor could seek his fortune in a foreign land as several of them did: Aldridge, Smith, Molyneaux, Arneaux. Or they could retire altogether in frustration as did Alice Franklin.

Whether they stayed home or went overseas, black Shakespeare actors faced an enormous hurdle which was seldom if ever imposed on their white counterparts. That hurdle required them to make their stage debuts in leading Shakespearean roles without serving a period of apprenticeship in subordinate roles with a reputable company, since no company would have them. That so many black actors, faced with this enormous obstacle, still persisted and survived their debut performance as Othello or Richard or Hamlet or Lady Macbeth is in itself an achievement of a kind. Why then were there so few all-black Shakespeare companies in which black actors could find a home? And those that did exist, why were their life spans so short? Answers readily come to mind.

As previously shown, white audiences in America were unwilling to accept blacks in dramatic portrayals. Toward the close of the century the *Washington Post* gave its opinion on this issue:

It is doubtful if the Negro will ever shine in the Shakespearean drama, excepting possibly the character of Othello. It seems more probable that if the Afro-American proves acceptable in serious roles he will develop a drama of his own, and not content himself with wearing the secondhand attire of the Anglo-Saxon stage. Undoubtedly there are depths and phases of Negro life and character which have never been adequately portrayed in play form, not even in "Uncle Tom's Cabin."[19]

The writer was correct in calling for a black drama of more complex characters, but to suggest that Afro-American actors were unfit for Shakespeare (and by extension any nonblack dramatic role) seems in retrospect to be utterly ridiculous. The image of blacks on stage that had been cultivated and promoted through Negro minstrelsy for over half a century had preconditioned white audiences to ridicule black actors in the legitimate drama, including Shakespeare. On the other hand, black playgoers were not numerous enough to sustain dramatic companies and, because of segregated seating in the regular play-houses, those who could best appreciate Shakespeare often chose not to attend the theater. Moreover, the first-class houses that catered to legitimate drama were reluctant to book black productions, citing a lack of audience support. The few black theatrical managers who existed found it more profitable to handle minstrel, vaudeville, or musical shows which had a popular following and could be put on the theatrical circuit with a fair chance of success. Recruiting a company for a vaudeville show was a comparatively simple exercise—an advertisement in a black newspaper would produce a host of eager and talented performers—but finding a group of properly trained black actors to play Shakespeare was another matter. Finally, the cost of keeping a Shakespeare company together without an assured box-office income was prohibitive. From every point of view, the new century promised a bleak future for black Shakespeare actors in America.

5
Challenge of a New Century

ARTICIPATION BY BLACK ACTORS in any type of Shakespearean performance diminished markedly in the early part of the
twentieth century. Several factors are responsible for this decline. First and chiefly, the professional solo elocutionist who was so
prevalent in the closing decades of the previous century had become
anachronistic in the twentieth. Those reciters who remained sought
to join black theater companies and appear in full-scale stage presentations, but few of these companies produced Shakespeare. Another factor was the emergence of black musical comedy and operetta
troupes, which became immensely popular, especially after the success of Williams and Walker's production, *In Dahomey* (1902), which
had a four-year run, including a tour in Britain with a royal command
performance on the lawn of Buckingham Palace. These troupes with
their black-face comedians, scintillating music, singing and dancing
chorus girls, all fashioned around flimsy plots, played to white audiences and were fast replacing the old discredited minstrel shows as
the most attractive type of popular entertainment available in the
public theater. Because these productions offered professional expo-
sure and fairly steady employment, many talented black artists who
might otherwise have chosen the dramatic theater turned instead to
the musical stage.

Another feature of the early twentieth century was the establishment of black stock companies attached to playhouses in major cities around the country. The Pekin Theatre of Chicago, founded in
1904 by the black entrepreneur Robert Motts, the Crescent, Lincoln, and Lafayette theaters in Harlem, and the Howard Theatre in

Washington, D.C., were only the best known of a growing number of playhouses located in black communities. They accommodated stock companies that performed vaudevilles and musical comedy sketches as part of a live variety program, but no Shakespeare was presented. The Lafayette Players of Harlem, which commenced in 1915, was the most reputable of the dramatic groups. It presented condensed versions of current Broadway successes and revivals of well-known nineteenth-century romantic melodramas, such as Dion Boucicault's *The Octoroon*. The players wished to demonstrate to the public that black actors could in fact perform in straight dramas as competently as their white counterparts downtown. But, again, they never performed Shakespeare. The group eventually dissolved in Los Angeles in 1932, a casualty of the Great Depression.

The advent of the motion-picture industry and the establishment of black film companies also provided new jobs for Afro-American actors. By 1914 it was estimated that there existed in America between 950 and 1,000 licensed motion-picture houses, a substantial number of which were previously vaudeville or playhouses that now offered both movies ("photo plays") and live acts. Thus in the first two decades of the twentieth century the black actor had more lucrative work opportunities in the professional theater than at any previous time in history. Lester A. Walton, dramatic critic of the *New York Age*, remarked on this situation in his column of March 26, 1908: "Thousands and thousands of dollars are made each year by Negro performers. In fact, the stage is today (the temporary presence of hard times being considered) giving the Negro an opportunity to make more big money than in any other form of livelihood."

It must be admitted, however, that while there were more jobs for black performers and attractive salaries for the most talented among them, there was at the same time little change in the attitude of white producers, critics and audiences concerning the roles in which black actors were acceptable. Shakespearean and other serious dramatic characters were taboo; interracial casting was the rare exception rather than the rule, and then only when blacks appeared in servile, comic roles. Indeed, even in musical comedy the tendency of white promoters was to insist on a plantation setting, thus relegating blacks in their stage life to a condition of servitude from which they had been liberated in real life. In this regard, Lester Walton in 1907 reported an attempt made by an Afro-American in New York to place a sizable presentation in one of the large vaudeville circuits. He wished to present a thirty-minute sketch with music and comedy, which would also involve elaborate costumes and stage settings, but he was told by the booking agent: "What we want is a coon act—a darkey plantation act with darkies dressed in old plantation costumes—that or nothing." Walton's comment on this incident is apposite:

Newspaper critics are largely responsible for the pro and con sentiment where the Afro-American actor is concerned. Publicity is a great thing in the show business. Managers make money when their show is given plenty of space and favorable comment. When it comes to putting on Afro-American shows many of the managers, knowing the prejudices of most of the white critics, fail to display any backbone and will collaborate [in] something that they believe will be accepted by critics and public.[1]

Walton cited other instances when white critics decried black productions "because they did not see colored performers with their faces blackened cake-walking and using language of the ante-bellum days, entirely foreign to those on stage, thanks to education and environment, but in accordance with some white man's ideas of what the Negro should be." He reminded his readers that white actors with blackened face have for years assumed black characters in serious parts and done so creditably; and he argued that the black actor likewise should be at liberty to portray characters other than his race, the only criterion being the quality of his acting.[2] It is no wonder that black intellectuals soon began to condemn the comic song-and-dance image that Afro-Americans were forced to adopt in the white-controlled professional theater and to call for the creation of a new black theater that would, in the words of W. E. B. DuBois, "loose the tremendous emotional wealth of the Negro and the dramatic strength of his problems through writing, the stage, pageantry, and other forms of art. We should resurrect forgotten ancient Negro art and history and we should set the black man before the world as both a creative artist and a strong subject for artistic treatment."[3]

According to this program, Shakespeare could wait until the black dramatic actor had established himself securely in his own theater on material shaped from the experiences of his race. Then with the self-assurance and conviction that he had mastered his craft and developed his unique style of performance, untrammeled by the demands of an alien marketplace, the black actor could begin to interpret the great dramatic works of other cultures. The problem with this theory, idealistic as it may be, is that the artistic material based on black heritage was not accessible in dramatic form, but Shakespeare was. As a result, whether they were fully professional, semiprofessional, or amateur, whether close to New York's Broadway theater or away in distant cities, black performers across the land continued to look to Shakespeare as the hallmark of achievement when they sought to establish themselves as serious dramatic actors.

Several fragmentary notices of black Shakespearean productions appear in the period from 1900 to 1916, the latter date marking the tercentenary of Shakespeare's death. A summary of these reports will show that, while black professionals were not allowed to act Shakespeare in the major playhouses, nevertheless a black Shakespeare repertoire was kept alive in different parts of the country by a variety of performing groups. Manuscripts written for the Writers' Program of the Federal Theatre Project in New York in 1939 give a tantalizing reference to a theater group organized between 1900 and 1902 that performed in the auditorium of the Church of St. Benedict the Moor on Fifty-third Street. In his essay entitled "The Negro Theatre Movement in New York," Claude McKay writes that this group presented *Othello* and *Richard III*, but that "this new movement in the drama did not last long."[4] Further substantial evidence of the work of this company awaits discovery.

In 1900 the *Colored American Magazine* carried an article on the Brooklyn-based Greater New York Dramatic Company under the management of A. B. Quetrell and Alonzo Skrine. Quetrell, an 1892 graduate of Norfolk (Virginia) Mission College, was both manager and leading actor of the company, which he organized to present plays "of a prominent character" throughout the state. Among its successful productions up to that time were *Julius Caesar* and *Richard III*.[5] Another Virginian from Norfolk, James C. Stith, an artist and dramatic reader, was characterized in 1901 as an "enthusiastic Shakespearean student [who] has rendered his conception of some of the great bard's characters before the most cultured audiences of the South, notably at Old Point, Virginia, where he appeared as Richard III before the guests of the Hotel Chamberlain."[6] A. L. Harris, born on a farm in Pike County, Ohio, formed the Harris Dramatic Company of Columbus. He managed to secure elocution training in Boston and Chicago and for several years played leading roles with amateur companies in such plays as *Othello*, *Richard III*, *Hamlet*, and *Julius Caesar*. In 1902 Harris wrote a four-act play set in Haiti and organized a stock company of young men to produce it, with the hope of putting it on the road if it proved to be successful.[7] Yet another report of a Shakespeare pioneer comes in 1902 from across the country. C. Henry Tinsley, "one of the best known colored actors on the Pacific Coast," was stage manager of the Shakespearean Stock Company of San Francisco, California. According to the report, Tinsley had few equals among his race in either tragic or romantic acting, his most successful Shakespearean role being Shylock in *The Merchant of Venice*. "He possesses rare versatile talent and is an ardent student in classical literature and the drama," concludes the notice.[8]

About this time black colleges began to encourage play production among their students. As already indicated, Tuskegee Institute had in 1898 appointed a professor of drama and elocution who was himself a classical actor. In 1905 Atlanta University initiated the custom of presenting a Shakespeare play by the graduating class. *The Merchant of Venice* was performed alfresco that year, followed by *The Taming of the Shrew*, *The Tempest*, *As You Like It*, and *Twelfth Night* in successive years. Directing these productions was a colored woman,

C. Henry Tinsley

Mrs. Adrienne McNeil Herndon, who had been invited to teach elocution at the university in 1894. Mrs. Herndon took her assignment seriously. She spent several summers and a winter's leave of absence studying at the Boston School of Expression, completing the course with distinction. At the conclusion of her studies and under the stage name of Anne Dubignon, she gave a one-woman public reading of one of Shakespeare's plays, during which she impersonated twenty-two different characters, receiving generous praise from Boston critics for her performance. On another leave of absence in 1907, Mrs. Herndon entered the School of Dramatic Arts in New York City, where she graduated a year later, winning the Belasco gold medal for excellence in expression.[9]

Mrs. Herndon's pioneer work at Atlanta received new impetus some decades later when Anne Cooke was appointed instructor in English and drama at Spelman College, one of the cluster of colleges that form Atlanta University. Miss Cooke, an Oberlin College graduate who had spent a year in New York at the American Academy of Dramatic Art, launched a series of striking productions with the University Players. *Macbeth, Richard III, The Merchant of Venice,* and *Julius Caesar* were produced as part of the regular season of plays in successive years from 1931 to 1934. When Miss Cooke left Spelman

Atlanta University students in The Merchant of Venice, *1905.*
Percy Williams as Shylock and Fannie M. Howard as Portia.

Adrienne McNeil Herndon

in 1942, she continued her inspiring work, first at Hampton Institute, Virginia, then as professor of drama at Howard University, Washington, D.C. Howard, in fact, had started a dramatic club much earlier, in 1909, and in 1911 the university staged a production of *The Merry Wives of Windsor*, followed in 1915 by *The Merchant of Venice*. By 1921, under Professor Montgomery Gregory, a Harvard graduate, Howard University began offering college credit toward a degree for production work. The objective of this new development is worth noting: "Professor Gregory believes that the Negro can win a broader recognition of his rights and responsibilities as a citizen by demonstrating his ability as an artist. He hopes to train actors and producers who will be able to organize groups of Negro players in some of the bigger cities, and give plays in theatres in and outside Negro districts, catering to both white and colored patrons."[10] Whatever the future might hold for those student actors who aspired to be professionals in the years ahead, college-educated black men and women were coming to grips with Shakespeare on stage at a critical period of their preparation for adult life. This initiation was essential to broaden the potential audience for black Shakespeare.

Not to be outdone by mere college students, the Washington Dramatic Club produced *A Midsummer Night's Dream* in 1912 and the next year staged at the downtown Howard Theatre *The Merchant of Venice* with Nathaniel Guy as Shylock and Mrs. Janifer Taylor as Portia. The records reveal no further productions by this group. In New York, a company of twenty-four talented players was brought together under the direction of Charles Burroughs, himself a Shakespeare reader of repute, to present a Shakespearean pageant for the benefit of the Detention Home for Colored Girls. Scenes from *Macbeth, The Merchant of Venice,* and *Othello* were enacted at Young's Casino in 1912. Burroughs played the Moor with Fred Hogan as Iago; A. L. Halsey took the part of Macbeth, while Minnee Brown was Lady Macbeth. Shylock was played by Fred Hogan with Mrs. Daisy Tapley as Portia. Although the brief report of their performance considered them to be "a proficient company of actors and actresses of the semi-professional grade,"[11] several of the principals were already practiced performers, while others would become career actors in new stock companies like the Lafayette Players.

The two most celebrated black professionals of this period possessed widely different talents but had one thing in common: neither ever appeared in a fully professional production of one of Shakespeare's plays. One was a black-face comedian of exquisite artistry; the other was a dramatic reader of great authority with a finely tuned vocal instrument. The first was West Indian–born Egbert Austin (Bert) Williams of the previously mentioned Williams and Walker Company that flourished from 1900 to 1908. After Walker's early retirement because of ill health, Bert Williams was invited in 1910 to join the Ziegfeld Follies. He remained with the show for eight seasons as the only black actor in an otherwise all-white company. Offstage Williams was a tall, well-poised, handsome and sensitive figure with clear, eloquent diction, but in performance he became the slouching, inept, dialect-speaking Negro known as the "Jonah Man" for whom everything went wrong. With infallible timing and pausing, shifts of emphasis, subtle irony, and wryly spoken asides, he succeeded as singer, dancer, and comedian, although he had had to work hard to acquire these skills. "Art knows no color line," wrote the *New York Age* of April 30, 1908, "and it is simple justice to say that our stage has no white comedian so good as Bert Williams."

Williams was one of the most highly paid stage artists in America,

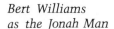

Bert Williams as the Jonah Man

yet he was known to express regret at never having a role in a straight dramatic production. When, however, at the top of his profession he was asked by the theatrical impresario David Belasco to consider appearing in a dramatic play, he was overcome by diffidence and gave as an excuse that he was still under contract to Ziegfeld. Hard as it may seem, this was probably a wise decision. A professional of Williams's standing would no doubt be expected to appear in a major dramatic role. If in Shakespeare, he would be required to make the transformation from the droll clown that he had played all his life in a contemporary style to a tragic or romantic hero of classical proportions. The burden might have been too much to carry. The nearest Williams came to Shakespeare was in a travesty sketch of *Othello* that was presented in the Follies of 1916 in honor of the Bard's tercentenary. The *New York Times* review of the show made special mention of Williams: "You should see the scene from 'Othello' with Bert Williams not to be outdone by any Frank Tinney as the Moor. He chokes his Desdemona (who has been flirting with one Vernon Cassia) till he is tired and then beats her with a sledgehammer, but it only irritates her. . . . This is the only amusing moment in the Shakespeare revue."[12]

At his death in 1922, Williams was universally mourned. There was a profound feeling that the theater had lost a great star, and for once the word "genius," applied to him in obituary notices, seemed well merited. Along with the posthumous praise there was sober reflection. Several writers echoed the sentiments of the *Literary Digest* of March 25, 1922, when it wrote under the headline "Genius Defeated By Race": "There was a tragedy in Bert Williams' career. The Negro comedian who has just died at less than fifty achieved a high position on the American stage, but not the position he craved, nor the one he felt his talents best fitted him to fill." Perhaps W. C. Fields's comment on Williams's career said it best: "He is the funniest man I ever saw and the saddest man I ever knew."[13]

Unlike Bert Williams, Richard B. Harrison was a practiced Shakespearean reader who never had the chance to perform his favorite characters in professional productions. Harrison was born in 1864 in Ontario, Canada, the son of fugitive slaves who had fled there from the United States. As a boy he was noted for his poetry recitations for which he won prizes at school. He liked going to the theater and would save up his earnings as a newspaper delivery boy in order to buy tickets. When he was seventeen, his father died and, as the eldest male child, he took on the responsibility of family provider. He began working in hotels in Windsor, Ontario, and then moved to Detroit where he was a bellhop at Russell House and other inns. Occasionally he would receive free passes to the local theater and opera and was able to see such actors as Henry Irving, Edwin Booth, and Lawrence Barrett performing the classics. Harrison began to memorize the parts he had seen acted and he so impressed Charles Hull, a theater manager, that he worked to get Harrison accepted as a student of elocution at the Detroit Training School of Art. He graduated from this school in 1887.[14]

Attempts to gain employment as an actor in a professional company failed, but Harrison began to give public readings, including in his repertoire selections from Shakespeare, narrative poems, and dialect pieces. Besides Shakespeare, his preferred author was the Afro-American poet Paul Laurence Dunbar, one of his closest friends. Income from his readings was never adequate and he often went penniless and hungry. He began to work as a railroad porter and once, on the Santa Fe line, he was befriended by a railroad official who got him hired as a reader with a Lyceum Bureau in Los Angeles. Performances for the bureau took him on tour to the southern states, Canada, and Mexico where he appeared on lecture platforms and in churches and colleges.

That these tours were anything but glamorous is evident in Harrison's own report of his experiences at the time: "Sometimes I found myself walking miles from one town to another because the committee in charge did not take in all their receipts before time for me to leave." Nevertheless, the rewards were also memorable, even though they could not be measured in monetary terms:

> The strangest thing about it all is not that I dared to do it, but that I got audiences of my own race and kept them awake while doing Shakespeare—taking all the parts, moving from side to side of the stage or hall without letting people see that I was moving, holding them without any let-ups between bits of dialogue. I did that for twenty years all over this country, keeping at the last, seven plays and more than 100 recitations in my mind.[15]

In 1923 Harrison was a drama instructor at the Agricultural and Technical College at Greensboro, North Carolina, from where he made trips to New York to give readings in Harlem churches and schools. When in 1925 Garland Anderson held a backers' audition in

*Richard B. Harrison receiving the Spingarn Medal from Herbert H. Lehman,
lieutenant-governor of New York, March 22, 1931.*

Richard B. Harrison as De Lawd in The Green Pastures, *1930.*

New York for his new play, *Appearances*, which was to become the first full-length dramatic work by a black man on the Broadway stage, it was Harrison who read the script to an audience of six hundred guests in the grand ballroom of the Waldorf-Astoria. On one occasion Harrison accepted a brief engagement at the Lafayette Theatre in a slight melodrama titled *Pa Williams' Gal* by Frank Wilson. He was spotted by a casting agent who recommended him for the only major role he ever had in a regularly produced play. And what a role it was! When Richard B. Harrison walked onto the stage of the Mansfield Theatre in New York City that wintry evening in 1930, it was in response to one of the most stupendous entrance cues ever uttered in the history of the theater. The Angel Gabriel appeared at a fishfry before a large crowd of picnickers and announced in commanding tones: "Gangway, gangway, for De Lawd God Jehovah!" As the critic Brooks Atkinson wrote subsequently in the *New York Times*, "Who could meet the challenge of imposing words like those?" Mr. Atkinson continued:

> We soon found out. For just at that moment Mr. Harrison stepped quietly from the wings in the black frock coat and white bow tie of a country preacher and with a look of paternal benignity. He stood there like a man apart from the common breed. Although his speech was familiar his manner was slightly reserved; he conducted himself like one who understood completely and expected to take full responsibility. He lost none of his artless

majesty by personal association with the creatures of heaven and earth, for he was set apart by grace. We shared his emotions; we regarded his judgments as final. Our hearts weeped when the sin of the world grieved him, for we believed in him implicitly. That was a glorious performance on the opening night of the play.[16]

Harrison was De Lawd in the all-black production of Marc Connelly's *The Green Pastures*, which played to 2 million patrons for 1,657 performances over a period of five years. He was sixty-five years old when cast, and he never missed a performance. Eventually, when the production returned to New York in 1935 after a four-year national tour, his health broke. He was simply worn out by overwork. No other actor in America, it was alleged at the time, could have played the part of De Lawd without creating a suggestion of irreverence. Harrison received many honors. He was granted honorary degrees by several colleges and in 1931 was awarded the Spingarn Medal, which is given annually by the National Association for the Advancement of Colored People for the highest achievement by a black American. On the occasion of the award presentation, W. E. B. DuBois commented: "By the breadth of a hair and half-turn of a phrase, by a gesture and a silence, [Harrison] guided a genial comedy into a great and human drama."[17] Harrison, who Marc Connelly once said possessed the humility of a great artist, was never heard to complain of the circumstance that forbade his appearance in a professional production of Shakespeare with the leading players of his day, but it was clearly his major unrealized ambition. One is left to surmise what this tremendously affecting actor might have done with a Prospero, a Shylock, a Lear, or, in his younger days, a Hamlet or Coriolanus. Richard B. Harrison was not allowed to play Shakespeare on Broadway; he died playing God.

April 23, 1916, marked the three-hundredth anniversary of Shakespeare's death. The occasion, celebrated in theatrical capitals around the world, generated a spate of Shakespearean productions and exhibitions in New York early in the year. The *New York Times* devoted six special supplements to Shakespeare, there were three home-grown professional productions of *The Merry Wives of Windsor*, *Macbeth*, and *The Tempest* respectively in the city, while visiting English and German companies also offered seasons, along with college productions by New York City College and Fordham University. The festive spirit inspired an ambitious production of *Othello* by an all-black cast that opened appropriately on April 24 (the 23rd being a

PROGRAMME

The Elite Amusement Corporation

LAFAYETTE THEATRE

EUGENE ELMORE, Manager

7th Ave. & 131st St.

Phone : 1811 Morng.

EDWARD STERLING WRIGHT

Presents His Own Company in

William Shakespeares Immortal Drama

" OTHELLO "

UNDER the DIRECTION of R. VOELCKEL

In Five Acts

Under the Personal Stage Direction of A. C. WINN

DRAMATIS PERSONNEL

Duke of Venice...Joseph Aloston
Brabantio, a Senator...P. A. McDougal
Grathianos..,..............Oliver Foster
OTHELLO, The Moor................. ....Edward Sterling Wright
Cassio, his lieutenant...................... ....Otto Foster
Iago, his ancient....... .... John H. Ramsey
Roderigo, a Venetian gentleman................................... Frank Brown
Montano, Othello's predecessor in the government of Cyrus,....I. H. Whiteman
Desdemona, daughter to Brabantio, and wife of
        Othello............ ....Marion Toney
Emelia, wife of Iago..... ....: ....Vincent Bradley
      Sailors, Messengers, Heralds and Officers

SYNOPSIS OF SCENES

Act I — Scene I A Street in Venice—Midnight
    Scene II A Street
    Scene III The Senate Chamber
Act II   The Castle at Cyprus
Act III   Scene I A room in the Castle
    Scene II A Street
Act IIII   A room in the Castle
Act V   Desdemona's Bed Chamber

Selections by

LAFAYETTE LADIES ORCHESTRA

Under The Leadership of Miss Marie Lucas

Overture......" Othello " from G. Verdi's Opera " ....Theo. Tobani
Selection......" Carmen '' from George Bizets Opera............ "   "
En Tre - Act......" Dance of the Hours " from Ponchielli's Opera
    b)   Thelma...... Intermezzo....... ....Neil-Moret
Selection, " Three Dances," from Henry VIII,...................Edward German
    Exit - " Broadway Fox Trot "..Wm. Jones

Next Week " THE WOLF "

Another Big Broadway Production

TWO SHOWS DAILY

MATINEE 2:15   NIGHT 8:15

SUNDAY

Continuous Big All Star Vaudeville

And Photo Plays

Playbill for Edward Sterling Wright as Othello at Lafayette Theatre, Harlem, 1916.

Sunday) for a short engagement at the Lafayette Theatre in Harlem. The company consisted of Shakespearean students and college graduates, few of whom had had much practical stage experience. Their leader, Edward Sterling Wright, was no novice, however. He had graduated from a school of oratory in his native Boston, where he was known for many years as a lecturer and song recitalist. In 1916 he held the position of dramatic lecturer for the New York City Board of Education. The production, with Wright in the title role, was staged by A. C. Winn, a white director and stage manager for the Harlem-based theater who had worked previously with the Lafayette Players.

One of the visiting English companies under Sir Herbert Beerbohm Tree, a renowned Shakespeare actor, was then playing a repertory season in New York. Tree and other dignitaries were invited to attend a vaudeville bill at the Lafayette on Sunday night, during which it was proposed to stage an act from *Othello* in his honor. However, a Sunday law that permitted vaudeville houses to open but prohibited appearances in costume with stage scenery made it impossible to pre-

Edward Sterling Wright

sent the act as planned and forced Wright to substitute a solo recital of the accusation scene before the Venetian Senate, which he performed in evening dress. After the performance Tree addressed the audience on Shakespeare and discussed the character of Othello, complimenting Wright on a powerful reading of the Moor.

The Lafayette performance of *Othello* was reviewed in three columns in the *New York Age*.[18] The production was felt to be on the whole meritorious, although there was room for improvement, partly due to the inadequate time allowed for rehearsal. A packed audience was sympathetic and appreciative. The stage settings, especially designed for the show, were beautiful if somewhat unorthodox for Shakespeare; costumes, however, were rich and historically correct. Lighting effects were fine, and a ladies' orchestra under Miss Marie Lucas rendered appropriate music. Of the principal actors, Wright, a short man, compensated for his lack of physical stature by his keen intelligence. His line readings were clear and illuminating, while his interpretation of the diverse phases of the Moor's character showed careful study. Desdemona was charmingly played by Miss Marion Toney, who also delivered her lines clearly and with understanding, although she lacked the requisite power called for by the role and evinced some slight awkwardness in the use of her hands during emotional scenes. John H. Ramsey was a clever and crafty Iago who excited an audible response from the audience in his diabolical plotting, while the Emilia of Vincent Bradley (a stage name for Mrs. James Allen of Boston) "reached the heights of emotional stress that thrilled and vitalized the people into spontaneous outbursts of applause." Mrs. Allen was one of the few members of the cast with previous experience as both an actress and a playwright, having several original plays to her credit.

Lest it be thought that this review in a black Harlem newspaper was too uncritical to give a true assessment of the production, it is appropriate to cite part of the notice that appeared in the *New York Clipper* of May 6, 1916:

> The Elite Amusement Company, with Eugene Elmore as house manager, has something to feel proud of in the production of *Othello*, as given by Edward Sterling Wright and his players last week at that house. Also A. C. Winn, the white stage director of the theatre, can say that he has accomplished something in producing this production with an entire negro cast. . . .

Othello was produced after only two weeks of rehearsal by a company of novices. The players were astonishingly capable and the performance, considering the difficulties that faced the actors, needed litle improvement.

Miss Vincent Bradley, as Emilia, the wife of Iago, was a revelation and her death scene in the fifth act was nothing short of remarkable. To say that her work as a whole was excellent would be putting it mildly. . . . When she entered the bedchamber after the murder of her mistress the actress rose to an emotional height that would have gained the same thunderous applause had she been playing to a sophisticated Broadway audience.

The *New York Tribune* noted that in spite of the fact that the players were amateurs, the performance itself was by no means amateur and there were scenes "when even the most supercilious critic would have forgotten to find fault." It hoped that the courageous Mr. Wright "will be able to play *Othello* at the head of his own company in an extended tour through cities where there are theatres for the colored race."[19] After a week's engagement at the Lafayette Theatre, Wright did take his youthful company to Boston, back to New York, and then to Philadelphia.

By the time they opened at the Grand Opera House in Boston, the players had obviously settled into their parts, for the reviews were very encouraging. One interesting comment concerned the possible dilemma faced by an all-black company in presenting a play whose plot rests on color distinction:

The audience wondered a little at first how they were going to recognize Othello when he made his appearance. As it turned out, there was no difficulty. Mr. Wright's make-up as the Moor was as unmistakable as Sir Henry Irving's or Salvini's, or Sothern's. He followed traditions of the part in the cut of his beard, and somehow, as the play wore on, you got the impression that he came nearer to the ideal that Shakespeare had when he created the part than a good many distinguished actors have come.

It wasn't merely that his make-up was genuine. The character was equally genuine, and in this fact and in Mr. Wright's capability lay the real merit of the performance. . . . His acting throughout was finished and efficient, and in the final great scene in which Othello murders the fair Desdemona, he rose to a height of dramatic acting that was more than ordinarily dramatic.[20]

Other actors—John H. Ramsey as Iago ("hardly the passionless, intellectual Iago of Edwin Booth but on the whole a more likeable villain") and Vincent Bradley as Emilia ("she made a great Emilia")—came in for their share of honors in Boston. Marion Toney as Desdemona fell short of her illustrious predecessors, but even she moved through the play with grace and sweetness of expression and altogether made a pleasing picture. The next week the company performed at the York Theatre, Lenox Avenue, New York City, and the week after that at the historic Walnut Street Theatre in Philadelphia, where they were hailed as the only Shakespearean production in the city during that anniversary season. Margaret Brown, replacing Marion Toney as Desdemona, was simple, appealing, and effective. The settings for the show received special compliments, one reviewer expressing his relief that the production was free from "those idiosyncracies of scenery which obtained in the last Shakespearean performance given at the Walnut Street several seasons ago, when portions of the pictorial background for *Macbeth* were New England farmhouse views presumably left over from Denman Thompson's ultimate production of *The Old Homestead.*"[21]

The only sour note in the general euphoria over the heroic efforts of this neophyte company occurred on their return to New York. The *New York Telegraph* of May 13, 1916, greeted the advent of black players in Shakespeare at the York Theatre with a sneer: "And now Darktown is to take a whack at the Shakespeare tercentenary thing. . . . Razors may be checked at the door." This is an instance of the kind of biased press directed against black performers by certain writers in the major papers. It is refreshing to report that the *Telegraph* theater critic who reviewed the show three days later was less churlish. While chiding Wright for overgesticulation, the critic conceded that "sincerity, dignity and admirable intentions mark the performance as one of which the colored race may well be proud." Wright had expected to use the production of *Othello* as a basis for establishing a black repertory theater company devoted to producing serious drama. His amateur players were not, however, quite ready for such a commitment, and the group disbanded. Wright continued to act with stock companies in the Harlem theaters.

Another short-lived but innovative effort in Shakespearean production was attempted by the Ethiopian Art Theatre of Chicago under the direction of a white named Raymond O'Neil. The company had been sponsored by the All-American Theatre Association of Chicago, an organization composed of both black and white members who believed that "the Negro has as great and original gifts to bring to the drama as he has already contributed to music and the dance."[22] The association aimed to establish similar theaters in other cities and eventually a theater school for Afro-American actors, designers, and other theater practitioners. The first production took place in February 1923, the play chosen for the company's debut being Oscar Wilde's Salome. By April the company announced that its repertory consisted of six established dramatic plays, including The Comedy of Errors and The Taming of the Shrew, a Molière farce, and a number of Afro-American folk plays, both comic and tragic.

Raymond O'Neil came from Cleveland and had worked for some years at the Cleveland Playhouse. He then studied in Berlin, where he became attracted to the directorial techniques of Max Reinhardt. Reinhardt, for instance, had presented The Taming of the Shrew in 1909 "as if produced in the supposedly crude Elizabethan manner by a company of blundering barnstormers"[23] in order to match the broadly farcical plot with equally broad exaggeration. Emulating this approach, O'Neil sought to adapt his plays to the perceived talents of his Afro-American actors. He had trained his players for twelve months, he wrote, "not in imitation of the more inhibited white actors but to develop their peculiar racial characteristics," which he identified as freshness and vigor of emotional responses, spontaneity and intensity of mood, and freedom from intellectual and artistic obsessions.[24] Whether these are racially ingrained characteristics of Afro-Americans is certainly open to question.

With three productions in place (a one-acter and two longer plays), the Ethiopian Art Theatre opened at the Frazee Theatre in New York on May 7, 1923, having played previously in Chicago, Washington, D.C., and at the Lafayette Theatre in Harlem. The one-act play, entitled The Chip Woman's Fortune by Willis Richardson, would be remembered as the first dramatic work by a black playwright to be seen on Broadway. The second play was Salome, chosen to display the range of the company's talents and probably because of its undercurrent of primitive passion, so evident in Herod's desire for Salome, her dance of the seven veils, and her ungovernable and destructive fascination for Jokanaan. The third production was Shakespeare's *The Comedy of Errors*, which was staged in a novel jazz version, the setting for which is described below:

> The action takes place on a rude platform in a circus tent and the absurd scenes are shifted by clowns under the crack of the ring-master's whip. A jazz band plays, not only for the scene shifters but for Dromio himself when he is most furiously clowning. Several of the leading characters are broadly burlesqued. The Duke of Ephesus becomes a squeaking mandarin and the Sheriff a doddering booby. But somehow the pinnacles of the higher fancy remain unscaled.[25]

Of the three productions, the company seems to have fared best in Richardson's honest and sympathetic tale of charity among the dispossessed poor. It was reminiscent of Lady Gregory's Irish folk plays at the Abbey Theatre. The production of *Salome* had received rave notices in earlier performances, mainly on the strength of Evelyn Preer's sensitive and appealing interpretation of the title role. The New York critics, however, were divided in their responses, some feeling that the production taken as a whole was dignified and impressive, others calling for more restraint and greater consistency in performance.[26] Sidney Kirkpatrick as Herod was singled out for special praise: "As this king watched the development of Salome's sadistic purpose his distorted features and fascinated eyes showed a horror and revolt that were not so much moral and religious . . . as they were expressions of the savage heart of darkness, of fetish-worship and devil-fears. . . . Seldom on any stage has there been a more torrential flood of words, more deeply felt and justly phrased, than in his final entreating of Salome."[27]

When director O'Neil conceived his jazz version of *The Comedy of Errors*, he was responding to calls for a Negro drama that would utilize the resources of the race as expressed in the folk arts of song, dance, and pantomime. These attributes were nightly on display in the sparkling new black musical comedies, such as *Shuffle Along*, that had captured Broadway audiences. These exhibitions, however, were tainted by their affinity with Negro minstrelsy—their comedians still wore blackface—and what was now needed was to incorporate the inherent racial arts in the legitimate drama. The theory was not advanced solely by black leaders. Max Reinhardt himself, O'Neil's artistic mentor, visited New York in the 1923 season and was captivated by the black musical comedies. When asked for his views on them, he responded:

> It is intriguing, very intriguing, these musical comedies of yours that I have seen. But, remember, not as achievements, not as things in themselves artistic, but in their possibilities, their tremendous artistic possibilities. They are most modern, most American, most expressionistic. They are highly original in spite of obvious triteness, and artistic in spite of superficial crudeness. To me they reveal new possibilities of technique in drama, and if I should ever try to do anything American, I should build it on these things.

Reinhardt argued that at every fresh period of creative development, drama turns to some aspect that had been previously subordinated or neglected. In his day pantomime was that aspect that would provide the fresh development. This art was the "special genius" of the Afro-American. "At present it is prostituted to farce, to trite comedy—but the technique is there and I have never seen more wonderful possibilities. . . . Somebody must demonstrate its fresh artistic value."[28]

O'Neil attempted to do so, but his effort did not win critical approval. Only John Corbin of the *New York Times* sensed the existence of a valid directorial idea behind the production, which, however, creaked at the hinges. Other reviewers of the established press were less sympathetic, calling it faddish and absurd, although everyone agreed that Charles Olden, doubling as the two Dromios, was peerless. It should be mentioned that W. E. B. DuBois found that the actors played Shakespeare with vigor and truth. He approved of the jazz interpretation as an attempt to bolster an old play that was not particularly funny to a modern audience, and he wondered "if this new thing had come out of France with a European imprint" whether New York would not have gone wild in praise of its daring originality. There is an unsavory footnote to the Ethiopian Art Theatre's adventure onto Broadway. The *New York Times* of June 11, 1923, reported that the director, Raymond O'Neil, thirty-three years old, had been arrested in Harlem for having appropriated monies advanced to him to pay his actors, some of whom claimed that they had received only a dollar or two each. Such are the uncertainties of a life in the theater!

6
Novelty Shakespeare

W HEN A LITTLE-KNOWN theater tucked away in a Pennsylvania valley hired a black actor for the role of Othello in 1930, it must have known that it was creating history.[1] The Hedgerow Theatre, a converted mill-house located in the Rose-Moyland Valley of Pennsylvania, was founded in 1923 by Jasper Deeter, who had firsthand knowledge of Afro-American actors on stage. As a member of the New York–based Provincetown Players in 1920, Deeter had insisted that none but a black actor play the title role in Eugene O'Neill's now celebrated drama, *The Emperor Jones*. It was he who had picked Charles Gilpin for the part, and the startling result of that particular combination of actor and play had made theatrical history. Not only had Gilpin's performance surpassed all expectations— the Drama League named him one of the ten most important contributors to the American theater in 1920—but, more significantly, a black man had taken the leading role in a white production before white people, and neither actors nor audience had expressed dismay over the event.

In 1926 Deeter was recalled by the Provincetown Playhouse to direct their production of Paul Green's *In Abraham's Bosom*. Again with black actors in starring roles in an interracial cast, the play was a great success on Broadway and won the Pulitzer Prize. Now Deeter was inviting a black actor to play the lead in a Shakespeare play with a white professional company, and that too marked a first in American theater annals. Though long overdue, the innovation would not set a trend—the Hedgerow was too insignificant to affect theater practice in the major cities—but it created one more avenue for the Afro-

American dramatic actor to gain access to mainstream professional theater.

The Hedgerow's *Othello* opened on April 21, 1930. The actor chosen for the lead was Wayland Rudd, of whom little is known beyond the fact that he was a salesman and belonged to an amateur theater group in Philadelphia when Deeter offered him his first professional part at the Hedgerow as Brutus Jones. After one or two more engagements with the company he was entrusted with the role of Othello. Rudd's future career, however, foreshadowed in a curious way the eventful life of a much greater black actor, Paul Robeson, who had also been a notable Emperor Jones and who would himself make theatrical history as Othello. When Rudd is next heard of, he is a citizen of the Soviet Union, where, according to the *Daily Worker* of February 1, 1939, he had settled as an actor "about ten years ago." He appeared on the Soviet stage under the direction of Vsevolod Meyerhold and was cast in the Soviet motion picture version of *Tom Sawyer*. He also wrote a play about mining in the southern United States titled *Andy Jones* that was based on Angelo Herndon's autobiography *Let Me Live*.

Wayland Rudd

Not even the perceptive Jasper Deeter could have predicted that, a few years ahead and burdened with the disastrous economic slump brought on by the Great Depression, black actors and other theater people would receive their greatest impetus toward a productive life in the theater. The government-sponsored Federal Theatre Project was established in 1935 to provide work for some 25,000 idle and impecunious theater workers, at least 3,000 of whom were black. So-called Negro units of the project were formed in some twenty-two cities across the country. New plays were written under the aegis of the project, and many established plays were produced with black casts, some of the scripts being altered to accommodate eager but fledgling talents. One of the project's Negro units in New York, directed by John Houseman and the gifted if unpredictable Orson Welles, staged a number of impressive productions. None was more heralded than *Macbeth*, directed by Welles and designed by Nat Karson, which opened at Harlem's Lafayette Theatre on April 9, 1936. The production, with a cast of one hundred, was led by Jack Carter as the murdering thane and Edna Thomas as his overly ambitious wife. Finding a striking parallel between Macbeth's story and that of Haiti's King Christophe, one of the leaders of the slave revolution who ruled the country tyrannically before committing suicide, Welles decided to set his production on the West Indian island, using authentic witch doctors and jungle drums, and transforming the witches into voodoo priestesses. As a result, the production came to be known as the "voodoo" *Macbeth*.

With only four professional actors in the cast, Welles radically revised the script and may have tried to compensate for acting deficiencies by emphasizing the spectacular effects, both visual and aural. The production was a great hit with the public. It ran for fourteen weeks in New York and toured the country for thirteen more. It attracted audiences numbering close to 120,000 but secured only a mixed critical reception. The Harlem press was generally complimentary, as much in defense of the Negro Theatre unit that had provided work for black artists as with pride at the novelty and magnitude of the undertaking: "Crowds milled, mounties charged, cameras ground and flashed while a band played. Hallie Flanagan, national theatre director, and Philip W. Barker, regional director, must have felt proud of their protege after it was all over. We were. Federal subsidizing of art had been justified. The theatre lives again! Hurrah!"[2] Nevertheless, the major New York critics were less than enthusi-

Edna Thomas as Lady Macbeth, 1936

Jack Carter as Macbeth, 1936

astic, the prevailing view being that the play was beyond the assembled talents of the largely amateur cast, the text had been unforgivably mutilated, and the production as a whole was undeserving of serious artistic criticism as authentic Shakespeare.

In a recent article in *Theatre Journal* on two of Welles's Shakespearean productions, John S. O'Connor characterized the response of reviewers to the voodoo *Macbeth* as racist. He argued that in 1936 black performers were not taken seriously and that many critics viewed the production as another Harlem spectacle comparable to such materials as *Run Little Chillun* and the later *Swing Mikado,* or to "exotic" shows like *The Emperor Jones* or *Bassa Moona.* "For Negroes to play *Macbeth,*" O'Connor concluded, "was a significant change from a long line of stereotyped roles and comic dialect, and it was difficult for critics to view them as Shakespearean actors rather

*Maurice Ellis as Macduff and Wardell Saunders as Malcolm
in a scene from* Macbeth, *1936.*

than awkward Blacks in fancy costumes."[3] On the other hand, the
audiences that flocked to the show by the thousands were free of the
preconceptions that allegedly inhibited the appreciation of the critics. They had neither seen nor read much Shakespeare; they were a
fresh and eager audience; and, as Welles himself observed, "one has
the feeling every night that here were people on a voyage of discovery
in the theatre."[4]

John Mason Brown of the *New York Post* thought that Welles had
an exciting idea but wasted it in execution. He wondered "why Mr.
Welles, having had inspiration enough to imagine voodoo witches for
a Negro cast, lacked imagination enough to adapt the language of the
play to the locale he had selected for it and the actors who were to
speak it."[5] In other words, the dean of American theater critics was
suggesting that Welles should have completely rewritten the play,
presumably in some form of appropriate dialect, for his all-black cast.

On the fairly widespread complaint that the actors lacked the ability to speak Shakespeare's verse, John Houseman relates in his autobiography, *Run Through*, that Welles had made a conscious artistic
decision to avoid the declamatory tradition of Shakespearean performance and to work for a simpler, more direct, and rapid delivery
of dramatic verse.[6] While this objective is admirable, years of ex-

perience with amateurs demonstrate that untrained and unpracticed actors are likely to have difficulty speaking Shakespeare's lines for the first time. Welles's statement to a reporter of the *New York Times* that "these Negroes have never had the misfortune of hearing Elizabethan verse spouted by actors strongly flavoring of well-cured Smithfield. They read their lines as they would any others" suggests that this company's inadequacy in coping with Shakespeare's language may not have been unjustly criticized. Nevertheless, the popular if not critical success of the voodoo *Macbeth* encouraged other Negro units of the Federal Theatre to produce Shakespeare. Los Angeles responded with an African version of the play and Seattle brought forth a musical adaptation of *The Taming of the Shrew* (both of which will be discussed later).

Only one member in the cast of the voodoo *Macbeth* was subsequently seen in a featured Shakespearean role. The part of Banquo had been taken by Canada Lee, who, nine years later, was offered the role of Caliban in a production of *The Tempest* that played first at the Colonial Theatre in Boston and opened on January 25, 1945, at the Alvin Theatre in New York. It was directed by American-born Marga-

Canada Lee as Banquo in Macbeth, *1936*

ret Webster, daughter of British actors and at the time one of the foremost directors of Shakespeare in America. The choice of Canada Lee was not determined by his performance as Banquo. In 1941 he had appeared as Bigger Thomas, the ghetto youth of Richard Wright's powerful novel, *Native Son*—in a production by Orson Welles—and achieved stardom. The *New York Times* review of March 30, 1941, captured something of the actor's compelling stage presence: "In his dark muscled body there flows a restless torrent of strength. His ears are cauliflowered, his nose is broken, one of his eyes is off center, and yet when one watches him one never notices these things. One watches only how he moves with an unpredictable and animal grace, loose and powerful." Lee had been a prizefighter and jockey before turning actor, and he carried the scars of those hazardous occupations. Now he was to appear on stage as Caliban, playing opposite Arnold Moss as Prospero and the ballerina Vera Zorina as Ariel.

If *Othello* can be labeled Shakespeare's American play because of its racial overtones, then *The Tempest* is his colonial one, dealing as it does with the master-slave relationship on an island in the Western Hemisphere. In this view Prospero represents the European colonizer who has conquered the island by force and enslaved two of its inhabitants whom he uses to provide for his and his daughter's needs. When the establishment theater slowly began to overcome its opposition to interracial casting in Shakespeare, Caliban was one of the first roles offered to black actors. Indeed, as one critic observed of Margaret Webster's production, "Caliban is a perfect role for a Negro."[7] That this type of casting is not without its racial significance was clearly apparent to Webster. In the February 1945 issue of *Theatre Arts* she explained her choice of Canada Lee:

> In picking the Negro actor for the role, Miss Webster made it clear that she meant to exploit his particular intensity, his power to come to grips with character, and not the pigmentation of his skin. "I do not intend," she insists, "to make Caliban a parable of the current state of the American Negro." Yet her willing eyes discover a ready parallel. "Prospero has taught Caliban the words of civilization but kept him a slave. Throughout the play—in his worship of a false god and 'celestial liquor' and in his final discovery that freedom cannot be acquired from without—Caliban is groping, seeking after freedom. This is in large part what *The Tempest* is about. Caliban's—and Ariel's—search for freedom."

It is true that to the medieval and Elizabethan mind, blackness was associated with evil and, hence, with the devil, the "prince of darkness" who personifies evil. Prospero calls Caliban "a devil, a born devil" and "a thing of darkness." Since, as we are told in the play, Caliban was fathered by the devil, it can be argued that he should be played black. However, there is no tradition of playing the role in blackface or of using a black actor prior to the mid-twentieth century, and from a modern viewpoint there is no logical justification for casting a black actor as Caliban (a name that is usually accepted as an anagram for cannibal) when the counterpart role of Ariel is given to a sylphlike white actor or, quite often, actress. Since both of these creatures are in bondage to Prospero, the fact that Caliban is a slave cannot be advanced as a reason for casting him alone as black. Shakespeare's text makes it clear that Caliban's mother was a foul, blue-eyed witch called Sycorax, who, pregnant with him, had been banished from Algiers to an uninhabited island somewhere near the Bermudas, probably in the Caribbean basin. Although Frank Kermode has argued that the term "blue-eyed" alludes not to the iris but to the eyelid, where blueness was regarded as a sign of pregnancy,[8] the fact remains that the reference is to a fair rather than a dark complexion. Sycorax was therefore either European or Mediterranean in origin, and her ill-formed son, who Shakespeare tells us is freckled, must have shared his mother's ethnic pedigree.

The delicate Ariel, on the other hand, was found on the island by Sycorax and imprisoned in a cloven pine until freed by Prospero, who promptly enslaved him as his personal genie. Though unhuman and free of the elements, Ariel inhabited the island prior to the arrival of foreigners and is presumably indigenous to the Caribbean—in any case, hardly European. These considerations have been traditionally ignored in filling the roles. Ariel, the creature of the air native to the Caribbean, is white. Caliban, the savage and deformed monster from the Mediterranean, is black. It is beauty and the beast all over again, with white equating beauty and black, bestiality.[9]

Canada Lee survived his casting as Caliban in Margaret Webster's production, although not all the reviews were as complimentary as John Chapman's in the *New York Daily News*: "Canada Lee's portrayal of the monster, Caliban, is one by which I shall measure all other readings in the years that are left. It is most beautifully spoken; it is one more evidence that Mr. Lee is a thoughtful, ambitious and resourceful actor."[10] In a contrary view, other critics found both Lee and Zorina's Ariel to be inadequate in speaking Shakespeare's verse, while Caliban's grotesque costuming came in for its share of censure.

Lee's next major classical role was not Shakespeare's but one of his contemporary John Webster's, whose tragic tale of blood and pity, *The Duchess of Malfi*, in an adaptation by the poet W. H. Auden, was presented at the Ethel Barrymore Theatre, New York, in October 1946. The play is not often performed professionally; its horror and implacable evil seem too extreme to be captured on stage realistically, and it is no accident this was its first time on Broadway. With Elisabeth Bergner in the title role, Lee was cast as the villainous spy Bosola, whose job it was to report the Duchess's amorous affairs to her brothers. When she secretly marries and has children, the brothers and Bosola arrange her torture and death. The most memorable detail of this production, which even the most sympathetic of the critics felt was uneven and often tedious, was the fact that Lee played his role in whiteface. With pink-colored greasepaint, a thick wig, bushy eyebrows, a goatee, and a putty nose, wearing a high collar and gloves, Lee was still a shade more credible than most others in the cast. Brooks Atkinson of the *New York Times*, who had not seen Lee for four years, disliked the makeup but could only "express delight over the way in which a good elemental actor has acquired mastery of the stage."[11]

Like most black actors of the legitimate theater, Lee wished to play Othello. He had attempted a section of the tragedy in an experimental version in the spring of 1944. It was not well received, and he longed for another chance. It came in 1948 in a summer theater production, directed by Henry Jones, which was staged at the New England Mutual Hall, Boston, from July 12 to 17, followed by further performances at Saratoga Springs, New York, and in East Hampton, Long Island. Clare Luce was his Desdemona and Wesley Addy his Iago. The consensus seemed to be that in his portrayal of the Moor Lee lacked both the physical stature demanded by the role and the fluent delivery required of Shakespeare's verse.

As his acting career developed, Lee began to choose roles in plays with a message. In 1946 he starred in Maxine Wood's *On Whitman Avenue*, dealing with housing discrimination, and in 1950 he went to South Africa to appear in the film version of Alan Paton's *Cry, the Beloved Country*. This was at a time when the House Committee on Un-American Activities was actively investigating alleged communists in the entertainment world. Lee's commitment to socially relevant theater and his open friendship with outspoken radicals caused him to be ostracized from work in radio, television, and film. In poor health that was aggravated by financial distress, he died in 1952 at the age of forty-five, robbing the theater of a unique and exciting talent.

From the period of the English Restoration, when Sir William Davenant's operatic version of *Macbeth* with flying witches held the stage, up to the present, playwrights, actors, producers, and directors have tried to shape Shakespeare to the fashion of their times and to their particular idiosyncracies. That his plays survive these assaults and continue to challenge dedicated artists to seek out their truths in less bizarre interpretations is a measure of their enduring greatness. Black Shakespeare has also had its fling at experimentation and popularization—witness Raymond O'Neil's jazzed-up *Comedy of Errors* and Orson Welles's voodoo *Macbeth*. Those experiments, whether or not they succeeded in practice, were at least informed by thoughtful aesthetic considerations. Given a black cast untrained in a conventional Shakespearean acting style but with unique strengths of its own, the directors believed that their particular interpretations would make Shakespeare more accessible to the public while largely respecting the integrity of the text. Not all other adaptations would be so thoughtfully conceived or so respectful of the script.

In Chicago the Federal Theatre Negro Unit No. 2 made its bow before the public at the Ridgeway Theatre on April 1, 1936, in an adaptation of *Romeo and Juliet* renamed *Romey and Julie*. The play was written by Ruth Chorpenning, once an actress with the Theatre Guild of New York, and James Norris, with music by Margaret Allison Bonds. It was directed by Robert Dunmore. Set in Harlem, the action of the play developed from a feud between native Afro-Americans and newcomers from the the West Indies, the latter group believing themselves to be of a social class superior to the native blacks. Romey, a Harlem youth, crashes a party at a nightclub, falls in love with Julie from the Caribbean, climbs to her fire-escape balcony by standing on an ashcan, gets into a street brawl that results in the death of Mercuti and Tybalt, and is banished to Hoboken, New Jersey. Friar Lawrence appeared as an avuncular Harlem preacher and the apothecary became an itinerant dope peddler. The major addition to Shakespeare's plot occurred in the epilogue. Here the lovers approach the gates of heaven but are forbidden entry by St. Peter because of their sin of suicide. They are reunited in hell, where they are joined by a number of sympathetic characters and some defecting angels. The angels have stolen a harp and journeyed below where they expect to have more fun than in their staid heavenly abode.

The performance of *Romey and Julie* was disappointing for several reasons. The script, it was alleged, lacked wit and drew its comedy mainly from the "rough clowning of old time blackface afterpieces."[12] Lyrics were dull and the music surprisingly free of any recognizable Afro-American idiom. The production itself was so hurried that the cast was obviously ill-prepared on opening night. Finally, the stage platform was much too small for the free action required by the script, while the flat-floored auditorium restricted the view of the pocket-size stage by the audience. Despite all these deficiencies, the idea of translating and updating Shakespeare's most celebrated tragedy of young love to an American urban setting was clearly an inspired one. Years later, in 1957, script writer Arthur Laurents, lyricist Stephen Sondheim, composer Leonard Bernstein, and choreographer Jerome Robbins would combine their talents in the spectacularly memorable production of *West Side Story*, which pitted two New York City street gangs against each other. The "Jets" were regular city toughs and white, while the "Sharks" were newly arrived Puerto Rican migrants. The initial production of *West Side Story* ran for 732 performances at the Winter Garden Theatre in New York. It was turned into a successful movie, and remains one of the important American contributions to the contemporary stage.

Taking its cue from the success of New York's voodoo *Macbeth*, the Los Angeles Negro unit of the Federal Theatre Project came forward with an African verson of the tragedy which opened in July 1937.[13] Jess Lee Brooks was a heavy-set Macbeth and Mae Turner played his primly dressed but bloody-minded wife. The voodoo *Macbeth* had been inspired by the story of the Haitian king Henri Christophe, but Brooks had already appeared as Christophe the previous year in the Los Angeles Negro unit's production of an original drama, *Black Empire*, by Christine Ames and Clarke Painter. Now as an African Macbeth using Shakespeare's lines Brooks would be able to deepen his interpretation of a tyrannical black monarch. His performance must have been impressive. Following *Macbeth* he was invited to play the Prince of Morocco in the 1937 Federal Theatre production of the *Merchant of Venice* by the white unit of Los Angeles, a develop-

Jess Lee Brooks as Macbeth and Mae Turner as Lady Macbeth in a production by the Federal Theatre Project, Los Angeles, 1937.

ment in interracial casting that was considered sufficiently innovative to warrant special mention in the local press.

In the African *Macbeth* a jungle atmosphere was conveyed by using a scrim to create mysterious, shadowy shapes and figures and by African motifs on flats that were constructed with bamboo posts. Costumes were modeled after garments worn in Madagascar, the Congo, and Abyssinia. They were ornamented with beads and animal teeth carved from wood, and with cloth tubing that simulated metal bracelets and collars. Headdresses were of elaborate design topped with plumes. As in Welles's version of the play, supernatural elements were emphasized. Music and sound effects consisted of savage rhythms, sibilant tom-toms, and pistol shots, with speeches that were punctuated by shouts and cries from off-stage. The staging was swift and animated, as writhing bodies and clutching hands of groups of shadowy apparitions moved from side to side, heightening the melodramatic effect.

Here again, as with the New York production, critical reaction indicated that poetry had been sacrificed to spectacle. While the acting of the cast was generally praised, their lack of proper diction was deplored. One contemporary reviewer was bothered by the fact that savages were addressing each other by such fine Scots names as Banquo, Macbeth, Duncan, and Macduff, while another critic commented that although the play had received "the most spectacular staging lately seen in any Federal show, if not in any productions outside the movies," it was nevertheless "a magnificent failure." Far better, he thought, to present a story native to the background of the African people than a hybrid version of what he termed "an Anglo-Saxon show."[14]

In 1938 George Abbott, working with an all-white company, had successfully translated *The Comedy of Errors* into a spirited musical comedy called *The Boys from Syracuse*. Now Louis Armstrong and Benny Goodman, a most unlikely pair of Shakespeare expositors, decided to capitalize on that success by producing a musical version of *A Midsummer Night's Dream* with a primarily black company. With book by Gilbert Seldes and Erik Charell, scenery based on Walt Disney's cartoons, and choreography by Agnes de Mille, the frolic opened at the Center Theatre in New York on November 29, 1939. If only for its exotic casting, this musical adaptation, called *Swingin' the Dream*, merits attention.

Bottom the Fireman was played by Louis Armstrong, whose mag-

Louis Armstrong as Bottom and Maxine Sullivan as Titania in
Swingin' the Dream, *1939.*

ical trumpet it must be presumed was partly responsible for the transformation of Shakespeare's characters into gyrating jitterbugs. Butterfly McQueen made a cute Puck, Flute the Iceman was effectively
shambled by Oscar Polk, and Quince the Midwife was commandeered by Jackie "Moms" Mabley. Maxine Sullivan was a golden-
voiced Titania, queen of the pixies; Oberon was regally played by
Juan Hernandez (later hailed for his moving performance in the film
version of *Intruder in the Dust*); and the little pixies were the three
Dandridge sisters: Vivian, Dorothy, and Etta. The Benny Goodman
Sextet appeared along with singers, dancers, the Rhythmettes, and
the Deep River Boys. Altogether it was a riotous array for a swinging
midsummer-night's revel set in a New Orleans canebrake at the close
of the last century. John Mason Brown, who had asked for a total
transformation of *Macbeth* for the Federal Theatre production, was
still not satisfied. He liked the show only for the first hour:

> For that length of time it is charming. It has great vigor and origi
> nality. . . . It is at its best and a delightful best that is, when

Shakespeare is being pushed offstage by its dancers and musicians. It is at its happiest when he is being irreverently dealt with. . . . Unfortunately in their second act they turn "Bardolaters" at least to the extent of following in too great detail the tedious story of the lovers. When they do this, they may please the school marms, but they silence Mr. Goodman and Mr. Armstrong for too long a while, and they prevent the dancers so admirably directed by Miss de Mille and Mr. White from having their rhythmic say. All of which is something of a major pity.[15]

Brown found the second act increasingly boring, and his smiles turned to yawns. The production played for only thirteen performances before closing.

One other black melodic adaptation of Shakespeare was attempted in the decade of the 1930s. The sponsor on this occasion was the Federal Theatre Negro unit in Seattle, Washington, whose version of *The Taming of the Shrew* opened on June 19, 1939, at the Metropolitan Theatre in that city. The adaptation was prepared by Joseph Staton and Herman Moore; original music was composed by Howard Biggs, who conducted the fifteen-piece orchestra; and staging was by Richard Glyer, a white director. A prologue set in 1589, in the Mermaid Tavern, London, introduced the character Shakespeare in conversation with a barmaid. Then the scene changed to contemporary New Orleans and Texas, where a modern Kate was tamed by her ebony-hued beau to the accompaniment of some dozen songs interspersed with dialogue.

The company, it turned out, was 80 percent amateur, and diction was so poor that speech had to be slowed down for clarity, thus ruining the swift flow of the action required in farce-comedy. However, when the actors were allowed to ad-lib their lines, they were riotously funny. As the director explained in his written report on the production, "the Negro must have comedy written in his own language, or he cannot clearly put over the meaning."[16] The director felt that the actors in the group completely lacked a sense of timing, but since he also confessed that he was "unacquainted with negro temperament and was not equipped to handle the group," it is possible that some serious difference had developed between him and the cast that prevented him from extracting the best performances from his players. The settings were designed in cartoon style and typified the broadly caricatured acting. A huge flower, hanging center like an open mouth with a wagging tongue, symbolized Kate, while a

Joseph Staton as Petrarch, Sarah Oliver as Kate, Robert A. St. Clear as the Preacher in the wedding scene from the Seattle Negro Repertory Company's production of The Taming of the Shrew, *1939.*

ridiculous-looking prizefighter figure sculptured in chicken-wire and papier-mâché was set downstage of the proscenium to represent Petruchio. In the picture illustration of the wedding scene, Pete's outfit consists of a bowler hat, football shoulder pads, a sleeveless tunic, and knee-high rustic-looking breeches, below which peep out his suspenders holding up calf-high socks. The apparently zany interpretaton of the play had its moments of hilarity, although very little of Shakespeare's original comedy was retained. Much of the comedy was physical, as the staging contained a goodly amount of roughhouse action: "Pete—Petruchio to Shakespeare's students—the man who had stayed ten seconds with Joe Louis, took on the Herculean

task of taming Sarah Oliver's Kate. But he did it. And how he did it!
... It went through hair-pulling matches, cane fighting, kitchenware
throwing, mud wrestling, and even a good old custard-pie barrage. It
went from New Orleans to Brownsville, Texas, and back to New Orleans—all in a midget automobile."[17] The director's final words affirmed his conviction that if only their version of *The Taming of the
Shrew* could be produced with a black company of professionals, it
would surely be a grand success.

In many ways the 1930s proved to be a turning point in the relationship of Afro-Americans to Shakespeare's plays. Hitherto that relationship existed only on the level of "higher art." Shakespeare was
studied in colleges and performed by and for the cognoscenti. His
was an aristocratic theater. Black folk attending his plays did so as
much out of duty to their cultural uplift as in recognition of the
fact that Afro-Americans were as talented as Caucasians and could
achieve success in the highest form of dramatic production. The
1930s changed those perceptions, or at least expanded them, by de-
mocratizing Shakespeare. His plays were brought closer to a black
mass audience than ever before. It mattered little that what these
audiences saw was not pure Shakespeare according to the academi-
cian or critic. Whatever forbidding halo had previously surrounded
his name and kept people away from his plays had now vanished.
Shakespeare's dramas became not merely accessible but enjoyable.

Of course the work of the Federal Theatre Project was largely responsible for this change. Hallie Flanagan, national director of the
project, had approached her assignment with a sense of mission: "No
person can work effectively in the theatre unless he cares increasingly about the theme engaging science and industry today, that is, a
better life for more people," she had declared. Flanagan believed in
a multicultural America and felt that ethnic minorities, if given opportunities to develop and exhibit their particular artistic gifts to the
highest level possible, would help to dispel racial bigotry. In keeping
with this belief, a French theater was started in Los Angeles, a German theater in New York, and an Italian theater in Boston, in addition to the Negro units. Training programs for apprentices in all areas
of theater practice were begun. The project called for a theater that
would be free of racial prejudice. It refused to support plays that
presented degrading images of blacks and abolished segregated seating at all its productions. Those reactionary forces who view con-
structive change as a threat to entrenched privileges and powers be-

came alarmed. The House Committee on Un-American Activities saw in the Federal Theatre program evidence of subversive activity, the committee's chairman declaring that "racial equality forms a vital part of the Communistic teachings and practices."[18] In 1939, after four years of vigorous and productive activity, the Federal Theatre Project was by act of Congress discontinued.

7
Broadway and Beyond

U NTIL THE 1940s the established professional theater in America failed to accommodate a black actor in a major role from the Shakespearean repertoire. Indeed, a book published in 1939 entitled *Shakespeare in America* by Esther Dunn does not mention a single black performer. It is therefore not surprising that the announcement in 1942 that Paul Robeson would play Othello in a Theatre Guild production raised great expectations and some concern in theatrical circles. Robeson at this time was a concert singer of world renown, while his stand on political and racial issues had already made him a controversial figure. He was born at Princeton, New Jersey, in 1898, the son of a former runaway slave who became a Methodist clergyman. After attending public school, he won a scholarship to Rutgers College, from which he graduated in 1919. His college career was exceptional. As an athlete he won thirteen varsity letters and was named All-American for two successive years. He also won the debating championship in each of his four years, gained Phi Beta Kappa honors, and was valedictorian of his class. Upon leaving Rutgers, he took a law degree at Columbia University, but within months abandoned the legal profession for a career on the concert stage, in the theater, and in films.

As a dramatic actor, Robeson had first come to prominence when he assumed the lead in a revival of *The Emperor Jones* presented by the Provincetown Playhouse in 1924. The role had been created by Charles Gilpin, whose performance was so compelling that the major critics had reached for superlatives to describe it.[1] If there was any doubt about Robeson's ability to match Gilpin's achievement, it was quickly dispelled on opening night. The *New York Telegraph* of May 7, 1924, recorded the event:

> For one hour and a half, with only a few minutes for scene-shifting, the atmosphere kept alive by the steady throb, throb of a tom-tom, Robeson held his audience—enthralled is the word. He was dragged before the curtain by men and women who rose to their feet and applauded. When the ache in the arms stopped their hands they used their voices, shouted meaningless words, gave hoarse throaty cries. Canes were thumped on the boards of the floor. The power of the play had much to do with the emotion fired—that must be admitted—but the ovation was for Robeson, for his emotional strength, for his superb acting.

Robeson may not have achieved all the subtleties in performance of the more experienced Gilpin, but his magnificent presence, organlike voice, and vigorous energy seemed to overflow the limited space of the small off-Broadway stage and completely engulf the audience with the passions and fears of the fallen black emperor.

His success in this role convinced the Provincetown group to go ahead with a production of *All God's Chillun Got Wings*, O'Neill's tragic melodrama of miscegenation, with Robeson in the role of Jim Harris, a black law student, playing opposite the white actress Mary Blair. The announcement of the production had brought vigorous opposition from across the country by people who, whipped up by the Hearst newspaper syndicate, objected to the portrayal of miscegenation in the public theater. The idea of a mixed marriage displayed on stage seemed to such people to be a forecast of utter damnation. This public expression of bigotry coming so early in his theatrical career might well have helped to set Robeson on a course that would make him, for most of his adult life, the victim of political harassment in his home country, notwithstanding his distinguished international career on stage and screen.

With his accompanist Lawrence Brown, who remained with him for over thirty years, Robeson embarked on his celebrated career as a concert vocalist, featuring Negro spirituals and work songs, that took him throughout the United States, to Britain, Europe, Africa, and the Soviet Union. He sang at the front lines for republican soldiers fighting against General Franco's fascist forces in Spain and made many speeches in support of the working class and against racial prejudice. During this period he appeared intermittently in stage

Paul Robeson as Othello and Peggy Ashcroft as Desdemona,
London, 1930.

plays and films, appearing for the first time as Othello in London, England, in 1930. It would be the only Shakespearean role he would attempt, and he would play it in three separate productions.

A young and talented English cast had been assembled by Maurice Brown, who presented the show at the Savoy Theatre on May 19 under the direction of Ellen Van Volkenburg. Peggy Ashcroft had the role of Desdemona, Sybil Thorndike was Emilia, and Ralph Richardson played Roderigo, with Brown himself appearing as Iago. Three of these actors would later be honored by the queen for their contributions to the English stage: Richardson received a knighthood and Misses Ashcroft and Thorndike were named Dames of the British Commonwealth. Not since the 1880s had a black American actor played Othello in Shakespeare's own country, and as Paul Robeson was already an established stage artist of repute (he had appeared successfully in *The Emperor Jones* and *Showboat* on the London stage), this new production of *Othello* aroused considerable interest. It was for Robeson a personal triumph. He overcame all obstacles, not the least of which were the heavy sets of James Pryde, a fine artist with little stage experience, whose designs pushed the action too far upstage. On opening night Robeson took twenty curtain calls.

Of his performance, most reviewers in the London dailies seemed to agree with the *Morning Post* that "there has been no Othello on our stage certainly for forty years, to compare with his dignity, simplicity and true passion."[2] The reviews in several contemporary London papers were summarized in the *Boston Evening Transcript* of June 7, 1930. For instance, Ivor Brown in the *Observer* noted Robeson's occasional awkwardness of movement and stance due to his relatively short stage career, but found that this very awkwardness proved a strength in that it helped to emphasize Othello's isolation from the mannered world of Venice and allowed his inner dignity to shine forth free of ceremony, convention, or acquired rank. Being lonely in this foreign court increased the value of Desdemona's love for Othello and made completely understandable his relapse to a barbaric rage when that love appears to be destroyed. The *London Times* found Robeson's interpretaton different but consistent within itself.

Maurice Brown as Iago and Paul Robeson as Othello,
London, 1930.

Despite occasional blemishes, it was nowhere seriously flawed; he "plays thrillingly upon the nerves and knocks at the heart" with a tranquil dignity and a melancholy infinitely sad. "It is a sadness that never lifts from the stage while Mr. Robeson is upon it; it grows as the tempest of fury, scorn, and hatred draws to its full, possessing our minds and giving a kind of noble plainness to the tragedy." The *Daily Telegraph* critic felt that by reason of his race, Robeson was able to surmount the difficulties that English actors generally have with Othello to make his sudden passion seem genuine and credible. He had a fine presence and a beautiful voice that gave the poetry its best quality and conveyed a sense of nobility. His only fault—and that not an insistent one—was a certain monotony of delivery in the passionate speeches. In the light of such praise by the major London critics, it is difficult to give much credence to J. C. Trewin's later dismissal of the performance with the comment that Robeson, "paying out the speeches with sonorous monotony, wanted any real command."[3] Robeson at this time was thirty-two years old. This, his first attempt at Shakespeare, was clearly a success, and negotiations were begun to take the production across the Atlantic. Sentiment against mixed casting still ran high in America, however, and the idea of a transfer to Broadway was shelved. It would take twelve more years before Robeson received the Theatre Guild's invitation to portray the noble Moor in the United States. It came in January 1942.

Associated with this new venture, in addition to the experienced Shakespearean director Margaret Webster, were other reputable stage figures. The designer was Robert Edmond Jones, who had worked with the Provincetown Players in their experimental productions and had also directed and designed the Company of Colored Players in a Broadway production of three Negro plays by the poet Ridgely Torrence in 1917. José Ferrer was cast as Iago and his wife at that time, Uta Hagen, was Desdemona. Webster had decided to test her production in try-out theaters before bringing it to New York. For the opening performance, in August 1942, she selected the Brattle Street Theatre in Cambridge, near Harvard University, "because it seemed likely that in this atmosphere the production would get a fair hearing. This stand in Cambridge was . . . a test case. It was undertaken to prove that a Negro actor is acceptable, both academically and practically, as Othello."[4]

How acceptable was Robeson's Othello with a white professional cast to a Cambridge audience? Boston theater critic Elliot Norton

Paul Robeson as Othello and José Ferrer as Iago in Othello, *1943.*

was present at the opening night's performance, and many years later, speaking at the annual convention luncheon of the New England Theatre Conference (at which Miss Hagen was presented the conference's major award for outstanding creative achievement in the American theater), he recalled the event:

> I remember vividly several things about that opening night, which was a test case. Only two American managers had had the courage in that year to put on this production with Robeson. The rest were scared to death. The whole Broadway community was hiding in closets when the subject was brought up. Nobody knew what would happen when the first black actor in American history walked on stage to play Othello, which he had every right to play. . . .
>
> I remember when Paul Robeson bent down for the first time to kiss his Desdemona, there was a thrill of excitement in the theatre. No black actor, believe it or not, had ever kissed a white actress on the American stage before that time. And when Robeson, tall, handsome, with that magnificent voice, made the speech to the Ducal council, one of the greatest of all Shakespeare's speeches, there was an enormous feeling of excitement in the theatre. . . .
>
> I remember when the innocent, vulnerable Desdemona prepared for bed, that magnificent scene, the tension was enormous; and when he strangled her, it was pretty close to unbearable. At the end, there was a moment of absolute silence, unlike almost anything I've ever seen or heard in the theatre. And then absolute pandemonium by that first audience in Cambridge, overwhelming acceptance, an historic occasion. . . . They had done something wonderful and everyone knew it and everyone rejoiced.[5]

The *New York Times* review characterized Robeson's performance as heroic and convincing, despite a disturbing tremolo in his voice, and added that the students "began to stamp their feet in the steady swelling stomp which is the undergraduates' traditional salute and the highest kind of acclaim."[6]

The production moved to Princeton, New Haven, and Boston before confronting the traditional barriers of Broadway, where it opened at the Shubert Theatre on October 19, 1943. It was a stupendous hit. At forty-five Robeson was at the top of his powers and able to make the necessary vocal adjustment from concert singer to Shakespearean

Uta Hagen as Desdemona and Paul Robeson as Othello, 1943.

tragic hero. This new production of *Othello*, as John Chapman made clear in his review for the *New York Daily News*, "with a Negro in the title role making love to a white Desdemona," was no theatrical trick. There was nothing cheap or titillating about it. Rather, the production presented a black man of dignity and intelligence in the role of a black man of dignity and intelligence.[7] Louis Kronenberger, a perceptive critic, was reminded that Othello is a difficult role that has taxed the abilities of three centuries of actors. Kronenberger found the performance not rich enough for his taste, yet

> physically, and not in look alone, but in bearing, in voice, in grandeur of manner, Paul Robeson is all that Othello could ever hope to be. Here stood revealed Shakespeare's most passionate and noble hero, though not—as Othello is—his most poetic one. Mr. Robeson has moderated the undue violence with which he played the role in Cambridge, and he gives a better reading to most of the great speeches. To the last two great ones, indeed, he brings a kind of magnificence. But he is a less moving figure than he ought to be, and not all his big scenes and speeches come off entirely right. There is a tendency at times to confuse solemnity with grandeur, and to assert his power by force of will rather than force of character. But where shall we find an Othello to equal him?[8]

Most of the New York critics were struck by Robeson's physical qualities and looming stage presence. These characteristics, together with a resonant voice of considerable range, gave to the role a majesty and power that had seldom if ever been seen on the American stage. Robeson's Othello was indisputably the dominant figure of the drama, while Iago was a subsidiary agent of evil who engineered his downfall. In the toppling of this giant figure, one felt both pathos and terror. For all his tremendous force, Robeson succeeded in giving the part a fully human quality. This was the view of Lewis Nichols in the Sunday *New York Times*. He called the performance "electrifying."[9]

The previous record for continuous performances of *Othello* in New York was 57; for any Shakespeare play in America, the record at that time was 157 performances. Robeson's *Othello* played for 296 performances on Broadway. The barricades had been breached. Thereafter no one could argue with impunity that the theater-going public would not accept a black actor as leading character in a racially integrated professional production of an established drama. Protests from what might be called the hard-core segregationist element were not unexpected. When *Life* magazine published a picture spread of Robeson's *Othello*, it engendered harsh letters to the editor denouncing the production in terms that exposed the virulence of antiblack feeling in certain parts of the country.[10] A South Carolina reader, for instance, wrote: "The time is not ripe, if ever, for the actual social mingling of the two races. Such pictures, in my humble opinion, have a tendency to create in some Negroes a longing for something that cannot be theirs and can only lead to a feeling of frustration." From Kentucky, another correspondent was not concerned with the merits of the production but with "the horrible, indelible, undeniable and terrifying fact that there are white men with so little respect for themselves that they would cause to be printed the picture of a Negro man with his arm around a white woman in a love scene." One letter writer from Denver lodged a protest of a milder sort. He wished the editor to know that Robeson was not the first black to play Othello in America and sent along a photograph as evidence of a 1938 production by the Negro Fine Arts Club of Denver, obviously an amateur group, in which Thomas Henderson was Othello and Harold Baliff played Iago, both actors being Afro-Americans. The photograph was generously reproduced in *Life*, neither the editor nor Henderson and Baliff knowing that a score of black actors had previously appeared in these roles.

In 1959 Robeson took the stage for his third portrayal of Othello, this time in Stratford-upon-Avon, to open the celebration of the one-hundredth anniversary of the Shakespeare Memorial Theatre. The occasion should have been the highlight of his stage career. It was not. Robeson was sixty-one years old and had been weakened by a serious attack of bronchitis in the Soviet Union. He had endured many years of political and professional ostracism in the United States as a result of his avowed left-wing beliefs. In addition, by this time, as Herbert Marshall has shown,[11] Robeson was becoming disillusioned with the Soviet Union as a defender of subject peoples. The trauma of de-Stalinization was exposing the crimes of that regime, and Robeson's political beliefs were being shattered. Moreover, the production of the tragedy by Tony Richardson was deemed gimmicky and the casting of Sam Wanamaker as Iago and Mary Ure as Desdemona was less than felicitous. The *London Times*'s dramatic critic thought that Robeson did his utmost to show that Iago's error lay in his miscalculation of the flood of strange primitive passion that his malicious tamperings with Othello's soul released, but that he was handicapped by an overclever production, the circumstances of which worked against this interpretation. As a result, while Robeson's performance was occasionally exciting, it hardly ever touched the heart.[12] Nevertheless, he received fifteen curtain calls on opening night, and W. A. Darlington, writing in the *New York Times*, ranked his performance as the second best of all he had ever seen, inferior only to that of the English actor Godfrey Tearle.[13]

It would be gratifying to report at this juncture that the floodtide of success that greeted Robeson's 1943 *Othello* in America had swept away all obstacles and ushered in a new era of hope for the black Shakespearean actor. Such, regrettably, was not the case. More than fifteen years later conditions were still so unyielding that Actors' Equity Association was moved to sponsor a special Integration Showcase performance at the Majestic Theatre in New York, the purpose of which was to call attention to the continuing exclusion of black actors from the professional stage. The playbill for that performance on April 20, 1959, spotlighted the issue with the following admonition: "We call upon all responsible creative elements of the theatre arts to grant freedom of choice, to cast aside preconceptions regarding the casting of Negro artists, to extend their scope and participation in all types of roles in all forms of American entertainment."

Among the black performers participating in the showcase were Harry Belafonte, Diahann Carroll, Ossie Davis, Ivan Dixon, Lou Gossett, and Ellen Holly, with Lloyd Richards directing. Robeson's *Othello* was proof that a trail had been blazed, but much still remained to be done. If black actors were to be readied for the new opportunities that lay ahead, they had to be properly trained. Several black community theater groups had attempted to start acting schools as part of their programs, most notably the American Negro Theatre of Harlem in the 1940s under Abram Hill and Frederick O'Neal. These efforts were, however, short-lived, and the most consistent training available to blacks was to be found in the traditional black colleges and universities, to which some reference has already been made.

One of the black educators who was responsible for several memorable productions of Shakespeare's plays was Owen Dodson, playwright, poet, play director, and college professor.[14] Dodson, a Phi Beta Kappa graduate of Bates College, took a Master of Fine Arts degree at the Yale School of Drama in 1939. He then taught drama at a number of black institutions, including Spelman College in Atlanta, Hampton Institute in Virginia, Lincoln University in Missouri, and, finally, at Howard University, where he served for over twenty years, retiring as chairman of the department of drama. Among his many productions of established modern and classic plays were several of Shakespeare's, such as *Richard III, Macbeth,* and *Julius Caesar,* but it is for his three separate productions of *Hamlet* over a period of nineteen years that he is endearingly remembered by his students and co-workers.

At a conference of Black Theatre Program members of the American Theatre Association, Dodson recalled his work with the three *Hamlets.*[15] He saw the tragedy, in general terms, as a "spy play." Everyone was always spying on someone else. The plot supports this interpretation. Polonius sends Reynaldo to spy on Laertes in France and Claudius recruits Rosencrantz and Guildenstern to spy on Hamlet. Polonius and Claudius spy on Hamlet and Ophelia to discover if their love is chaste or carnal. Hamlet and Horatio secretly watch not the play but Claudius's reaction to it, and Hamlet spies on the king at prayers. Dodson also saw *Hamlet* as a nighttime play and felt that particular attention should be given to creating an atmosphere of darkness in which evil lurks. Thus, when in the play scene Claudius calls out "Give me some light," his cry becomes a symbol for light in a world where darkness reigns. In the first scene the presence of evil is sensed even by the subordinate characters, as indicated by Francisco's line, which becomes thematic for the whole play: "For this relief much thanks. 'Tis bitter cold / And I am sick at heart." If the tough old soldier Francisco is disturbed by the conditions at court, how much more so will they distress the philosopher, poet, playwright, and lover Hamlet.

Dodson's first production of the play took place in 1945 at Hampton Institute as part of a summer theater festival. Taking the role of the somber Danish prince was a talented twenty-two-year-old student actor of Hampton, Gordon Heath, whose Ophelia was Marion Douglas, herself the granddaughter of two famous black theater personages, the composer Will Marion Cook and his wife, the actress Abbie Mitchell. This Hamlet was a haughty and passionate prince. He spoke Shakespeare's verse beautifully but could also be emotionally explosive when the occasion required. He was genuinely in love with Ophelia, with whom he had already slept, and had given her presents as a pledge of their union. Hamlet had become totally dis-

Marion Douglas as Ophelia and Gordon Heath as Hamlet, 1945.

traught upon realizing that the queen his mother and her new husband were both false and guilty of his father's murder. They wanted
the trappings of royalty, were prepared to kill to secure them, but
were indifferent to the responsibilities that attended kingship. When
the student who was cast as Claudius dropped out, Dodson himself
took the role of the sensuous usurper (the older Hamlet, a pompous
and unaffectionate king had caused his wife to seek love elsewhere).

Dorothy Carter played Gertrude as a subdued and remorseful queen. One of the touching moments of the production, as Dodson remembered it, was when the mad Ophelia ran up a flight of stairs, disappeared behind a curtain, and the audience heard her disembodied voice calling piteously, "Where is the beauteous majesty of Denmark?" Dodson said from that moment one knew Ophelia would kill herself. There was death in her speech.

The second *Hamlet* production by Owen Dodson occurred at the Howard University Theatre in 1951. In the title role was Earle Hyman, then twenty-five and a free-lance actor in New York who had studied acting with Eva Le Gallienne at the American Theatre Wing. Born in North Carolina, he moved with his parents to Brooklyn, New York, where he attended public school, but he was shipped back to his grandparents' farm in the South for the long summer vacations. On leaving school, Earle joined the American Negro Theatre of Harlem and at seventeen was cast as the young man Anna loves in the company's sensational hit drama *Anna Lucasta*. "I played it off and on for 1,500 performances," Hyman recalled, "New York, Chicago, for nine months, London for two years. London was a big influence on my life. I did a good deal of studying there—Shakespeare and speech and voice. All the big people in London were very kind to us; they encouraged us instead of saying, 'What are *you* going to play in Shakespeare?' "[16] How he got to play Hamlet for Owen Dodson provides an interesting anecdote. Dodson was a family friend and, on visiting the Hyman home, he was invited by Hyman to listen to recordings of several actors reading selections from *Hamlet*. Dodson recognized John Gielgud's voice, then Barrymore's and Maurice Evans's, but there was one impressive reading he could not identify. It turned out to be Hyman himself, who, having never before acted a classical role, had prepared carefully for the chance to play Hamlet. His industry was rewarded with the part, and he played the prince "as a tortured youth. It had a quality of such beauty," Dodson said, "that all Washington came out to see it. We turned away 500 people from our little theatre on the last night." In his view, Earle Hyman's Hamlet was equal to or better than all the professional Hamlets of the age. It was meditative and of deep understanding. The feeling of inner torment was conveyed by the actor's speaking of the soliloquies almost in a whisper. This gave a mystical quality to the performance and had a strong effect on the audience. Dodson emphasized that this interpretation was Hyman's own decision, of which he, as director, approved. So rapt was the audience in the fate of the hero that at the end of the play when Horatio pronounced the benediction in the words "Goodnight, sweet prince, and flights of angels sing thee to thy rest," everyone in the house spontaneously crossed themselves "because they knew that Hamlet was nobility itself and greatness."

The third production, also at Howard, took place in 1964. Again Dodson was lucky to find an unexpected Hamlet. He had never been impressed with St. Clair Christmas, then a Howard architectural student and theater follower (he finally graduated with a degree in drama), whom Dodson dubbed "a giggler." Then one evening at a preliminary reading of the play, Christmas was asked to take a small part. Suddenly his apparent levity dropped like a mask, and he spoke the lines with such authority and conviction that Dodson cast him in the title role. Christmas was an athletic Hamlet. "When he dashed across the room with his cloak flying behind him, you knew he meant it," said Dodson. In his speech to the Players, he impressed upon them the need for absolute clarity in performance. He didn't want his play muddled up with gimmicks. For the play scene he changed his clothes from inky black to purple, since he was already convinced that his mousetrap scheme would be successful. Christmas also extracted all the humor there was in this scene and throughout the play. The giggling youth became the mordantly humorous Hamlet with the physical presence and athletic ability to be a dangerous adversary as well.

What these three Hamlets demonstrated to Dodson was how much the individual actor can contribute to a role when he is working with a character as complex as those Shakespeare has created. Each of his Hamlets was convincing, each had combined his individual concept of the role with his particular personality and experience to present a fresh and appealing interpretation of what Dodson called "the most beautiful and wondrous play that I know." When Dodson was asked why of all Shakespeare's plays he was so strongly attracted to *Hamlet*, he spoke first of its universality, its dealing with decisions that all people have to face as they go through life. He believed that hardly a day passes without a performance of the play occurring somewhere in the world. Then he spoke of the particular infusion that oppressed minorities could bring to this play—a deep and profound suffering born of humiliating experiences that stretched endurance to its limits. Each of his Hamlets had this quality in varying degrees, and the largely black audience empathized with it immediately. By a sad coincidence, the mothers of two of the Hamlets had died during rehearsals of the play and this personal sorrow, combined with the pain suffered as a result of racial bigotry, gave their performances an extra dimension of poignancy, particularly in the Hamlet-Gertrude scenes.

Of the three Hamlets, two went on to become professional actors, while the third, St. Clair Christmas, now deceased, became a drama instructor at Howard University, where he taught and designed scenery and costumes and continued to perform periodically in college productions. Gordon Heath capped his appearance as a student actor at Hampton with a starring role on Broadway and the West End, London. In 1945 he was cast as Brett Charles, the returned war veteran, in D'Usseau and Gow's *Deep Are the Roots*, a moving analysis of racism in the southland immediately after World War II. Heath undertook the part of Othello in a 1951 touring production for the Arts Council in England, and four years later he repeated the role on BBC television, probably the first time that a black actor was seen as a major Shakespearean character on public television in the English-speaking world. Commenting on the effect of viewing Shakespearean tragedy on the intimate television screen within the privacy of one's own home, the London *Times* critic found the production overpoweringly realistic. The English director Tony Richardson was praised for bringing "this smouldering unbearable play to life in a more concentrated and detailed form than any previous Shakespeare produced on television."[17] The advantages offered by the television camera were noted: rapid pacing of the scenes, close-ups of hands and faces, inventive details such as Othello observing Cassio and Bianca through a fishnet. Inevitably some of the poetry was sacrificed to superficial realism. Though not a powerful verse-speaker, Heath made of the Moor such a visually attractive if naive romantic, arrayed in plumes, that his Othello was likely to stick in the memory when more technical performances were forgotten. Rosemary Harris was a remarkably mature and poignant Desdemona, and Paul Rogers brought a peasant earthiness to Iago. Heath is also a professional folk singer, and in 1949 he opened his own club in Paris, where he resides, performing there, in London, and in New York. Periodically he directs and acts in plays, and in 1970 he appeared as Oedipus at the Roundabout Theatre in New York City.

Earle Hyman developed into an actor of quality, being as proficient in Shakespeare and the classic repertoire as in modern plays. After his Howard University *Hamlet*, he played a summer season at the

Earle Hyman as Othello in the Shakespeare Guild Festival production at Jan Hus Auditorium, New York, 1953.

Antioch, Ohio, Shakespeare Festival, where he first performed Othello. In New York he appeared at the Jan Hus Auditorium in 1953 as the Prince of Morocco in the Shakespearewrights' production of *The Merchant of Venice*. This was followed by his second appearance in *Othello*, this production staged by Luis Martinez for the Shakespeare Guild Festival Company. For this, his initial New York performance of the role to which all black actors aspire, Hyman at twenty-seven years of age received such flattering reviews that his professional career seemed solidly grounded. He was, according to the *New York Times*, "a magnificent Moor, a figure of great stature and power at one moment, a weak and tortured victim of suspicions and tempers in the next. . . . [He] is a performer of consummate skill [who] can move with force and distinction in any company."[18]

In the years immediately ahead, Hyman would have plenty of opportunity to test his histrionic skills against other experienced actors. In 1955 the American Shakespeare Festival Theatre at Stratford, Connecticut, was established, and Hyman was invited to join the company. Over a period of five summers he appeared in eleven roles at the theater, among his most important parts being Melun in *King John* with Morris Carnovsky and Fritz Weaver (1956), Othello with Alfred Drake as Iago and Jacqueline Brookes as Desdemona (1957), Autolycus in *The Winter's Tale* (1958), and Caliban to the Prospero of Carnovsky in *The Tempest* (1960). Other appearances included Horatio to Fritz Weaver's Hamlet, Philostrate in *A Midsummer Night's Dream*, and Alexas in *Antony and Cleopatra* with Robert Ryan and Katharine Hepburn in the principal roles. Not all these productions were critically applauded, nor was Hyman uniformly good in all his parts, though his Caliban was rated a considerable achievement, having a sullen, barbarous point of view that balanced the sunniness of other parts of the play.[19] Yet, no other black actor in America had previously been offered the chance to work with such distinguished peers in so wide a range of Shakespearean roles. Credit for this courageous approach to casting must go to the early directors of the American Shakespeare Festival Theatre, chief among whom were John Houseman and Jack Landau. Houseman, of course, had been associated with the New York Negro unit of the Federal Theatre Project in the 1930s, when his impartiality and willingness to nurture theatrical talent regardless of race had been well demonstrated.

While playing Shakespeare with the summer festival theater in Connecticut, Hyman performed a range of classic and contemporary roles in the winter months. A summary of these will illustrate his versatility at an early stage of his acting career. In New York he played the lieutenant in *No Time for Sergeants* in 1953; the title role in a dramatization of Joyce Cary's novel *Mister Johnson* and Dunois in Shaw's *Saint Joan*, both in 1956; Vladimir in *Waiting for Godot* and Antonio, the steward and husband of the ill-fated Duchess of Malfi, in 1957. In London he played the lead roles of rebellious young men in Errol John's Caribbean drama *Moon on a Rainbow Shawl* (1958) at the Royal Court Theatre and in Lorraine Hansberry's *A Raisin in the Sun* (1959) at the Adelphi Theatre. Among these parts his most notable success was Mr. Johnson, the irrepressible yet tragic African civil servant who is trapped between admiration for the British and the pull of his own native culture. Hyman was unanimously praised by the critics for a portrayal that was characterized as "superb," "brilliant," "fabulous," and "clearly the best of the season."[20]

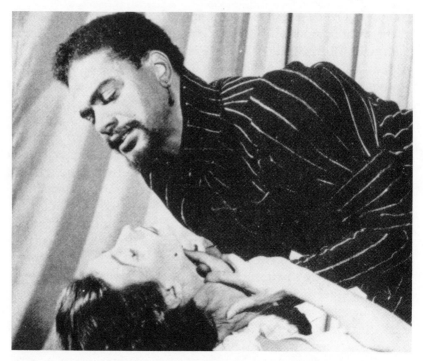

Earle Hyman as Othello and Jacqueline Brookes as Desdemona in the
American Shakespeare Festival Theatre production directed by
John Houseman, 1957.

When Hyman came to act Othello for the third time in the Stratford, Connecticut, season of 1957, he explained to an interviewer the meaning that the role had for him. As an alien in Venetian society, Othello was a nonplaced being who had constantly to prove himself. Similarly, Hyman, a young southern black shipped up to Brooklyn for public-school education in a white society, felt a goading pressure to place himself: "It was only six years ago that I came to realize that my placement depended on myself. Where I used to want to lose difference between myself and the people around me, I now believe that it's just that difference that's important. For me, this is the same apotheosis Othello undergoes after he has killed Desdemona."[21]

The production, directed by John Houseman, was visually striking, with original sets and costumes by Rouben Ter-Arutunian, but *New York Times* critic Brooks Atkinson was disappointed in the performances. He thought that while the acting was intelligent and agreeable, it lacked the fire, passion, and size of a Shakespearean tragedy. Hyman's Othello was "without depth" and the Iago of Alfred Drake was "mainly romantic."[22]

A completely different appraisal is given by Caldwell Titcomb of Brandeis University, a Shakespearean scholar who has made a special study of Othello on stage. In an extensive review of the Stratford, Connecticut, production, Titcomb found Hyman to be ideally suited to the role, if still a bit young. Handsome and tall at six feet three, he properly cut a figure of great physical and moral stature. He possessed a rich, sonorous voice, complemented by an extraordinarily expressive face. Most Othellos, in Titcomb's view, make the mistake of getting enraged too soon, with the result that as the play progresses their bellowing becomes unintelligible and meaningless. Hyman avoided this error. For instance, when Othello says of his wife, "I'll tear her all to pieces,"

> most actors would here face the balcony and bellow their guts out. But Hyman, realizing that at this point in the drama Iago has not yet fully drawn out Othello's latent bestiality, delivers the line at medium volume and with his back to the audience! But he underscores the thought by extending his right hand overhead and pulling it down to his side like a claw grating on glass. That is real artistry; the effect is electric. And he makes the most of the poetry in the role. . . . Just as Richard Burbage was the great Othello of Shakespeare's day, David Garrick the great Othello of the 18th century and Tommaso Salvini of the 19th century, Earle Hyman bids fair to be the great Othello of our century.[23]

On January 30, 1978, at the Roundabout Theatre in New York, Hyman once again opened in *Othello*, reviving a role he had first attempted over twenty-five years earlier and had since played repeatedly. The critics again divided sharply in their opinions. Richard Eder in the *New York Times* felt that while Hyman's performance was lucid enough, it lacked depth and passion. This view was essentially shared by some reviewers. On the other hand, Edith Oliver in the *New Yorker* found Hyman's speeches to be fresh and spontaneous in an otherwise lackluster production; Clive Barnes in the *New York Post* considered Hyman to be one of the finest interpreters of Othello, while William Glover, writing for the Associated Press, found Hyman to be "in masterful control of a portrayal that from a quiet start builds until with juggernaut force it explodes into emotional

Earle Hyman as Othello and Nicholas Kepros as Iago in the Roundabout Theatre Company production, directed by Gene Feist, New York, 1978.

immolation. . . . Hyman's long enthrallment with the role appears simply and grandly to have created a concept of definitive, intricate power."[24]

Mr. Hyman's appearances have not been limited to America. He has played in Norway, speaking the two official languages used in the theaters of that country,[25] and he has appeared also on the stages of Sweden and Denmark, where he spoke Norwegian while the rest of the players spoke their native tongue. In 1965 he was honored in Oslo for the best performance that year in the title role of *The Emperor Jones*. It cannot be denied that the repeated engagements Hyman enjoyed with the American Shakespeare Festival Theatre in Connecticut, coming early in his career, had a profound influence on his development as an actor of remarkable scope and variety. He has never been limited to black parts and, quite possibly, has performed as many Shakespearean roles as any black actor since Ira Aldridge.

While these encouraging developments were taking place in America, the situation in England, where traditionally there was no bar to the employment of black actors in Shakespeare, was becoming increasingly difficult. During the Second World War thousands of black servicemen and women from America and the Caribbean had gone to Britain, and many eventually settled there. The Caribbean influx continued in the postwar years, with skillful writers, artists, and performers seeking professional training abroad and a metropolitan market in which to display their art. With a growing community of black actors such as had never previously existed in Britain, interracial casting continued to be a rare event, the London and provincial producers seeming to ignore the presence of black performers of talent in their midst.

Edric Connor as Gower in Pericles, *directed by Tony Richardson, at Shakespeare Memorial Theatre, Stratford-upon-Avon, England, 1958.*

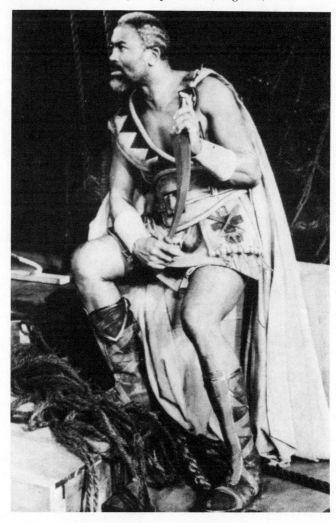

Two notable exceptions to this exclusionary practice were Gordon Heath's previously mentioned touring and television Othellos and the 1958 Stratford-upon-Avon production of *Pericles*, directed by Tony Richardson. This was Richardson's first stage production of Shakespeare—he had previously won acclaim for directing John Osborne's *Look Back in Anger* in London—and he was assigned a play that is not only episodic in structure and improbable in story, but also seldom performed. Richardson decided to make Gower, the chorus who is "to sing a song that old was sung," into a veritable balladeer whose purpose it would be to narrate the old tale for a modern audience. For this role he cast Edric Connor, the Trinidad-born concert singer. As Gower, Connor opened the play seated in a galley ship with rowers chanting the words of a sea chantey. He sang and spoke Gower's linking narrative to the intimate audience of boatmen, supported by "nautical choruses and eastern music recorded from shawms, Syrian reeds, Egyptian pipes and a great assortment of other ancient and exotic instruments."[26] This innovation, for which Richardson was critically commended, translated into theatrical terms the dramatic intention of the chorus and also helped to overcome the slow-moving first two acts of the play. The engagement did not lead to further roles for Connor, however, which is just as well. He was a concert artist with a richly textured voice of considerable power and a fine exponent of Caribbean folk songs and Negro spirituals. But he was not a dramatic actor and a very unlikely Shakespearean.

8
How Relevant Is Race?

WHEN IN 1954 the U.S. Supreme Court ruled that separate educational facilities were inherently unequal and, a year later, called upon school districts to desegregate "with all deliberate speed," the stage was set for a comprehensive attack on all forms of discriminatory practices against racial minorities. The demand for equal rights in every area of employment reached into the entertainment industry. An increasing number of college-educated and academy-trained black actors and actresses sought entrance into the professional theater and clamored for roles in nonblack plays, requiring a more venturesome policy in casting Shakespearean productions. True, opportunities had been provided for Robeson and Hyman to appear on the public stage in Shakespeare, but an array of black talent remained essentially invisible. This was particularly true of black actresses, who were never considered for any of Shakespeare's heroines, since, apart from Cleopatra—a role that was seldom if ever thought of as black—nonwhite female characters do not exist in his plays. Casting black women in Shakespeare, except as silent ladies-in-waiting or other supernumeraries, seemed to pose insuperable problems for producers, despite the fact that many of the actresses were so lightly complexioned as to be almost white. More than one actress has been known to complain bitterly of the predicament she has experienced by reason of skin color: "I've just always been too white to be black or too black to be white, which, you know, gets to you after a while, particularly when the roles keep passing you by."[1]

This was the state of affairs when Joseph Papp made his spectacular entrance in the producing arena of New York City with the novel idea of a summer season of free Shakespeare in Central Park. Papp had actually begun his Shakespeare work in 1953, two years before the Stratford, Connecticut, festival got underway, and had given his first modern dress productions of several of Shakespeare's plays in a Lower Eastside church in 1955. So daring was his proposal for free public theater in a commercially oriented metropolis like New York, it took some time to persuade the authorities and secure the funding to get his project firmly established. By 1957 Papp had settled into the Belvedere Lake Theatre (later rebuilt and renamed the Delacorte Theatre) of New York's Central Park, and Shakespearean productions began to roll from his shop with assemblyline precision: two, three, four, and sometimes five productions a season.

Papp's aim was to popularize Shakespeare, to make his plays accessible to all New Yorkers, but principally to the disadvantaged and ethnic minorities who seldom if ever went to the theater. To achieve this aim more completely, he introduced a school program in 1960 and a mobile theater four years later, operating them in addition to his principal productions in the Central Park theater during the summer season. Then in 1967 Papp established the festival unit in a permanent home at the old Astor Library landmark building on Lafayette Street, lower New York City. He converted the premises into his Public Theatre, which houses five performing spaces where a variety of plays, including new and contemporary works, is presented year-round.

With three trailer trucks to serve as a portable stage and dressing rooms, the first mobile theater production was a handsome *Midsummer Night's Dream*. It played fifty-eight performances in small parks, squares, ballfields, and other spaces, celebrating, as it were, the fourth centenary of Shakespeare's birth by bringing his plays to the nonplaygoing American public. Howard Taubman in the Sunday *New York Times* found an interesting comparison between Shakespeare's original audiences and those who flocked to Papp's first mobile theater production:

> Watching a performance of this itinerant "Dream" in Harlem, I had the feeling that it might have been something like this in the inn yards when the strolling players of Shakespeare's time toured the countryside. . . . The rude mechanicals and hempen homespuns of Shakespeare's time probably did not appreciate all

the subtleties of their playwright's flowery diction, but you may
be sure that they howled with joy at Bottom and his cronies, at
the confusion of the lovers and at the good-humored mischief
and confusion of Robin Goodfellow. So it was in Harlem.[2]

Taubman ended his review with words of praise for the imaginative
producer.

Papp was astute enough to realize that in a cosmopolitan city like
New York, popular theater would need to be multiracial in order to
have the broadest possible appeal. It also made good practical sense
for a project, constantly in need of funds, to cast its net widely so as to
attract greater public and foundation support. He explained his production philosophy in these words: "Whenever you do a classic, you
recreate life in the terms that now exist, both politically and socially.
If you try to reproduce a play the way it was done originally . . . it becomes a museum piece. You have to draw from what exists. What
exists in New York, and all throughout the world are different colored
people. And you can't deny their existence."[3] The approach, essentially sound, would lead Papp into some questionable interpretations
of Shakespeare, but for the moment it was opening doors that had
been long bolted against black actors appearing in major Shakespearean roles. By 1974 Papp's festival theater enterprise had produced all
but one of Shakespeare's plays, many of them several times. In the
process he had employed dozens of black actors, some in principal
and others in supporting roles, completely disregarding the tradition
that gave most of Shakespeare's leading roles to white actors. For the
first time in the history of professional production in America, plays
were cast on the basis of an actor's presumed ability to portray a role
without regard to skin color. In racially integrated productions, Afro-
American women began to perform parts from which they were previously disqualified. Two such actresses who played several roles in
Papp's companies were Ellen Holly and Jane White.

A New Yorker by birth, Ellen Holly gained a bachelor's degree
at Hunter College, where she appeared in school productions. Then
she pursued further studies in acting at the Perry Mansfield Theatre
School in Colorado. Her first professional role with the New York
Shakespeare Festival was, strangely enough, Desdemona to William
Marshall's commanding Othello in a 1958 production directed by
Stuart Vaughan. Here was an ironic twist to the whole question of the
relevance of racial ancestry in acting Shakespeare. Ellen Holly, by

Lance Cunard as Charles VI, Ellen Holly as the Princess Katherine, and Robert Hooks as Henry V in King Henry V, *directed by Joseph Papp, presented by the New York Shakespeare Festival's Mobile Theatre, 1965.*

conventional standards a member of the black race despite her light skin, and therefore subject to the historic inequities that have beset black people in America, playing the leading white female role in a racially integrated production of *Othello!* And no walls came tumbling down. Holly was apparently not experienced enough for the role. Her performance was deemed pleasant but elementary; in her first attempt to act Shakespeare, she failed to extract all the nuances in the character of the unjustly abused Desdemona.

Holly's next role for the New York Shakespeare Festival was Iras in *Antony and Cleopatra* (1963). In the following three years she appeared in a series of Mobile Theatre productions for the festival, touring the city parks and schools for several months as Titania in *A Midsummer Night's Dream* (1964), as Katherine, Princess of France, in *Henry V*, which played in repertory with her Kate in *The Taming of the Shrew* (1965), and as Lady Macbeth to the Macbeth of James Earl

Jones (1966). In her various roles Miss Holly became more competent and accomplished as each season advanced. An attractive woman of delicate proportions with a mellifluous voice, she has a quick kinetic sense, and some of the resonances of Shakespeare's verse often seem to escape her. At her best, however, she can be irresistible on stage, as may have been the case with her Princess of France in *Henry V*. The *New York Times* review of that production, referring to the English lesson scene between the princess and her lady-in-waiting, found it to be "perhaps the funniest, and certainly the most charming scene . . . a pair of lovelies played with wit and grace."[4] The *Macbeth* production was not especially distinguished, and reviewers noted that a quality of broad playing was necessary for the outdoor park audiences. Yet at least one critic held that Holly gave "some degree of darkness to the character that impelled her to conspire with her husband at murder" and that this contrasted nicely with "a hint of softness, a touch of uncertainty that brought on her insanity as the killings mounted."[5]

More important perhaps than a critical examination of the work of the players in Papp's Mobile Theatre operation is the effect it had on city audiences, which were made up almost entirely of middle- and lower-income groups, most of whom had never before seen live theater. A detailed report on audience reaction to *A Midsummer Night's Dream* showed that when the play was presented in a predominantly black neighborhood, the interracial casting was noted with surprise and approval.[6] The experience, as one observer put it, was "a valuable object lesson in democracy, a good one to bring to the troubled neighborhoods of the city."[7] Taking shows to the people in this way made them realize that Shakespeare was not only for the upper classes or the college educated, but for everybody. On one occasion when *Macbeth* was being performed in Washington Square, a heavy shower of rain scattered the audience of 1,600. Twenty minutes later, when the shower had subsided and the stage was mopped, the spectators returned in soaked clothing, again as intent and appreciative as they had been before the downpour. Occasionally the raucous behavior of audiences unnerved some of the actors to the extent that the report concluded it may become necessary to recruit and train actors with a sense of mission for such presentations. Finally, the Mobile Theatre was seen as a force that could be instrumental in bringing new audiences into the professional theater. For all these reasons, then, Holly's contribution to the touring program deserves recognition. In

1973, after an absence of some years, she returned to the New York Shakespeare Festival to play the part of Regan in *King Lear* at the Delacorte Theatre in Central Park. That production will be discussed later in reviewing the work of James Earl Jones, who played Lear.

Jane White, daughter of the late Walter White who served as secretary of the National Association for the Advancement of Colored People, presents a clear example of the frustrations that in the past have besieged the Afro-American actress. A graduate of Smith College, Miss White got an early start in professional theater playing on Broadway as the female lead in *Strange Fruit* opposite Mel Ferrer. This was in 1945, a year after she left college. That lackluster production, based on Lillian Smith's novel about a black woman passing for white, did not help Miss White's professional aspirations, although the more discerning critics found her personable on stage and capable of better things. There followed intermittent engagements on and away from Broadway. These included White's first Shakespearean role as Katherine in *The Taming of the Shrew*, together with that of Barbara Allen in *Dark of the Moon* for the Hayloft Theatre in Allentown, Pennsylvania, in 1949. She had the title role in an Equity Li-

Jane White as Volumnia in a scene from Coriolanus, *directed by Gladys Vaughan, presented by the New York Shakespeare Festival, Joseph Papp, producer, at the Delacorte Theatre, 1965.*

Jane White as the Queen and Sam Waterston as Cloten in Cymbeline, *directed by A. J. Antoon, presented by the New York Shakespeare Festival, Joseph Papp, producer, at the Delacorte Theatre, 1971.*

brary Theatre production of *Lysistrata* at the Lenox Hill Playhouse in 1956 and in 1958–59 she appeared in two Phoenix Theatre productions, but a decade went by before she was cast in another Shakespeare play, and then it was a repetition of the shrewish Kate for the New York Shakespeare Festival in 1960. By 1964, after almost twenty years of uncertainty, Jane White decided to go abroad. "I had the feeling I didn't have much of a future here in America,"[8] she once said, looking back on those times. She married and moved to Rome with her husband.

Some months prior to leaving for Rome, Miss White was cast in the New York Shakespeare Festival 1965 productions in Central Park. She was the Princess of Navarre in *Love's Labor's Lost*, took the commanding role of Volumnia, mother of the proud Roman patrician Coriolanus played by Robert Burr, and she also had the part of Helen of Troy in *Troilus and Cressida*. Here in a single engagement, hard on the heels of her decision to emigrate, was the unique chance to play three of Shakespeare's woman characters, each very different from the other, the type of roles for which she had become an actress. Of the *Coriolanus* production, which was directed by Gladys Vaughan, Judith Crist wrote in the *New York Herald Tribune*:

> Mr. Burr and Miss White bring a fiercely contemporary note to their roles. . . . [She] exhibits a will as rigid as her backbone, but manages always to combine with her tone of the super Roman matron the neurotic nagging of the voracious mother, the widow who lives vicariously. . . . This *Coriolanus*, sparked by Mr. Burr and Miss White, is more than a theater piece; it is exciting and absorbing theater.[9]

Howard Taubman in the *New York Times* called Miss White "a passionate and eloquent Volumnia," and it seemed appropriate that she should be chosen to receive the *Village Voice* Obie award for her performances in the park that season. Abroad Miss White appeared in productions of American plays in Paris and Rome, but her heart remained in her native New York. She returned to the city in 1967, succeeding Irene Pappas in the role of Clytemnestra in Michael Cacoyannis's production of *Iphigenia in Aulis*, and took the part of the Queen in *Cymbeline* at Central Park in the summer of 1971. In the 1975 season of the American Shakespeare Festival Theatre in Stratford, Connecticut, she played Goneril to Morris Carnovsky's Lear, a performance that elicited high praise from Peter Saccio, writing for *Shakespeare Quarterly*:

> She has power, a superb sense of style, and a marvellous speaking voice: a richly musical contralto containing more tones than one thinks possible, capable of either diamond brilliance or velvet warmth regardless of what volume she chooses to work at. . . . This fine technical equipment was at the service of a fine intelligence. . . . Here was a Goneril first commanding the lusts that drove her and then devoured by them, so that the woman ultimately vanished in feral chaos. Miss White gave us experiential knowledge of some of the things Shakespeare was writing about.[10]

While waiting for greater acting challenges, Miss White acquired a new career as a cabaret singer in her husband's restaurant in New York City.

Papp's policy of casting blacks as leads in racially mixed productions extended to male actors as well. As a result, a number of Shakespearean heroes that had never before been professionally played by

*Jane White as Goneril in a scene from the American Shakespeare Festival
Theatre production of* King Lear, *directed by Anthony Page, 1975.*

*Robert Hooks as King
Henry V in a scene from
the production directed by
Joseph Papp, presented by the
New York Shakespeare Festi-
val's Mobile Theatre, 1965.*

black performers were now being offered to them. A few examples
will suffice. Staged by Papp himself, Frank Silvera appeared as King
Lear with Roscoe Lee Browne as his wistful Fool (1962). Silvera had
been attracted to Shakespeare's tragic king since 1948 when, between
his performances in *Anna Lucasta* in London, he had visited the
Hammersmith Theatre to watch Donald Wolfit play the role in a performance that was adjudged the definitive Lear of the age. Though he
was an actor of considerable skill in contemporary drama, Silvera
lacked the bravura approach required by this part, his low-key acting
being most effective only in the final scenes with Cordelia, which
were genuinely moving. One could have wished that Silvera did not
have to perform what is perhaps the most demanding tragic role in all
of Shakespeare with so meager a preparation for it. Then Robert
Hooks appeared as King Henry V in 1965, confusing the critics who, it

seems, had some difficulty in judging his performance objectively. "King Henry was especially good, combining fiery grace with an almost tragic sensitivity" is a far cry from "Mr. Hooks strains a little and wears a perpetually worried-angry look, as if the cares of Knighthood and the demands of the role were a little beyond him." Another reviewer saw it as an act of courage on Papp's part "to put a Negro in the role of Henry V," suggesting that for the writer it may likewise have been an act of courage to review it.[11] Yet a third example was the casting of the 1965 *Troilus and Cressida* that saw Roscoe Lee Browne as Ulysses, James Earl Jones as Ajax, and Al Freeman, Jr., as Diomedes. This was Browne's seventh appearance with the festival company in ten years, and while most of his parts were secondary, at least he was serving an apprenticeship in Shakespeare that would one day make him the superlative craftsman that he is.

A "pop" version of *Hamlet* with Cleavon Little in the title role illustrates the lengths to which Papp was prepared to go in his eagerness to make his productions relevant and accessible to a mass public. Produced for a four-week touring program in the city parks in 1968, this adaptation turned the world's most admired tragedy into an interracial political comedy ninety minutes long:

> Cleavon Little . . . is a black, lithe, monomaniacal Hamlet, scheming to overthrow his white stepfather, who, as played by Ralph Waite, looks like a cross between Fidel Castro and the Late Late Show's Barton MacLane. In this context, too, Anita Danglee is a provocative Queen Gertrude, an aging red-haired beauty who probably once hustled in a Havana bar and who now, most likely, tipples behind the Citadel arras. Unfortunately, however, Shakespeare was not writing about either Caribbean politics or biracial societies, nor did he write the outline for an absurdist comedy, which is the way this *Hamlet* winds up.[12]

The show played primarily for laughs, most of them gratuitous, and one cannot but hear the words of Hamlet cautioning the players about stage business that makes the unskillful laugh while the judicious grieve. Papp's response would be that he deliberately set out to "shatter the play, to fragment it, and to turn it inside out," his justification being that it would be more meaningful to the current generation. "We got more young people coming to *Hamlet* than came to *Hair*" was his proud boast.[13] That what they saw was in fact not *Hamlet* didn't seem to bother him.

Jonelle Allen as Silvia and Clifton Davis as Valentine in a musical version of
Two Gentlemen of Verona, *adapted by John Guare and Mel Shapiro, directed
by Mel Shapiro, presented by New York Shakespeare Festival, Joseph Papp,
producer, at Delacorte Theatre, 1971.*

With yet another adaptation of Shakespeare devised for touring and produced with a biracial cast, Papp scored, if not a critical, certainly a commercial success. This was John Guare's musical version of *Two Gentlemen of Verona* (1971), one of Shakespeare's plays that, unlike *Hamlet*, it is probably no travesty to fool around with. Mel Shapiro directed, and Galt MacDermot, fresh from his triumph with *Hair*, supplied the music. In the production, Proteus and Julia were Hispanics (in exciting moments Julia would break out in Spanish dialogue), while Valentine, Silvia, and Silvia's father the Duke were all played by black actors, the rest being Caucasian. While some of the critics quibbled about the nonsensicality of the innovations, it was all tolerable fun, and no one had anything but a rave notice for the Silvia of Jonelle Allen, whose performance was little short of sensational. Walter Kerr called her "an untamed enchantress" with "manic feet" and an "electrified profile" whose body "quivers when she is standing absolutely still."[14] The show was the first of Papp's productions to move to Broadway, where it enjoyed a respectable run and eventually won the Tony and Drama Critics Circle Awards as Best Musical of the season.

The civil-rights movement of the 1960s had adopted a Gandhian philosophy of nonviolent protest in order to dramatize the harshness of southern discriminatory laws that existed in defiance of federal law, as well as the de facto segregational practices that obtained in targeted northern cities. In the 1960s and '70s radical elements of the movement, frustrated by the slowness of effecting reform measures that had become bogged down in legal wrangling, abandoned nonviolence in favor of militant confrontation. They called for immediate action to abolish all forms of racial discrimination, demanded reparation for centuries-long oppression of Afro-Americans, sought equal access to jobs and other opportunities for education and advancement. Much of this militancy occurred on college campuses around the nation, but in a more violent form it was manifested in street rioting, burning and looting in the inner cities, and shoot-outs with police and law officers. This domestic upheaval was played out against the backdrop of a seemingly endless conflict in Vietnam that had seriously split the country and was not without its racial overtones. The most powerful Western nation was waging terrible war against an impoverished third-world country half a globe away in order to save the world from communism.

Resident regional theaters and festival producers who were involved in staging Shakespeare responded to the pressures of the times in various ways. Since most of them were dependent on government or foundation subsidies to balance their budgets, they could not afford the charge of being racist or insensitive to black aspirations. With the apparent success of Papp's varied experiments clearly in mind, some producers decided to deal with the racial issue head-on by slanting their productions, wherever possible, to highlight racial attitudes and conflicts. Others sought for the first time to add a few black performers to the composition of their companies and to offer them black or nonblack roles. Special financing was enlisted for hiring black actors, with the result that when those grants expired, black performers were no longer employed, and the situation was returned to the status quo. Still others found a simpler way of dealing with the problem temporarily. They decided to stage those Shakespearean dramas that include black characters or characters that were conventionally played by black actors—Othello, the Prince of Morocco, Aaron the Moor, Caliban, and Kate the Shrew—thereby justifying the inclusion of a single black in their traditionally all-white companies.

The Washington, D.C., Summer Shakespeare Festival is a case in point. In 1968, the year in which civil-rights leader and Nobel Peace Prize winner the Rev. Martin Luther King, Jr., was gunned down by a white assassin, the festival chose *Romeo and Juliet* for production at its outdoor Sylvan Theatre, situated on the slope of the Washington Monument grounds. The director Philip Burton cast the two feuding houses as if racial antagonism was the issue, Juliet's family being black and Romeo's white. The setting was moved from Verona to New Orleans, and the ball scene became a part of the Mardi Gras festivities. Burton felt that his innovations were natural and obvious and was pleased that he could "put the current racial conflict to good use." The part of Juliet was played by Janet League, a graduate of the Goodman School of Drama in Chicago, whose previous experience included performances with the Lincoln Center Repertory Company and the American Shakespeare Festival Theatre in Stratford, Connecticut.

Reviewing the production for *Shakespeare Quarterly*, Lynn K. Horobetz found that it lacked both significance and focus and that it sidestepped the racial issue which should never have been raised. Overall, the verse speaking was devoid of lyrical delicacy, and the balcony scene was played for laughs, with Romeo jumping up and down

trying to touch Juliet's hand. Juliet herself "was altogether credible and winning as a high-spirited, volatile adolescent just emerging
from the schoolroom. Her reactions were as sudden and tempestuous
as a child's. . . . What the love of Romeo and Juliet lacked in depth
was balanced by the fragile intensity of their relationship. They fell in
love like two children discovering an exhilarating new game, reck-
lessly and enthusiastically."[15] The maturation of this love was well
depicted when Juliet learned she was to marry Paris. As Capulet raged
and the Nurse counseled ineffectively, it was clear that the roles had
been reversed: the adults were behaving like children, and Juliet,
with fierce determination, had assumed the maturity her elders had
surrendered. William Vine was a fading bon vivant Capulet, and Damon W. Brazwell a sympathetic and heroic Tybalt, who was prodded
by Mercutio into a fight he never wanted. Horobetz found much to
commend in the production and regretted Philip Burton's attempt to
turn it into a morality play. She admitted that in the summer of 1968
the racial issue deserved far more than a token theatrical gesture,
which is all the production offered. Richard Coe in the *Washington
Post* was less disturbed by the racial aspect which, he thought, after
the opening street scene of Creole merchants and hawkers, tended to
become less noticeable from a distance as the play progressed. The
amplification made the voices very clear but they lacked lyricism,
and the acting of the principals was earnest but passionless. For Coe
the most attractive aspects of the show were the unaccustomed locale and the effectiveness of setting and costumes.[16] At the time,
Washington, D.C., had a population of over 700,000 people, two-
thirds of whom were black. A large number of the audience was no
doubt made up of this majority group, and the question arises whether their reactions to the production were in any way represented by
the official critics.

The 1970 *Tempest* at Washington's Sylvan Theatre, directed by
Nagel Jackson, was also somewhat innovative. Simple, unpreten-
tious, and basically traditional, as the production was, it contained
"a slight dislocation of Shakespeare's text and probably of his intention."[17] The innovation concerned the characters of Caliban and Ariel, both played by black actors. In the case of Caliban, Henry Baker
interpreted the savage as neither deformed nor servile, but rather
violent and arrogant. Keenly aware of how this portrayal might be
viewed by a Washington audience, Jeanne Addison Roberts writes in
Shakespeare Quarterly:

He was powerful and intractable from beginning to end. He never actually obeyed the command of his new master Stephano to kiss his foot. And even when he spoke of his fear of pinching, he did not cower. Most significantly of all, he never uttered the final resolve given him by Shakespeare that he would be wise hereafter and go seek grace. He admitted his folly in worshipping a drunkard, but, after rejecting the "dull fool," strode angrily off stage, an enigma reverberating in the memory.

In the minds of a modern American audience, Caliban might evoke guilty thoughts of the plight of the Native American, especially when he speaks of being dispossessed of his land. Seeing this role played by Baker with his black skin, flawed diction, and minstrel-type mouth painted on a greenish face, and combining that impression with the use of the word "slave" in the play, the Washington audience could not fail to identify him with the black American.

Ariel, portrayed with grace and gentle authority by Darryl Croxton, contrasted nicely with Caliban by being witty and amenable, even compassionate, although he was "such a light shade of black as to reinforce the vulgar prejudice that lighter is better." Roberts saw the casting of these two characters, both of whom resented being servants to an overlord, as symbolic of the idea that the black man could be either a threat or an instrument of salvation to white society. A crude analogy would be to consider Caliban a black militant and Ariel an Uncle Tom, but this scenario would forebode a further confrontation rather than reconciliation when they are left alone on the island at the end. In her review, Roberts emphasized that the black-white conflict was not allowed to become the central issue in the play but served merely to lessen the allegory in favor of realism. She felt that the production managed to maintain a delicate balance between being both Shakespearean and contemporary.

That the racial problem remained prominent in the minds of producers and directors for a number of years can be seen in another interracial production of *Romeo and Juliet*, this time by the Shakespearean Society of America at its intimate imitation Globe Playhouse in Los Angeles in 1977. The society, under the leadership of R. Thad Taylor, had embarked on a plan to produce the complete Shakespearean canon in monthly sequence. Having reached the halfway mark, it closed out the year triumphantly with *Romeo and Juliet*. This production was directed by Taylor who, from the plays' imagery

Morris Carnovsky as King Lear and Ruby Dee as Cordelia in the American Shakespeare Festival Theatre production, directed by Allen Fletcher, 1965.

of doves and crows, day and night, light and dark, drew the idea of casting the Montagues as whites and the Capulets as blacks (although Juliet's nurse was white). No significant changes were made in the text, but a type of Elizabethan "soul music" was added.

Calling the result "fascinating," the reviewer thought that Taylor's interpretation worked effectively on stage. The concept was supported by an excellent cast: "Eugenia Wright glowed as a very young, very wide-eyed Juliet. As Romeo, Ronald Morhous was pale and cerebral by comparison. . . . Yet his reserve complemented Ms. Wright's openness. The lovers were a harmony of opposites: light and dark, playful and somber. The effect was genuinely tragic—no mere gimmick. The supporting cast around them was solid."[18] The production was not without its directorial flaws. It was unconscionably slow-moving (it stretched to almost four hours), but it succeeded in making Shakespeare contemporary, it revitalized the play's imagery, and it explained the nature of the "ancient grudge" clearer than ever before.

If these companies reinterpreted Shakespeare in order to reflect the racial tensions in American society and concomitantly to provide acting roles for nonwhite players, there were other companies besides Papp's New York Festival Theatre that recruited black actors and offered them leading Shakespearean roles that in the past had been reserved to white performers.

The American Shakespeare Festival Theatre in Connecticut, having lost Earle Hyman in 1960 and conscious of the black talent regularly on display in the rival summer Shakespeare season in Central Park, woke up to its responsibilities and invited that engaging actress Ruby Dee, a graduate of Hunter College, to undertake her first full-scale Shakespearean roles. Dee had already won triumphs in contemporary plays such as *A Raisin in the Sun* and *Purlie Victorious* and would certainly prove a drawing card among the black community in New York and Connecticut. In the season she played Cordelia to a masterly Lear by Morris Carnovsky, bringing her own unique quality

Gloria Foster and Alvin Epstein double as Hippolyta/Titania and Theseus/Oberon in the Circle-in-the-Square production of A Midsummer Night's Dream, *directed by John Hancock, at the Theatre de Lys, New York, 1967.*

of warmth and tenderness to the final scenes of the great tragedy. She doubled this role with that of Katherine in *The Taming of the Shrew* to the Petruchio of John Cunningham in a production that was strangely conceived to be a performance by a group of strolling players dressed as Spaniards. Tumbling out of a wagon drawn on stage, the troupe lay to with a clamorous, restless will as if they intended to make up for the inadequacies of the script with unnecessary noise. Although Ruby Dee is not ideally suited to the role of the rebellious, man-hating Kate, her knockabout wooing scene with Petruchio was played with fiery spirit and her final speech on the duty a wife owes her husband was delivered with an amusing lightness.

Papp had cast Ellen Holly as Titania in his 1964 touring version of *A Midsummer Night's Dream*, so it was no novelty when Gloria Foster turned up doubling as a black fairy princess and a black Amazon queen to Alvin Epstein's Oberon/Theseus in a production directed by John Hancock. It was brought from San Francisco and opened off-Broadway at the Circle-in-the-Square in 1967. What was novel about the production was its conception and the outrageous divertissements incorporated in the show, which included a transvestite Hermia, a glowing codpiece on Demetrius, and a jukebox emitting Mendelssohn's score. Hancock was one of the very few blacks to direct a professional Shakespeare company since the first decade of the century. At least his direction eschewed the racial theme and opted instead for an absurdist interpretation after the Polish scholar Jan Kott. His spirit world was malevolent, while his humans were callous and lustful. The elves and fairies of the Athenian wood were presented as mysterious creatures under black light and phosphorescent paint that seemed to suggest eerie mischief, if not downright evil. Into this forbidding forest strode Gloria Foster as "a kind of Mae West Titania [or] as a sulky, leopardskin-clad Hippolyta. . . . It is unfortunate that any theatre man, although moved by a genuine desire to give contemporary meaning to Shakespeare, should be so trapped by gimmicks that he destroys the tone and the sense of the text,"[19] wrote one reviewer. And another wrote: "Mr. Hancock makes all the points he is out to make, but this prevents him from making the points that have kept the play alive since it was written."[20] Needless to say, this production was a director's piece, the acting, such as it was, being completely subordinated to the concept and theme.

Three different versions of *Macbeth*, all staged in 1977, offered the role of the power-drunk queen to a black actress. Two of the productions took place in New York, where Ellen Holly had previously toured in the part for the Shakespeare Festival. At Ellen Stewart's La Mama Experimental Theatre, a tightened version by the Lithuanian exile Jonas Jurasas emphasized the sensuality, lust, and greed of the main characters. In a highly ritualistic and symbolic production, soldiers moved in a stylized manner, primitive musical instruments beat rhythmically and the witches' ceremonial bowl contained a deep red frothing brew (it turned out to be real beef blood) that served as both blood and wine. Almost everyone's hands and Macbeth's severed head were immersed in it by the play's end. Barbara Montgomery played Lady Macbeth "beautifully, subtly, suggestively, an embodiment of sexuality and passion with a sense of evil that makes even the

Barbara Montgomery as Lady Macbeth and Tom Kopache as Macbeth in the La Mama Experimental Theatre Club's production, directed by Jonas Jurasas, 1977.

witches cower," wrote critic Ellen Foreman, who was deeply moved by the production. Yet she found one aspect troubling. Montgomery was the single black member of the cast; all the others were white except for one Oriental in the small role of the doctor. Since the interracial character of the production had been stressed in preperformance publicity, Foreman was moved to ask, "Was it intentional to link sexuality and evil with blackness? For what other purpose is the interracial aspect stressed?"[21]

The second production that year was a questionable attempt to resuscitate Orson Welles's 1936 voodoo *Macbeth*, setting it in an unspecified English-speaking Caribbean island, where the natives spoke in different dialects and the indigenous cultures appeared to be ridiculed. It was directed by Edmund Cambridge with an all-black cast for Henry Street Settlement's New Federal Theatre, and the producer, Woodie King, Jr., explained his reasons for reviving the 1936 success. King had been inspired by the work of the old Federal Theatre, which is why the new theater, founded in 1970, was given its name. When Welles's script, which was believed to be lost, turned up in 1974 in an airplane hangar in Maryland, King felt impelled to re-stage it. Despite an impressive set and effective lighting, the production, in the view of some critics, failed to generate the excitement of its progenitor. Esther Rolle, a popular television comedienne called upon to play Lady Macbeth, conveyed a certain regal bearing and had her moments in the sleep-walking scene, but apart from some primitive dancing and animated drumming, the production as a whole was tame, and Lex Manson as Macbeth was strangely resigned. What was it about Welles's original show that had created such a stir? Robert Hapgood researched this and came up with at least a partial answer:

> One could imagine Welles's boldest effects (all omitted from the revival): Hecate's twelve-foot bullwhip, the on-stage voodoo drummers, the giant mask of Banquo, the 18-foot drop of the cream-faced loon, whom Macbeth first shot and then kicked to the courtyard below. Sitting in the Library, I came to realize that I was finding there exactly the kind of theatrical excitement that I had missed in the theatre the night before.[22]

It is only fair to say that Edith Oliver in the *New Yorker* called the show "a tremendous artistic success." She saw the focal point as "Hecate's domain—the land of the supernatural," which actually enhanced Shakespeare by an inspired transformation of his setting.

Hecate presided over all and became the mysterious Third Murderer who, alone on stage at the end with upraised arm, closed the proceedings. The lilting Caribbean voices gave an extra gleam to Shakespeare's lines, Manson was an eloquent Macbeth and the production was lively and beautiful.[23]

The third black Lady Macbeth in 1977 was Yolande Bavan, who appeared in a production at the Cleveland Playhouse directed by John Dillon. This *Macbeth*, obviously influenced by Roman Polanski's film version, was described as theatrical and visually savage. It opened on a dumb show of the witches, who as three rag-picking hags stripped valuables from the body of a dead soldier whose neck had been pierced by an arrow. Banquo was murdered by having his eyes stabbed out; when his ghost appeared to Macbeth, the eye sockets ran with blood. Contrasting with this gore, Bavan's Lady Macbeth was strangely contained. This actress had worked with the New York Shakespeare Festival and the previous year had played Cleopatra to the Caesar of Clayton Corzatte at the Cleveland Theatre. She was therefore no newcomer to the stage and presumably was aware of the effect she sought to achieve. Her character was dressed "puritan-like in a dull robe and gray cap tied below the chin. . . . She spoke in an unrealistic, carefully enunciated elocutionary style."[24] Clive Barnes found her to be "an interestingly restrained Lady Macbeth, her envy and fury held down by a will that eventually breaks, leading to madness and death."[25]

Along with racially relevant interpretations of Shakespeare and nonracial productions that employed black actors in hitherto white roles, there was yet a third category of productions that were regularly undertaken in an effort to provide openings for leading black talent. These were plays that contained black characters, of which *Othello* is, of course, the most important. At least one writer has called it "Shakespeare's American Play."[26] In the 1960s and '70s numerous productions of the play took place in America and abroad, and many black actors, some of them admittedly unfit physically for the part or suited for it only physically, seized the rare opportunity to appear as the magnificent Moor. A few of these performances were indeed memorable and merit inclusion in the record.

In 1962 the American actor William Marshall portrayed the Moor at the Dublin Theatre Festival in a production that toured several European countries. This was one of those fortuitous opportunities that occasionally falls to black actors when an emergency situation arises. Hilton Edwards, the director, had cast the veteran Irish actor Anew McMaster as Othello. However, just before the production was due to open, McMaster died, and Edwards, urgently needing a replacement, recalled seeing Marshall act in Paris and learned that he had previously played Othello. Edwards immediately contacted Marshall and offered him the part. Actually Marshall had played the role at least three times earlier in America: in 1953 to the Iago of Lloyd Richards and Jane White's Desdemona at the Mother Zion A.M.E. Church in Harlem and to New York City schools; in 1955 for the Brattle Street Players in Cambridge (at the very theater where Robeson had begun his triumphant Othello thirteen years before), moving later to New York; and in 1958 for the New York Shakespeare Festival in Central Park. For none of these performances were his reviews wholly laudatory, but everyone remarked on his handsome, commanding figure and resonant baritone voice. Of the Brattle Theatre performance, John Chapman in the *New York Daily News* could not avoid the comparison with Robeson and found Marshall to be a more gifted actor, magnificent, with the intelligence of a stage craftsman.[27]

Marshall had been acting professionally since 1944 in theater and films, and television. He was an experienced, naturally gifted performer and after three encounters with Shakespeare's noble Moor in nine years he was ready for the fourth. He won a great victory. Ecstatic acclaim greeted him in Dublin, with the Irish critics hailing his performance as "a wonderful personal triumph"; "one of the highlights of this year's theater festival"; and as containing "chilling moments of truth."[28] Harold Hobson in the Sunday London *Times* called him the best Othello of our time:

> The American actor William Marshall is nobler than [Godfrey] Tearle, more martial than [John] Gielgud, more poetic than [Frederick] Valk. From his first entry, slender and magnificently tall, framed in a high byzantine arch, clad in white samite, mystic, wonderful, a figure of Arabian romance and grace, to his last plunging of the knife into his stomach, Mr. Marshall rode without faltering the play's enormous rhetoric, and at the end the house rose to him.[29]

Marshall was not through, however. There was no question of resting on his laurels, of avoiding a possible adverse experience in a role for which he had already won high praise. Drawing on his ability as a singer, he appeared in 1968 in a rhythm-and-blues musical version of the play called *Catch My Soul*, which was conceived and directed by Jack Gould and presented at the Ahmanson Theatre of Los Angeles. It was not happily received, and one shudders to think of Othello destroyed by a piano-playing Iago in a seventeen-piece band of rockers, two guitars, three percussionists, a bass, an organ, two drums, a seven-piece brass section, and a harp.

After that unfortunate diversion, Marshall returned to straight Shakespeare at the Old Globe Theatre in San Diego, where his Iago was John Devlin and his Desdemona Pamela Payton-Wright in a 1976

Pamela Payton-Wright as Desdemona and William Marshall as Othello, directed by Dan Sullivan at the Old Globe Theatre, San Diego, California, 1976.

production by the director Dan Sullivan. One is loath to rely too completely on a single critique of a performance, but when a Shakespearean scholar and avid playgoer chooses to devote five columns in a reputable journal like *Shakespeare Quarterly* to analyzing a performance, one is constrained to treat his views with respect. Stephen Booth of the University of California at Berkeley called Marshall's fifth portrayal of Othello "one of the most remarkable things I have seen on a stage." He had watched Marshall in the role twice before when the actor played Othello as a superman destroyed by circumstance, misjudgment, and Iago. Those performances had been easy to watch; one knew that Othello was imperfect and indirectly culpable. But this latest performance was different. Marshall was able to convince his audience that Othello could overwhelm his circumstances at any time, but that something minor and temporary had neutralized his capacities. Thus the early scenes were dominated by Iago:

> The unrealized but always imminent power of Marshall's full voice was to the voice we heard as his body was to his costume. That might suggest that his voice sounded repressed; it did not. Othello roared and rumbled in the early scenes, but one always felt that there was more—that one was hearing a man trying, a bit sleepily and reminiscently, to sound like himself. Marshall's gait and gestures had a similar effect; they were confident and grand, but they began a little late or concluded a little early. . . .
>
> At exactly the moment when Iago achieved his most complete mastery over the dramatized situation (the moment when Othello commits himself to the action Iago is trying to bring about) Othello took over the play—took command of the audience and became the center of its attention. . . . On "Farewell the plumed troops and the big wars / That makes ambition virtue," Othello became the godlike creature he had not quite been before. As the scene progressed Othello became increasingly awesome: on "Villain be sure you prove my love a whore," Marshall flipped his large, sturdily-built Iago across the stage with one hand. To summarize crudely, this production first presented a shadow Othello in a real world and then "the real" Othello in a false world.[30]

Booth made it clear that the production was not immediately pleasurable, since in the first half of the play the audience wished the actor to perform differently, more as a hero should, and in the second half the audience wanted the character to act differently in coping with the

Moses Gunn as Othello and Roberta Maxwell as Desdemona in the American Shakespeare Festival Theatre production, 1970.

situation. But Marshall made no compromises for incidental gratification, and the production was ultimately more satisfying as a result.

Marshall had been able to develop his interpretation over five different productions, but Moses Gunn gave one of the most impressive recent performances of Othello in his first and only portrayal. It took place at the American Shakespeare Festival Theatre in Connecticut in 1970 with Roberta Maxwell as Desdemona and Lee Richardson as Iago. The direction was by Michael Kahn. Gunn had been waiting for this opportunity for eight years, ever since he moved to New York in 1962 for his first major role in Genet's *The Blacks*. His earlier acting experience in Shakespeare had been at the Antioch Festival in Ohio in 1964 when he had played five roles in one summer—Prospero, Horatio, Jacques, Banquo, and Glendower. Then in three seasons with the New York Shakespeare Festival at Central Park, Gunn had been seen as the Provost in *Measure for Measure*, as Aaron the Moor in *Titus Andronicus*, and as Capulet in *Romeo and Juliet*. Asked how he felt about black actors performing traditionally white roles, Gunn replied soberly:

When Shakespeare is done in South America or in India, do you believe that anyone thinks of the parts as "white roles"? In school, everyone is taught about the universality of these roles. Yet when a black goes to the theater and sees an all-white cast, he is bound to feel "what does this have to do with me?" You cannot imagine the psychological damage that has been done to a group who on TV, films and the stage never saw themselves represented at all. When I played Capulet, several black kids came up to me after the show and one 15-year-old said: "I like that. We've never seen a black man play a role as commanding as that, and we could identify with you." It touched me.[31]

When Gunn was pressed further on the incongruity of Juliet's having a black father, he responded that people are more sophisticated nowadays and can accept that such a situation could exist. The question touched closer to home than his interviewer realized. Gunn's wife is white, and his daughter is the child of his wife's former marriage.

Although Gunn's previous Shakespearean roles were mostly supporting characters, the enthusiastic notices he received should have prepared one for the distinctiveness of his Othello. As Aaron the Moor, for example, he was not only the most evil but also the most human character in the play, "powerful, terrifying, and real." In 1968, two years before appearing as Othello, he was awarded an Obie for performances with the Negro Ensemble Company and was referred to as a rarity in the American theater—an actor with the physical discipline and the emotional depths to accomplish classical, realistic, and avant-garde roles with equal facility.[32] "Moses Gunn is the most moving Othello I've seen in all my years of theatre-going,"[33] trumpeted Richard Watts in the New York Post, while a fellow reviewer in that paper added, "one of the greatest and most pertinent to our time." Walter Kerr in the New York Times labeled the performance "a giant Moor." What was special about it?

Both Kerr and Clive Barnes attempted to define the uniqueness of the performance.[34] It was focused on Gunn's use of Shakespeare's language, which they both found supremely effective. Kerr called him the singing Othello in Connecticut and felt that Gunn tasted the words before releasing them: "They are savored not only for sense but for syllable, with each piece of a word given its separate, surprising value." In the same vein, Barnes noted that Gunn measured out his cadences "like a grocer with sugar, deliberate and sparing. The accent

—more West Indian than American—hits the play's poetry like a tor-pedo." Gunn's slightly affected speech added to the total effect, ren-dering an Othello of pain rather than passion. His "sensual-melodic" reading was not simply a mannered form of expression; it was built into the fabric of his characterization, and this enthralled Kerr:

> I have heard something like it twice in my life, and then at the very ends of the careers involved. I heard Margaret Anglin do it, and I heard Nazimova do it; in a sense, I have been starved ever since. I can only say that the "Put out the light" and the "Soft you" passages, as Mr. Gunn is reading them, are the two most beautiful moments to be savored anywhere on the Ameri-can stage just now.

Moving to another aspect of the performance, Barnes, who did not really approve of black actors playing Othello because "it is too obvi-ous," had to admit that Gunn went beyond his presuppositions: "Othello was written for a white actor in blackface. Mr. Gunn plays him black—plays him for the deliberate position of black conscious-ness. Even in its simplicity this portrayal is gratifyingly complex. . . . He gives the part magnificently, but gives it on his own terms and at his own distance."

Down in Atlanta, Georgia, the Alliance Theatre Company, in a conscious attempt to boost the number of its black patrons, chose *Othello* for the final offering of its six-play subscription season in 1978–79. Indicative of the progress achieved in race relations in the southern states, Bernard Harvard, the English managing director of the Alliance, expressed his view that someone other than a black ac-tor for Othello was unthinkable. Paul Winfield was engaged to play the Moor, Richard Dreyfuss was Iago, Dorothy Fielding played Des-demona, and Kristin Linklater was Emilia. Having Linklater in the cast was of strategic importance. An English-born professional voice-and-speech coach and author of the text *Freeing the Natural Voice*, she was of inestimable service in improving the projection and vocal clarity of several actors, including the principals. In the title role Winfield was not unknown to Atlanta audiences. He had received an Emmy nomination for his portrayal of Martin Luther King, Jr., in the television docudrama, "King." His previous experience in Shakespeare, however, was fairly limited. He had first played Othello at nineteen as a college student at the University of Portland in Ore-gon and had appeared in *Coriolanus* while he was artist-in-residence at the University of Hawaii. Then in 1974 he was Buckingham to Michael Moriarty's *Richard III* for the New York Shakespeare Festival in Central Park. Notwithstanding this limited background, his Othello was overpowering.

Winfield believes it is the actor's duty to find in the great characters of Shakespeare something pertinent to each new generation of auditors. He explained his approach to the role, which he hoped would be relevant to the 1970s and '80s: "*Othello* is not just about jealousy but about a loss of love. He really is an outsider, as far away from his roots as any American black. As his belief in Desdemona crumbles, so does his belief in culture and so-called civilization. He looks back to more savage ways. Killing Desdemona becomes a ritual he has to do, a tribal cleansing or purification."[35]

In keeping with this concept, Winfield presented a tormented Moor, wracked with pain and anguish, not self-pity, at the supposed infidelity of his beloved wife. His suffering built slowly, inexorably. At its peak, he tore from his neck the chain and cross that symbolized his acquired Western religion and sought comfort in the beliefs of his African heritage. Instead of falling into an epileptic fit as required by the text, a piece of stage business with which Winfield felt very uncomfortable, he substituted a ritual chant accompanied by rhythmic beating of the stage floor that produced a trancelike state. In the brothel scene, a symbolic raping of Desdemona was suggested when, both fully clothed, Othello lay on her on the stage floor, writhing in anger and agony toward his love. Then rising accusatorily, he spat out the words, "I took you for that cunning whore of Venice / That married with Othello." And in the final bedroom scene when Othello enters to the sleeping Desdemona, Winfield in bare feet and clad in a loose, flowing caftan silently performed a tribal-like ritual cleansing before approaching the bed to dispatch the wife whose virtue he believed had been ineradicably sullied. His performance was considered powerful, passionate, and convincing.[36]

The Alliance Theatre production was a signal success. Capacity houses induced the company to extend its three-week run to four weeks; box-office receipts jumped more than threefold from the immediately precedent production of *The Little Foxes;* special matinees were added for high school students; and two performances at the Piedmont Park Arts Festival, sponsored free to the public by the city government, drew an estimated audience of 20,000.

Undoubtedly one of the most prodigious talents exhibited on the professional stage in our time is that possessed by James Earl Jones, whose childhood experiences gave little indication of the talent that would eventually blossom forth.[37] Born in Arkabutla, Mississippi, Jones was raised on a farm by his evangelistic Methodist maternal grandmother who fed his infant imagination with tall tales spun for his edification and entertainment. He did not at the time know his father, an itinerant prizefighter and, later, a left-wing poet and actor, who had left his mother before he was born. When Jones was about five, the family decided to move to Michigan, leaving him with paternal grandparents in Memphis, but the boy stubbornly resisted going into a strange home and was eventually taken along with the family. His mother, however, remained behind in the South. The feeling of near-abandonment apparently had a traumatic effect on young Jones. He became introverted and developed a serious stutter which lasted until he entered high school. There, helped by a sympathetic English teacher, he followed an arduous program of speech training and took part in debates and oratorical competitions. His efforts were rewarded when, on the same day in 1949, he won both a public-speaking contest and a college scholarship. For the first time in his life he communicated with his father to convey the joyful news.

Jones entered the University of Michigan intending to become a doctor, but soon turned to drama, especially the study of Shakespeare's plays, which he found more to his liking. Graduation from college was followed by two years in the army. In 1955 Jones moved to New York City and enrolled at the American Theatre Wing, gaining his first off-Broadway role in 1957. A chance meeting with Joseph Papp in 1959 resulted in a small part in *Henry V*. Thereafter, his professional career moved quickly. Between 1962 and 1965 he received two Obies plus the Theatre World and the Vernon Rice awards for his performances on the New York stage. Then in 1969 he gained the Tony award for his uncanny evocation of the heavy-weight champion Jack Johnson in Howard Sackler's Pulitzer Prize–winning play, *The Great White Hope*. Jones has played an impressive variety of roles, classic and contemporary, and has worked on the stage, in movies, and in television. He has portrayed over a score of Shakespeare's characters, many of them for the New York Shakespeare Festival at Central Park or in its touring productions. He is not above appearing in a fringe theater for a challenging assignment, as he did in 1976 when he took the title role in a showcase production of *Oedipus Rex*, directed by David Gild, at the Cathedral of St. John the Divine

Ellen Holly as Regan, James Earl Jones as King Lear, and Rosalind Cash as Goneril in King Lear, *directed by Edwin Sherin, presented by the New York Shakespeare Festival, Joseph Papp, producer, at the Delacorte Theatre, 1973.*

in New York City. His portrayal of Paul Robeson in 1978 (despite the controversy that erupted over the authenticity of that biographical monodrama) left those who witnessed his essentially one-man performance of over two hours in no doubt whatever that they were in the presence of an extraordinarily gifted actor.

When Jones opened as Othello at the Winter Garden Theatre in New York in February 1982, it was the first time he had played the role on Broadway, but it was also his seventh Othello in nineteen years. In between his periodic wrestling with the noble Moor, he had appeared as King Lear, Macbeth, Timon of Athens, Caliban, and Oberon, along with a string of lesser supporting characters such as Macduff, Claudius, Ajax in *Troilus and Cressida*, the tribune Junius Brutus in *Coriolanus*, and others. As Caliban (1962) he was "a complete original . . . a savage, green-faced lizard darting his red tongue in and out, lunging clumsily at what he wanted and yelping when he was denied it."[38] The performance was singled out as one of the finest characterizations of Papp's early offerings in Central Park. Jones was a likably comic Ajax (1965) and exciting as Junius Brutus (1965), "roaring out his judgments with the power of self-righteousness."[39] The proverbial curse that haunts *Macbeth* actors was not banished from his touring production (1966), although audiences loved it, and one critic who waited out a rain shower was impressed with Jones's power and the splendid clarity of his readings. Jones gave one of his finest performances as King Lear, energetic and exciting, with Ellen Holly and Rosalind Cash appearing as his two ungrateful but singularly attractive daughters Regan and Goneril, while Lee Chamberlin played Cordelia with great tenderness. In this 1973 production Jones was directed by Edwin Sherin, who had directed him in *The Great White Hope,* and it was clear that "once again the actor and director were able to merge their talents in a highly rewarding collaboration." Mel Gussow in the *New York Times* captures a quality of the performance:

> There is a mellowness to the characterization—this is one of the most sympathetic Lears that I have seen—that is both unexpected and suitable. Carefully Jones charts Lear's descent into madness. We know when his mind cracks and when his heart breaks. As he charges through the wilderness, he sways like a tree toppling in the wind. And near the end when he recognizes Gloucester, we see a spark of sanity beneath the outraged madness. It is, after all, the world, not Lear, gone mad.[40]

Another aspect of the portrayal was seen by Michael Feingold: "Jones has found his cue in making Lear the most changeable of humans. He laughs and cries a good deal—reminding us how often both actions are mentioned in the text—roisters and mutters, bellows and pines. Even on the heath, he finds occasion to think of forgiving Regan and Goneril."[41]

As Othello, Jones possesses the three characteristics that Caldwell Titcomb believes are prerequisite for any actor undertaking the role. They are an imposing physique (six feet or over), a God-given organ-toned windpipe, and an extraordinary aura of personal magnetism.[42] Given the magnificence of his figure, however, which is immediately apparent in his heroic roles, Jones has acquired the art of undercutting its power to show us the vulnerable human being within the body. Both the majesty and the frailty were fully apparent in his 1982 Othello. The production had originally been presented by the American Shakespeare Theatre at its summer playhouse in Stratford, Connecticut, under the direction of Peter Coe. It moved to Boston, then to New York, with some casting and directorial changes in the process, but retained its two principals, Jones as Othello and

James Earl Jones as Othello and Christopher Plummer as Iago in the 1981 American Shakespeare Theatre production directed by Peter Coe. Somewhat revised, the production opened on Broadway in February 1982. (Copyright © Martha Swope, 1983)

Christopher Plummer as Iago. Plummer's performance was spell-
binding. He gave what Walter Kerr characterized as "quite possibly
the best single Shakespearean performance to have originated on this
continent in our time." The tendency of Iago to run off with the play,
especially when he is not guided by a firm directorial hand, is legendary, and it is to Jones's credit that an equitable balance was maintained. Walter Kerr supplies an instance of how this was achieved. He
is describing a moment in the thunderous strumpet scene when Desdemona has fallen to her knees in terror:

> And then—for a few mysterious seconds—the fever breaks. Des-
> demona, body curled double in despair and retreat, is already in
> near-foetal position. Looking down at her, and possibly seeing
> her for the bewildered, unformed creature she is, this Othello
> slowly and gently lowers himself, stretches out his massive mili-
> tary-man's arms, and draws the folds of his voluminous cloak
> over both of them. As his body shelters hers, conforms to hers,
> the two seem little more than children lost in a fairy-tale forest
> and falling asleep beneath a blanket of snow. Their love for each
> other, so rapidly being destroyed, is in the silence. The silence is
> finally broken with a surprisingly hushed, tender reading of a line
> that a hundred Othellos have read in a hundred different ways:
> "O Desdemona! Away! away! away!" Secretly, scarcely daring
> to let himself hear the words he is pronouncing, he sounds as
> though he were toying with the notion of an impossible flight
> that will bring her to safety, safety from the treacherous world
> into which he has stumbled, safety from himself.[43]

Moments such as this combined to make this *Othello* memorable.
There was, in addition, the inherent tension between a mercurial but
implacable Iago and a magisterial but vulnerable Othello. It mattered
little that the rest of the cast seemed pale by comparison. Jones has
still to reach his definitive portrayal in this role, but with each new
attempt he comes closer to his goal.

9
Toward the Future

BESIDES JOSEPH PAPP's New York Shakespeare Festival, two other organizations whose stated policy includes a commitment to interracial casting have produced Shakespeare within recent years. They are the Inner City Cultural Center of Los Angeles (also known as the Los Angeles Cultural Center) and Shakespeare and Company of Lenox, Massachusetts. As harbingers of what might yet become standard theatrical practice in America, these two groups deserve more than passing notice.

Since its founding in 1966, the Inner City Cultural Center has produced dozens of plays, many of them contemporary, original, and with special reference to the ethnic minorities that the center serves. In addition, it has staged dramas by well-known playwrights such as Molière, Chekhov, Garcia Lorca, and Tennessee Williams. It has also presented three Shakespearean plays, *A Midsummer Night's Dream*, *Macbeth*, and *Hamlet*, and two original pieces that were inspired by *Othello* and *Macbeth*. Established with grant monies in the wake of the well-publicized Watts riot of 1965, the center located itself in the heart of Los Angeles, in a neighborhood comprised of African, Hispanic, Asian, and Native Americans. Its stated purpose was "to create and maintain a multi-racial, multi-cultural approach to the arts."[1]

Its founder and executive director, C. Bernard Jackson, had taught music for the dance at the University of California in Los Angeles and, with James Hatch, had written the musical *Fly Blackbird* which had won an Obie award in 1962. Jackson started the center because as a Brooklyn ghetto youth his life was dramatically changed after he was encouraged to enroll at the High School of Music and Art. "The arts saved my life," he once said, and he wanted other disadvantaged young people to have a similar chance of finding themselves through involvement in artistic endeavors.

Activities at the center have encompassed much more than play production but it is this aspect of its program that primarily concerns us. The center began its first season with a company of professionals largely recruited from the East Coast under the artistic direction of Andre Gregory. Soon objections were voiced about the relevance of plays chosen for production and the practice of importing actors from the East instead of using local talent. By the end of the season significant changes had occurred. In the fourth and final production, *A Midsummer Night's Dream*, which opened on April 11, 1968, the cast of twenty-six, though still predominantly white, included several newly recruited actors, among whom were five blacks, an Asian, a Hispanic, and a Native American. The roles played by black actors were Theseus, Hippolyta, Titania, Snug, and Moth. The production was the most popular of the season. Directed by Malcolm Black, it was thought to be "less a blissful idyll of a dream than a mad, exuberant, drunken hallucination . . . immensely physical . . . with great leaps and bounds and sprawling falls."[2] The play had been produced chiefly for the center's school program and its emphasis on external action and horseplay was probably deliberate in order to appeal to the 35,000 tenth-grade students who would view it in matinee performances. By this time Andre Gregory had resigned and his place was eventually filled by Afro-American Hal Dewindt and Native American David Willy who served jointly as artistic directors. Thus the center extended its multiracial policy to management and artistic direction as well as to casting.

In its second season the center produced *Macbeth* with a multiracial cast in which black actors Yaphet Kotto and Beah Richards had the principal roles. (There was a second cast in which these roles were played by whites.) Kotto made a majestic Macbeth but his performance was amateurish and his diction poor. He left the production before the end of the run. As Lady Macbeth, Beah Richards wore an "afro" wig and interpreted her character in such a flippant manner that it produced a comedic effect to which some reviewers objected. However, in his review for the *Los Angeles Times* of February 16, 1969, Dan Sullivan felt differently:

It could be that Beah's Lady Macbeth will come closer to the black kids who will see it than a more "correct" performance. So this *Macbeth* may have a significance for these kids that, say, a performance by the Royal Shakespearean Company wouldn't have. . . . I think something artistically important is happening here, that this *Macbeth* for all its flaws is the starting point for something.

The center produced no further Shakespeare for several years until black director Ted Lange staged *Hamlet* in 1978 with Glynn Turman in the title role. Lange had offered a course in Shakespeare for students at the center's teaching institute and his message there was that Shakespeare could be fun and that there was no need to treat his plays with awe or reverence. Rather, one should think of him as "a hack writer from England."[3] According to Dan Sullivan, Lange's production was "a carnival of special effects and odd images but the ground technique isn't there—director's technique as well as actor's technique." There was, Sullivan felt, considerable energy in the cast, much of it misplaced. For instance, "Ophelia's soul-train funeral with minstrel-show pallbearers wiggling their hands" got lots of laughs and Glynn Turman was curiously unmelancholic for a bereaved prince, "truckin' on up to his mother's room after he's caught the conscience of the king. Whoo-ee! Again, you have to laugh."[4] Sullivan noted that the cast consisted of both black and white actors, but he did not regard the mix as disturbing and thought it might even have made a point about the forces in opposition in the play.

Executive director Jackson was aware that productions at the center did not always maintain high artistic standards. Casts containing professionals often had to be complemented with amateurs from the community. Jackson considered this situation part of the center's growing process. His first concern was to establish an institution that, in his words, "had the potential for long life." Only then, he felt, could the center's staff concentrate on making the institution "in artistic terms, one of the most important in the area." Despite his concerns over quality, Jackson is convinced that multiracial casting is "the only principle that seems to me to make any sense in America, because America is a pluralistic culture comprised of people from many different ethnic strains. . . . Certainly we have done productions 'straight' and will continue to do so, but we will also continue to search for a genuinely American theater, which I don't think we've found yet."[5]

In his attempt to produce plays of substance that at the same time reflected the acute feelings and concerns of his audiences, Jackson composed the drama *Iago*, which he adapted from the works of Giraldo Cinthio and Shakespeare. It was first produced at the center in 1979, played that summer at Lincoln Center in New York as part of the Black Theatre Festival, then toured extensively along the West Coast and through the Southwest. The point of the play is that Iago is not really the archvillain that Shakespeare created. Instead, he is a reasonable man who has been grievously maligned by history. Jackson makes Iago a black Moor like Othello, but keeps Cassio Italian. Othello elevates the inexperienced junior officer Cassio over the seasoned soldier Iago at a time of peril to the safety of his troops in order to appease his Venetian sponsors, and the injustice that occurs in employment situations where race becomes a factor is dramatically underscored. In Jackson's version, Emilia, who is also a Moor, has survived her husband and is obsessed with her self-imposed duty to clear his name, taking as her text Iago's own words: "Who steals my purse steals trash . . . / But he who filches from me my good name / Robs me of that which not enriches him / And makes me poor indeed."

The cast contained no more than seven actors, and during the run of the play at several venues, these have included blacks, Asiatics, and Chicanos. Using masks and playing multiple roles, the actors as entertainers performed all the characters in a large cast, often with a single character being presented by different players at various points in the play. The drama, which was directed by Jackson himself, carried its audience from the present day back to the Renaissance, frequently returning to the present. "This play," wrote critic Ivan Webster of the New York performance, "not only finds a fresh approach to familiar characters and ideas, it shakes up our assumptions about the way history lives. . . . Jackson has taken one of theatrical literature's most puzzling outsiders, Iago, and brought him and all his tribe inside—where all of us must claim some relation to him." Webster declared that no director in America had thought more about multiracial casting, or practiced it more assiduously, than Jackson. He felt that the presence of Asian actors in the small cast did not disturb the intensely European and African themes of the piece, but instead had quietly affirmed them. And he concluded: "We *are* a human family, in Jackson's reckoning, even though the configurations in which history has scattered us have to be respected before we can get beyond them."[6]

In the winter of 1982, the center mounted a musical adaptation of another of Shakespeare's plays under the title *Sleep No More*. Described in the program as "a black comedy inspired by Macbeth," this new version was written by Felton Perry (who also took the part of Macbeth in the production), with musical settings to Perry's lyrics by a young rock composer, Gary Brooks. Except for two members, the cast was all black. Once again, as in the earlier production of *Hamlet*, the tragic implications of Shakespeare's drama were transformed into a "madcap romp." Turning the drama inside out, playwright Perry chose for his central characters the two chamber grooms who, in the original play, are framed for the murder of Duncan. The events of the play were thus seen from the point of view of servingmen and kitchen wenches, and the Porter's role was considerably expanded. The battle with which the play opens became a peasants' revolt. Duncan was a petty tyrant who, during the victory celebrations, carried off Lady Macbeth and returned later tying up his pants. The songs were mostly funny and risqué, and the whole effect was that of a zany comedy. Despite a somewhat lame ending due to its unresolved plot, the production was apparently very successful in its two-month run at the center.

A commitment to the uplift of its multiracial community was a prime incentive to the establishment of the Los Angeles Center but no such consideration influenced the formation in 1978 of Shakespeare and Company. Located at The Mount, a neo-Georgian mansion built by the novelist Edith Wharton in Lenox, Massachusetts, the company gave a new dimension to summer entertainment in the culturally alive Berkshire countryside. Its declared purpose was

> to re-establish the universal appeal of classical theatre; its credo is that the power of Shakespeare and other classical playwrights can be regenerated by returning to the source: the word. . . . The emphasis is on the actor's art and the direct relationship between actors and audience. There is no pre-determined directorial concept when rehearsing a play; production values come from the actor's and director's experience of the text and are given form by the structure of the verse and the guidance of the director.[7]

Co-founders Tina Packer and Kristin Linklater were uniquely prepared to lead the company toward a realization of its goals. Britishers both and trained at English academies, they have had extensive experience in the professional theater as performers and instructors, with a concentration on classical material. Packer, the artistic director, has devoted considerable time to the study of Shakespearean acting and production in many countries, while Linklater, director of training and voice specialist, is recognized as a foremost practitioner in her field in the English-speaking world and has coached at some of the most prestigious theater companies on both sides of the Atlantic. With this company, training is an essential concomitant to performance and actors are required to undergo rigorous instruction with master teachers of voice, movement, stage combat, dance, and clowning, not only during the six-week rehearsal period of a play, but also at specially organized workshops which the group conducts in periods between its summertime performances.

Since 1978 the company has produced eight of Shakespeare's plays on its outdoor stage in the mansion's sprawling grounds. The audiences sit on the grass and actors play around and through them, among the trees, and even at times on balconies of the adjacent mansion. Of the plays presented, two were tragedies: *Romeo and Juliet* and *Macbeth*; two romances: *The Winter's Tale* and *The Tempest*; and four were comedies: *A Midsummer Night's Dream, Twelfth Night, As You Like It,* and *The Comedy of Errors.* From the first, certain aspects of the company's operation stamped it as unique. It does not, for instance, rely on the star system to attract audiences. A large proportion of its actors are young and have graduated from its own training programs or from earlier workshops conducted by Linklater. There is great fidelity to Shakespeare's text; the plays are usually performed in their entirety or with minimal textual excisions. Productions emphasize the aural theater as opposed to the visual— "at the forefront is the verbal, thrusting images out of the words" Packer has asserted[8]—and actors strive to achieve clarity with a high-speed delivery that calls to mind Hamlet's advice to the players to speak "trippingly on the tongue." A genuine love of language and a joy in speaking it are evident results of careful preparation and, as one reviewer in the *Boston Globe* of August 22, 1983, pointed out, the audience experiences a "voluptuous pleasure" in simply hearing the sound of the English language as it is spoken by actors of the company. In addition, actors bring an energetic physicality to their roles that is at once interpretative, enlivening, and delightful to watch. Finally, and most pertinent to our discourse, productions invariably include actors of different racial backgrounds.

One of the founding members and a consistent performer with the company is black actor Gregory Uel Cole, a Linklater-trained master teacher who has played in all but one of the productions. Cole graduated from New York University School of the Arts and has worked extensively off-Broadway. Joining the company in Lenox gave him the opportunity to extend his range and test his growth as an actor by regularly performing Shakespeare as part of a rigorously trained team. He has, so far, appeared as Oberon, Autolycus, Tybalt, Stefano, Duke Orsino, Jaques, and the Porter of Macbeth's castle. With evenly matched skills among the ensemble players, individual performances seldom merit particular attention, but Cole's Tybalt in *Romeo and Juliet* (1979) was picked out by one reviewer as "the best single performance of the show. He is everything, including fine swordsman, that Mercutio says of him: King of Cats."[9] As an instance of multiracial casting, this production had a Japanese Canadian, Natsuko Ohama, as Juliet; a Jamaican-born and Royal Shakespeare actor, Joseph Marcel, as her father, Capulet; Lady Capulet was played by Nancy Buttenheim, a Caucasian; and a black actress, Kaia Calhoun, was the Nurse. Several of these actors return to join the company for successive summers, thus keeping alive the sense of ensemble playing. Miss Calhoun has appeared for four seasons, playing Olivia in *Twelfth Night* (1981, 1982) and Phebe in *As You Like It* (1981), among other roles. Miss Ohama, a founding member, has also played four summers with the company.

Packer's policy of racially mixed casting is based less on sociological than on aesthetic considerations. She fervently believes that the universal truths and healing powers associated with classic drama such as Shakespeare's can be most effectively revealed by tapping into the root source of several cultures simultaneously. Hence her approach as a director of Shakespeare is to encourage each actor to find within himself and his culture those experiences and beliefs that inform and enhance the character under study. These experiences can then be presented with absolute veracity because they belong to the individual actor's particular background. Thus one critic writing of *The Winter's Tale* (1979) production found that "the speech rhythms of the actors are dictated not by their accents (which blend perfectly well—having the Old Shepherd played Texan and

John Hadden as Antipholus of Syracuse (L), Fran Bennett as Emilia the Abbess, and Michael Hammond as Antipholus of Ephesus in The Comedy of Errors, *directed by Tina Packer for Shakespeare and Company, 1983. Photo by Jane McWhorter*

Autolycus played, brilliantly, by Gregory Uel Cole as a street black, immediately illustrates class differences) but by what their character's function is within the scene."[10] That particular care is taken to underscore the resonances of interracial casting was evident in the 1980 production of *The Tempest*. In reviewing this play in the *Village Voice* of September 10, 1980, Terry Curtis Fox drew attention to the casting of a black Caliban (Joe Morton) which he found raised the troubling questions of bondage and servitude with which the play abounds. But Stefano was also played by a black actor (Gregory Uel Cole), which added yet another layer of meaning: "The servant who comes upon a captive monster and, in the name of freedom, makes the monster his own slave, is not just a fool but a representative of the unending chain of power society provides."

Perhaps the most daring piece of casting yet attempted by Shakespeare and Company occurred in its 1983 production of *The Comedy of Errors*. Four Afro-American actors appeared in the cast of nineteen. Two of them, Charles Halden and Brenda Thomas, were newly graduated apprentices who had been advanced to full status in the company and given the roles of Jailer and Courtesan respectively. A third black and an actor of experience, Neville Aurelius, was entrusted with the part of the Duke of Ephesus, while a fourth, Fran Bennett (who also served as the company's Director of Training in the absence of Linklater) took the role of Emilia, the Abbess. Toward the end of the play the Abbess turns out to be the mother of the Antipholus twins, who were played by white actors.

A measure of the success of this company's casting policy is that few critics have found it necessary to draw attention to the racial mixture except where it serves to underscore some meaning in the play. This is as it should be. Occasionally, though, a reviewer might be troubled by what seems to be an inexplicable incongruity. This was obviously the case with the syndicated critic who reviewed *The Comedy of Errors* in the *Norwalk News* of May 26, 1983. He found a jarring note introduced at the play's end and asked for an explanation of the rationale behind casting a black woman as the mother of twin white sons. Put this question, Tina Packer reaffirmed her decision by saying that she had cast the best actor for the role and ignored color. Moreover Miss Bennett, a Linklater-trained specialist of considerable vocal power, had given to the Abbess's long speeches a quality of revivalism, reminiscent of black Baptist preachers, that made them distinctive and enjoyable. Whatever may be the final verdict on its work, Kevin Kelly seems to speak for the majority of informed viewers when he says that Shakespeare and Company has the potential to become a permanent, significant, classical *American* company.[11]

The record of black actors in Shakespeare has been distinguished not simply by the few who have achieved renown, but also by the many who, despite overwhelming odds, have maintained a truly professional attitude to their work. With dedication to their craft and a passion for the great dramas of Shakespeare, they have persevered in their endeavor to attain the heights of their profession and to present ennobling images of their race. In this endeavor they have been aided by others.

It has been made manifest that opportunities for black performers to appear professionally in these productions have been largely under the control of white producers and directors who have had access to the resources and facilities necessary for mounting these plays. In the nineteenth century, William Brown's African Company of the 1820s and J. A. Arneaux's Astor Place Company of the 1880s were the

Roscoe Orman as Brutus and Gylan Kain as Cassius in Julius Caesar, *directed by Michael Langham, presented by the New York Shakespeare Festival, Joseph Papp, producer, at the Public Theatre, 1979.*

only permanent troupes of Shakespearean players that were controlled and directed by blacks. Other companies under black directors were short-lived or primarily composed of amateurs. In our own century, if we except college-sponsored presentations and those of the Inner City Cultural Center of Los Angeles, there were but two productions under black control (La Mama Experimental Theatre and the

New Federal Theatre, both staging *Macbeth*) and only two black directors employed (John Hancock for *A Midsummer Night's Dream* in 1967 and Edmund Cambridge in the revival of the voodoo *Macbeth* in 1977). Scores of other productions employing black actors and actresses were under white auspices. Even the Negro units of the Federal Theatre Project had white directors.

Generous praise is due to those who have pioneered in opening up the casting of Shakespeare's plays to ethnic minorities, but the fact that these decisions are invariably made by whites can only be a mixed blessing. White producers and directors often have quite different perceptions of reality from their black collaborators. This difference alone could lead to casting decisions and conceptual interpretations of the plays, often reached with the best intentions, that are inimical to black interests. True integration in the theater should mean not integrated casting alone, but integration at the level of decision making, producing, and directing, as well as in the areas of design and technical production.

On January 25, 1979, a new production of *Julius Caesar* opened at the Public Theatre in New York devoid of white actors. It heralded the latest venture of Joseph Papp's Shakespeare Festival Theatre—namely, a repertory company composed entirely of blacks and Hispanics, two of the city's principal ethnic minorities. Of course, the idea of an all-black Shakespeare company is not really new—such troupes have existed since the 1820s—but never before had they enjoyed the sponsorship of a major private producing organization with several theaters at its disposal. The company, recruited for the production but with no prior experience of working together, lacked the cohesiveness of a true ensemble, and the clash of different racial and regional accents was troublesome, but under the skillful staging of Michael Langham, a seasoned Shakespearean director, what might have been simply an interesting experiment approached an evening of exciting theater. Jack Kroll in *Newsweek* pointed to some of the problems:

> The American theater has never really known what to do with its black performers. As with the society itself, the theatrical culture has responded to the situation in desultory spasms of tokenism, integration and separatism. . . . Should Shakespeare with black performers be a classical production colored black, or should it be a *black* transformation of Shakespeare? This *Julius*

Roscoe Orman and Frankie Faison as Senators, Robert Christian as Tullus Aufidius, and Morgan Freeman as Coriolanus in a scene from the play staged by Michael Langham, presented by the New York Shakespeare Festival, Joseph Papp, producer, at the Public Theatre, 1979.

Caesar falls between these two stools, but always gets up to drive on with determination. . . . Langham hasn't been able to effect a real synthesis from his kaleidoscopic cast. But a project such as this needs a great deal of dedication and hard work, and *Julius Caesar* is the first step in a difficult process that's worth pursuing.[12]

As a whole, the critics, all white, were divided on which aspects of the production deserved to be commended and which were flawed. Nor was there unanimity about individual performances, though most reviewers were inclined to agree that Jaime Sanchez's Marc Antony was excitingly contemporary with a fascination all its own.

Langham also staged the company's next production, *Coriolanus*, which opened at the Public Theatre on March 14, 1979, with Morgan Freeman in the title role and Gloria Foster as his mother, Volumnia. Since the major parts in this production were all taken by black actors, the discrepancy of accents noted in the first play was partly eliminated. However, speaking difficulties persisted, suggesting that, laudable as the notion is of an all-black Shakespeare ensemble, uniformly high quality performances cannot be attained without a considerable period of careful preparation by and training of company members. Mr. Freeman's portrayal of the hero was judged to be rich and heartbreaking, brilliant in the final scenes, and by itself justifying a visit to the theater. Gloria Foster gave a spectacular display as Volumnia which, however, seemed to leave behind the rest of the cast.[13]

With worthy intentions, Papp had set out to bring Shakespeare within reach of the city's multiethnic populations, as audiences no less than as performing artists. Yet in deciding to form a black and Hispanic repertory company, he was focusing on certain racial minorities to the exclusion of others. He should not have been surprised, therefore, when in February 1979 the Public Theatre was picketed by a group of Asian-American actors who claimed that their interests had been overlooked and that the Public had employed too few of them in the past ten years. Characteristically, Papp responded with a headlined article in the *New York Times* of March 23, 1979, in which he announced that the black-Hispanic Shakespeare company would be transformed into an "emerging third world repertory classical acting company" to include Asian-Americans. The expanded group would begin with a budget of $1.2 million a year and would cost eventually between $2.5 and $3 million, or approximately half of the entire budget of the New York Shakespeare Festival. Papp invited a number of leading black and Hispanic actors in the country (many of whom had appeared previously in his productions) to join the company. He named several directors he planned to use, explaining "these are third world directors even though they are white. They are directors of artistic vision"; and he hoped to begin an apprenticeship program to train fifteen to twenty people in all aspects of the theater. To finance the program, Papp planned to solicit support from federal, state, and local agencies.

Remarkable as Papp's record was in providing employment for black theater artists, the announcement of his projected third-world company was greeted with dismay by leaders of the black theater community in New York City. Autonomous black theater companies and producers, many of whom existed precariously on marginal budgets, reacted with apprehension to what they viewed as Papp's growing cultural imperialism over black theater in their city. Their concerns, cogently summarized in a roundup of views published in the *Black Theatre Alliance Newsletter* of May 1979, were aroused not merely through self-interest and the fear that Papp's enormous influence would tend to diminish support for their own efforts, but also by what they saw as white paternalism in his announced decision to continue engaging white directors, with the promise of using black directors mentioned as an afterthought. "The final distinction in ethnic theatre is who makes the final decision about what is being done," said Douglas Turner Ward of the Negro Ensemble Company. "We must get funding sources to understand the need for the continuation of autonomous black theatre." Woodie King, Jr., producer of the New Federal Theatre, saw Papp's proposed company as a perpetuation of the white power structure in America, "a white concept in black face," while Ernie McClintock of the Afro-American Studio Theatre felt that "that kind of money could be better spent on the development of a black theatre of national prominence whose primary purpose would be to perform contemporary and traditional black theatre classics of Afro-American, African and Caribbean origin."

The overriding need for a national black theater is not relevant to this study (I have discussed it in another context).[14] Meanwhile, Joseph Papp's contribution to black participation in Shakespearean and other classical productions should not be disparaged. In our time he has been the greatest force in demolishing barriers that for too long have shut out black actors from appearing in all but a few of Shakespeare's plays. He has also been chiefly instrumental in gaining public acceptance of multiracial Shakespearean productions. An objective assessment of his efforts by Jack J. Jorgens, which appeared in a 1974 issue of *Shakespeare Quarterly,* can bear repetition:

> In giving a large number of actors a chance to play Shakespeare, many of them blacks and Puerto Ricans, Mr. Papp has done a great service to the American theater (we forgive him the embarrassing failures which occasionally resulted). If, like any Shakespeare festival, this one has been plagued by mediocre performances in major roles and even by some downright disasters, it can also boast many individual triumphs. . . .
>
> In straining to entertain, Papp's directors have sometimes shown an alarming tendency to reduce and simplify, to be cute and clever, in order to get the play across. But the one trait for which we must be eternally grateful is his insistence that Shakespeare is a playwright of lifelike characters and real emotions, not a composer of poems in Standard British English to the well-bred. . . .[15]

Recognizing Papp's work with ethnic minorities need not preclude acknowledgment of the legitimacy of black concerns over his plans for a third-world classical repertory company. These concerns raise questions of artistic autonomy and integrity that are crucial to the expression of the black experience in the arts, questions that deserve to be fully explored before huge sums of public money are committed to any new project involving the arts.

The danger of allowing control of Shakespearean production to remain exclusively in the hands of the dominant white society is easily demonstrable. In the 1980s, at a time of economic recession when social pressures for equal justice have eased and funding sources have dried up, the employment of black actors in Shakespeare companies has markedly diminished. Papp has apparently abandoned plans for a third-world company. A rough tabulation of Shakespeare offerings in America during 1981 furnishes revealing figures: thirty-one summer festival operations produced among them seventy-eight plays, and thirty-seven additional companies staged forty-nine plays. Altogether there were 127 productions of Shakespeare, none of which (from information currently available) was produced or directed by blacks. Of these 127 productions, the number of recognized black actors in principal roles was no more than four: two Othellos, an Oberon/ Theseus, and one Olivia. In addition, a Hispanic played Prospero.[16]

A crucial question implicit in this survey of black Shakespeare actors in America was pointedly asked by Stanley Kauffmann in an article written in 1966: "Must Negro actors be confined to plays about Negroes or to Negro characters in otherwise white plays?"[17] When the eminent French critic and man of letters Theophile Gautier saw Ira Aldridge play King Lear in St. Petersburg, Russia, in the nineteenth century, he was moved to assert that if a white actor could besmirch himself with bistre to play a black role, then a black actor could surely paint himself white to play a white role, always allowing for the necessity of a credible surface illusion being produced. In 1916 the black theater critic, Lester Walton, seeking to justify the Broadway repertory of the all-colored Lafayette Players of Harlem, made essentially the same observation.[18] Then in 1946 Canada Lee created history of a sort when he appeared in whiteface in John Webster's *The Duchess of Malfi* at the Shubert Theatre in Boston. Of this event, Boston drama critic Eliot Norton wrote: "Mr. Lee's performance . . . seemed to prove the point at issue, that a colored actor can portray credibly a white role, just as white actors, for generations, have personated people of the other races."[19]

Times have changed, happily. Audiences are more sophisticated now. They no longer seek cosmetic verisimilitude in the theater but are more concerned with the revelation of the human experience by means of the actor's craft and conviction. Stanley Kauffmann was therefore able to answer his own question in the following way: "All art lives by convention, which means factual unreality for the sake of larger truth. Now theatrical convention is being extended, so that the actor who is best for a role—in ability, temperament and physique— can be engaged, regardless of color. Skin tone soon becomes irrelevant in performance.[20]

Shakespeare, the greatest of all dramatists, has created roles that by and large do not depend on race for their depiction or theatrical impact. His characters speak to all of a common humanity and a shared destiny. Black actors and actresses have shown that they, like their white counterparts, have the skill and power to re-create these magnificent personages and, often, to throw a new light on our understanding of the human condition. In this cosmopolitan land of ours, the black actor should no longer be made to feel misliked for his complexion, "the shadow'd livery of the burnished sun," but should be fully invested into that wonderful coterie of players where talent is the only criterion and Shakespeare and his audiences the only true beneficiaries.

Notes

1 Shakespeare and the Black Actor

1 *Washington Post*, May 8, 1884.
2 Bernard Grebanier, *Then Came Each Actor*, p. 534.
3 *New York Age*, September 19, 1891.
4 Quoted in *Colored American*, March 19, 1898.
5 Ibid., March 16, 1901, and April 12, 1902.
6 *New York Age*, June 30, 1907.
7 Alain Locke, "Steps Toward the Negro Theatre," pp. 66–68.
8 Montgomery Gregory, "The Drama of Negro Life," *The New Negro*, p. 159.
9 See Paul Carter Harrison, *The Drama of Nommo*, pp. 182–89; Hoyt Fuller, "Towards a Black Aesthetic," in *The Black Aesthetic*, ed. Addison Gayle, Jr., pp. 3–11. The whole question is summarized in the introduction to *The Theater of Black Americans*, ed. Errol Hill.
10 See Laurence Hutton, *Curiosities of the American Stage*, pp. 322–23; and Charles E. L. Wingate, *Shakespeare's Heroes on Stage* (New York: Thomas Y. Crowell and Co., 1896), pp. 65, 335.
11 John K. Hutchens, "Paul Robeson," p. 582. For detailed interpretations of the role by six modern actors including Robeson and Earle Hyman, see Marvin Rosenberg, *The Masks of Othello*, pp. 189–205.
12 Hutchens, "Paul Robeson," p. 585.
13 See Eldred D. Jones, *The Elizabethan Image of Africa*, pp. 20–21. I am indebted to Professor Caldwell Titcomb of Brandeis University for this reference, as well as for the textual references to Cleopatra's blackness.
14 The debate on this topic through the nineteenth century is summarized in Horace Edward Furness, *A New Variorum Edition of Shakespeare*, vol. 6, *Othello*, pp. 389–96. For subsequent commentaries, see Philip Butcher, "Othello's Racial Identity," *Shakespeare Quarterly* 3 (1952):243–47, and Ruth Cowhig, "Actors Black and Tawny in the Role of Othello—and Their Critics," pp. 133–46.
15 *Letters of the Late Ignatius Sancho, an African; to which are prefixed Memoirs of His Life*, ed. Joseph Jekyll (5th ed., 1803; reprint ed., London: Dawsons, 1968).

16   For a complete description of this enterprise, see Herbert Marshall and Mildred
     Stock, *Ira Aldridge: The Negro Tragedian*, chap. 4; and Yvonne Shafer, "Black
     Actors in the Nineteenth Century American Theatre," pp. 387–400.
17   See Mary Henderson, *The City and the Theatre*.
18   George C. D. Odell, *Annals of the New York Stage*, 3:36.
19   Quoted in Marshall and Stock, *Ira Aldridge*, p. 36.
20   Odell, *Annals*, 3:36.
21   Quoted in Marshall and Stock, *Ira Aldridge*, p. 36.
22   *National Advocate*, May 8, 1824.
23   Odell, *Annals*, 3:536.
24   *American*, April 27, 1825; quoted in Marshall and Stock, *Ira Aldridge*, p. 37.

2   **Involuntary Exiles**

 1   Quoted in Marshall and Stock, *Ira Aldridge*, p. 26.
 2   *Era*, April 26, 1857.
 3   Quoted in Marshall and Stock, *Ira Aldridge*, p. 225.
 4   *Era*, April 26, 1857. This critic, admittedly, was reviewing not Shakespeare's
     Aaron but Aldridge's.
 5   T. Edgar Pemberton, *The Kendals* (London: Pearson, 1900), p. 42.
 6   Quoted in Erroll Sherson, *London's Lost Theatres of the Nineteenth Century*
     (London: John Lane, 1925), p. 13.
 7   See Marshall and Stock, *Ira Aldridge*, p. 312; Grebanier, *Then Came Each Actor*,
     p. 194; and Shafer, "Black Actors," p. 398.
 8   *New York Age*, January 25, 1890.
 9   Quoted in Marshall and Stock, *Ira Aldridge*, pp. 213–14.
10   Moncure D. Conway, "The Negro as Artist," pp. 39–42.
11   It is not known what other "coloured tragedians," if any, the reviewer had in mind
     when he wrote this in 1873. Aldridge had died in 1867 and Paul Molyneaux had not
     yet arrived in England. Only one other black actor is mentioned, and only once, in
     the records consulted for this period. He was Gustavas Allenborough who ap-
     peared as "the coloured tragedian" in *Othello* at Faversham in 1867. See *Era*,
     September 1, 1867.
12   *Era*, February 2 and April 28, 1872.
13   Quoted in ibid., July 29, 1866.
14   Marshall had appeared in *Hamlet, Julius Caesar*, and *Macbeth* at the Boston
     Theatre in 1855–56. In the 1857–58 season he alternated with Edwin Booth in the
     roles of Othello and Iago. Later he became manager of the theater from 1863 to
     1865. See Eugene Tompkins, *The History of the Boston Theatre, 1854–1901* (Bos-
     ton: Houghton Mifflin Co., 1908).
15   Diligent inquiries have failed to locate a copy of this volume.

3   **No Place Like Home**

 1 · Quoted in Charles H. Shattuck, *Shakespeare on the American Stage*, p. 134.
 2   These figures are computed from black newspapers of the period. The Theodore
     Drury Opera Company of New York City began in 1889 by giving concerts of

operatic selections. By 1900 the company was presenting full opera. See, principally, the *Colored American Magazine.*

3 For a short biography of J. A. Arneaux, see William J. Simmons, *Men of Mark*, chap.
65.

4 *New York Globe*, August 9, 1884.

5 Quoted in Simmons, *Men of Mark*, p. 488.

6 *New York Freeman*, February 6, 1886.

7 Preface to *Shakespeare's Historical Tragedy of Richard III*: Adapted for amateurs
and drawing room by J. A. Arneaux (New York: J. A. Arneaux, c. 1887).

8 Quoted in the *Cleveland Gazette*, February 14, 1887.

9 Simmons, *Men of Mark*, p. 489.

10 *New York Freeman*, October 3, 1885.

11 *New York Age*, December 26, 1885.

12 *Cleveland Gazette*, January 7, 1888.

13 *New York Age*, September 13, 1890.

14 *Colored American*, May 25, 1901.

15 *New York Age*, October 24, 1891.

16 *New York Freeman*, November 14, 1885.

17 *New York Age*, January 7, 1888.

18 See *Cleveland Gazette* of June 5 and July 31, 1886, for Wood's appearances as
Richard III "supported by Miss Ada Brown and a select colored company." His acting at this time was thought to be "of the Forrest, Barrett and Keene order."

19 Handbill, "A Life That Reads Like a Romance," in alumni records file at Beloit
College.

20 *Cleveland Gazette*, December 24, 1887, and January 21, 1888.

21 Edward Dwight Eaton, *Historical Sketches of Beloit College* (New York: A. S.
Barnes and Co., 1928), pp. 231, 233.

22 *New York Times*, March 24, 1935.

23 *Afro-American Ledger*, September 28, 1901.

4 From Artist to Activist

1 *Cleveland Gazette*, February 9, 1884.

2 *Washington Bee*, July 21, 1883.

3 *New York Globe*, August 4, 1883.

4 Ibid., March 29, 1884.

5 Ibid., May 3, 1884.

6 *Cleveland Gazette*, January 26, 1884.

7 Ibid., May 7, 1884.

8 *New York Globe*, May 17, 1884.

9 *Washington Post*, May 8, 1884.

10 *Cleveland Gazette*, November 7, 1885.

11 Ibid., March 10, 1888.

12 Quoted in *New York Age*, April 28, 1888.

13 Quoted in ibid., May 9, 1891.

14 *New York Freeman*, January 23, 1886.

15   Ibid., March 26, 1887.

16   *New York Age*, September 19, 1891.

17   Reprinted in ibid., April 4, 1885.

18   I am indebted to Professor Robert Hill, editor of the Marcus Garvey papers at the University of California, Los Angeles, for information concerning Miss Davis's political activities.

19   Quoted in *Colored American*, March 19, 1898.

5   Challenge of a New Century

1   *New York Age*, July 11, 1907.

2   Ibid., May 13, 1909.

3   *Crisis* 9 (April 1915):315.

4   Federal Theatre Project Writers' Program: Negroes of New York, 1939. Article no. 3, p. 2, in Schomburg Center for Research in Black Culture, microfilm 974. 7W, Reel 5.

5   *Colored American Magazine*, November 1900, p. 37.

6   Ibid., June 1901, p. 135.

7   Ibid., May 1902, p. 66.

8   Ibid., April 1902, p. 392.

9   Clarence A. Bacote and Hallie Beachem Brooks, "Theater at Atlanta University," pp. 18–21.

10   Kenneth MacGowan, "The Negro in the Theater" in *Shadowland*, July 1921, pp. 47, 63.

11   *New York Age*, November 21, 1912.

12   *New York Times*, June 13, 1916.

13   Mabel Rowland, *Bert Williams: Son of Laughter*, p. 128.

14   Andrea J. Nouryeh, "When the Lord Was a Black Man," pp. 142–46.

15   Jack Beall, "After Five Years As De Lawd." Quoted in ibid., p. 146. The article is in an unidentified clipping in the New York Public Library.

16   *New York Times*, March 24, 1935.

17   W. E. B. DuBois, "Beside the Still Waters," *Crisis* 40 (May 1931):168–69.

18   *New York Age*, April 27, 1916.

19   Quoted in *Crisis* 12 (June 1916):74–75.

20   *Boston Herald*, May 8, 1916.

21   *Philadelphia Public Ledger*, May 23, 1916.

22   Esther Fulks Scott, "Negroes as Actors in Serious Plays," p. 20.

23   *New York Times*, May 20, 1923, sec. 7.

24   Frazee Theatre Program for week beginning May 7, 1923.

25   *New York Times*, May 20, 1923, sec. 7.

26   See ibid., May 8, 16, and 20, 1923; *World*, May 9 and 16, 1923; *Nation*, May 23, 1923, pp. 605–6; and *New Republic*, May 30, 1923, p. 21.

27   *New York Times*, May 20, 1923, sec. 7.

28   Alain Locke, "Max Reinhardt Reads the Negro's Dramatic Horoscope," pp. 145–46.

6 Novelty Shakespeare

1 Information on the Hedgerow Theatre's production of *Othello* is taken from a release issued in 1977 by Gail Cohen, project director of the Hedgerow Theatre Collection, and from material supplied by the Hatch-Billops Oral History Collection, 491 Broadway, New York City.

2 *New York Age*, April 25, 1936.

3 John S. O'Connor, "But Was It 'Shakespeare'?: Welles' *Macbeth* and *Julius Caesar*," *Theatre Journal* 32 (October 1980):337–48.

4 *New York Times*, August 29, 1936.

5 *New York Post*, April 18, 1936.

6 John Houseman, *Run Through*, p. 201.

7 Otis L. Guernsey, Jr., "Brave New Shakespeare," *New York Herald Tribune*, January 26, 1945.

8 Frank Kermode, ed., *The Tempest*, 6th ed., Arden (London: Methuen, 1969), p. 27 n.

9 As late as the summer of 1979, the American Shakespeare Theatre of Stratford, Connecticut, in a production of *The Tempest* directed by Gerald Freedman, cast a mercurial white actor as Ariel, while the only black actor in the cast, Joe Morton, played Caliban as a bowlegged, barbaric creature with bared fangs. Only Mr. Morton's considerable energy and fine speaking voice saved his characterization from being a banal caricature worthy of the minstrel stage.

10 *New York Daily News*, January 26, 1945.

11 *New York Times*, October 16, 1946.

12 *Variety*, April 8, 1936.

13 Information on the Los Angeles African *Macbeth* is taken from Stephen M. Vallillo, "The Shakespeare Productions of the Federal Theatre Project," pp. 28–53.

14 *Los Angeles Evening Herald and Express*, July 15, 1937. Quoted in Vallillo, "The Shakespeare Productions," p. 41.

15 *New York Post*, November 10, 1939.

16 From literature supplied by Lorraine Brown, Associate Director, The Research Center for the Federal Theatre Project, George Mason University, Fairfax, Virginia.

17 *Seattle Daily Times*, June 20, 1939.

18 Ronald Ross, "The Role of Blacks in the Federal Theatre, 1935–1939," *Journal of Negro History* 59, no. 1 (January 1974):38–50.

7 Broadway and Beyond

1 Alexander Woolcott in the *New York Times* of November 7, 1920, called Gilpin's portrayal "an uncommonly powerful and imaginative performance, in several respects unsurpassed this season in New York." Heywood Broun in the *New York Tribune* of November 14, 1920, thought it was "a performance of heroic stature. It is so good that the fact that it is enormously skillful seems only incidental." Kenneth MacGowan in the *Boston Globe* of November 4, 1920, rhapsodized: "Gilpin's is a sustained and splendid piece of acting. The moment when he raises his naked body against the moonlit sky beyond the edge of the jungle and prays, is

such a dark lyric of the flesh, such a cry of the primitive being, as I have never seen in the theater."

2   *Morning Post*, London, May 30, 1930.
3   J. C. Trewin, *Shakespeare on the English Stage, 1900–1964*, p. 130.
4   *New York Times*, August 16, 1942.
5   *New England Theatre Conference News*, November-December 1980, p. 13.
6   *New York Times*, August 16, 1942.
7   *New York Daily News*, October 20, 1943.
8   *PM*, October 20, 1943.
9   *New York Times*, October 24, 1943.
10   *Life*, September 21, 1942, pp. 8, 11.
11   See *Bulletin of the Center for Soviet and East European Studies*, nos. 17–20, 23, 24, 26 (Spring 1976 to Spring/Summer/Autumn 1982).
12   *Times* (London), April 8, 1959.
13   *New York Times*, April 12, 1959.
14   For a summary review of Owen Dodson's career, see Bernard L. Peterson, Jr., "The Legendary Owen Dodson of Howard University," pp. 373–78.
15   Dodson spoke at the studio of the Hatch-Billops Oral History Collection at 491 Broadway, New York City, on August 16, 1982. A tape recording of his address was made available by James Hatch. Additional information was gleaned from Mr. Dodson in a personal communication.
16   *New York Times*, March 25, 1956.
17   *Times* (London), December 16, 1955.
18   *New York Times*, October 30, 1953.
19   Ibid., June 20, 1960.
20   See the *New York Post, Times, Herald-Tribune,* and *World Telegram* of March 30, 1956, and *Saturday Review*, April 14, 1956, p. 34.
21   *Saturday Review*, June 29, 1957, p. 23.
22   *New York Times*, June 24, 1957.
23   *Harvard Summer News*, July 1, 1957.
24   *New York Times*, January 31, 1978; *New Yorker*, February 13, 1978; *New York Post*, February 16, 1978; and Associated Press release dated January 31, 1978.
25   The official Norwegian languages are *Riksmal*, or the language of the realm, which was originally a combination of Norwegian and Danish; and *Landsmal*, a language constructed from the dialects spoken by people who live in the valleys and fiords of Norway. The intention is gradually to combine the two into a single Norwegian language.
26   *Times* (London), July 9, 1958. See also Muriel St. Clare Byrne's review in *Shakespeare Quarterly* 9 (1958):521.

8   How Relevant Is Race?

1   Jane White in *New York Post*, March 19, 1968.
2   *New York Times*, July 12, 1964.
3   Quoted in Floyd Gaffney, "In the Dark: *King Henry V*," pp. 39–40.
4   *New York Times*, June 29, 1965.

5   Ibid., June 29, 1966.
6   Alice Griffin, "The New York Shakespeare Festival 1965," *Shakespeare Quarterly* 16 (1965):335–39.
7   Marlies K. Danziger, "Shakespeare in New York, 1964," *Shakespeare Quarterly* 15 (1964):419–22.
8   See *New York Post*, March 19, 1968, and *New York Times*, March 25, 1968.
9   *New York Herald Tribune*, July 15, 1965.
10 Peter Saccio, "The 1975 Season at Stratford, Connecticut," *Shakespeare Quarterly* 27 (1976):47–51.
11 Gaffney, "In the Dark," pp. 36–41.
12 *New York Times*, July 4, 1968.
13 "Theatre Goes Public: New York Shakespeare Festival," *Players* 45, no. 2 (December-January 1970):60.
14 *New York Times*, December 12, 1971.
15 Lynn K. Horobetz, "The Washington Shakespeare Summer Festival 1968," *Shakespeare Quarterly* 19 (1968):391–92.
16 *Washington Post*, July 11, 1968.
17 Jeanne Addison Roberts, "The Washington Shakespeare Summer Festival, 1970," *Shakespeare Quarterly* 21 (1970):481–82. Other references to this production are taken from this review.
18 A. R. Braunmuller and William L. Stull, "Shakespeare in Los Angeles," *Shakespeare Quarterly* 29 (1978):259–67.
19 Mildred C. Kuner, "The New York Shakespeare Festival, 1967," *Shakespeare Quarterly* 18 (1967):411–15.
20 *New York Times*, June 30, 1967.
21 Ellen Foreman, "Two Macbeths," *Black American*, June 16–25, 1977.
22 Robert Hapgood, "Shakespeare in New York and Boston," *Shakespeare Quarterly* 29 (1978):230–31.
23 *New Yorker*, May 23, 1977, p. 84.
24 Lester E. Barber, "Great Lakes Shakespeare Festival," *Shakespeare Quarterly* 29 (1978):246–49.
25 *New York Times*, April 21, 1977.
26 John Lovell, Jr., "Shakespeare's American Play," pp. 363–70. The author traces the frequency of American productions of *Othello* and suggests that the play's popularity is due to "its dramatization of minority aspiration." He argues that "the battering down of insurmountable barriers has been a central part of the American dream."
27 *New York Daily News*, September 8, 1955.
28 Quoted in *New York Times*, September 28, 1962.
29 *Times* (London), September 30, 1962.
30 *Shakespeare Quarterly* 28 (1977):232–35.
31 *Time*, April 6, 1970, pp. 62–63.
32 *New York Times*, June 16, 1968.
33 *New York Post*, June 27, 1970.
34 See reviews by Clive Barnes and Walter Kerr in *New York Times*, June 22 and 28, 1970.
35 *Atlanta Journal and Constitution*, April 21, 1970.

36 Information on Paul Winfield's Othello was gleaned from a paper presented by Charles B. Lower at the annual convention of the American Theatre Association at San Diego in August 1980 and from Gully Stanford of the Alliance Theatre Company, Atlanta, in a personal communication on September 2, 1980.

37 See Michelle Green, "The Struggle to Be James Earl Jones," pp. 22–27.

38 Alice Griffin, "The New York Season 1961–62," *Shakespeare Quarterly* 13 (1962): 553–57.

39 *Village Voice*, July 22, 1965.

40 *New York Times*, August 2, 1973.

41 Ibid., August 12, 1973.

42 *Bay State Banner*, September 3, 1981.

43 Walter Kerr, "The Jones-Plummer 'Othello' Is Twice Blessed," *New York Times*, February 14, 1982, © 1982 by The New York Times Company. Reprinted by permission.

9 Toward the Future

1 Jay Bayete and Gloria Calomee, "The Inner City Cultural Center," pp. IC 1–8.

2 *Los Angeles Times*, April 13, 1968.

3 "Shakespeare in the Pluralism Stew," *Los Angeles Times*, Calendar, February 19, 1978.

4 *Los Angeles Times*, February 27, 1978, p. 11, sec. 4.

5 Ed Sakamoto, "Inner City At 12," pp. 44–46.

6 Ivan Webster, " 'Iago': Bright New Light On the Old Moor," *Encore American & Worldwide News*, July 2, 1979, pp. 41–43.

7 Program for "The Comedy of Errors" presented by Shakespeare and Company, 1983.

8 Fred LeBrun, "Shakespeare & Company: As You Like It, As He Wrote It," *Albany Times-Union*, August 5, 1979.

9 Tom Littlefield, "Shakespeare & Co. Taking Risks," *Kite*, August 8, 1979.

10 Terry Curtis Fox, "A Summer's Tale," *Village Voice*, September 3, 1979.

11 Kevin Kelly, "The Bard As You Like Him," *Boston Globe*, July 16, 1981.

12 *Newsweek*, February 5, 1979.

13 See Richard Eder in *New York Times*, March 15, 1979.

14 Errol Hill, Introduction, *The Theater of Black Americans*, pp. 1–11.

15 Jack J. Jorgens, "New York Shakespeare Festival, Summer 1974," *Shakespeare Quarterly* 25 (1974):410–14.

16 Information on 1981 productions of Shakespeare was extracted from issues of *Shakespeare Quarterly* for that year.

17 Stanley Kauffmann, "Enroute to the Future," p. 1.

18 *New York Age*, January 16, 1916.

19 *Boston Post*, September 29, 1946.

20 Kauffmann, "Enroute to the Future," p. 1. For a more recent discussion of the issue, including a contrary view by the critic John Simon, see *New York* magazine, February 23, 1981, pp. 6–7, and April 13, 1981, p. 7.

Selected Bibliography

Bacote, Clarence A., and Hallie Beachem Brooks. "Theater at Atlanta University." *Atlanta University Bulletin*. Series 4, no. 2 (September 1974):17–24.

Bailey, A. Peter. "BTA Responds to Papp's Move on Black Theatre." *Black Theatre Alliance Newsletter* 4, no. 5 (May 1979):5.

Bayete, Jay, and Gloria Calomee. "The Inner City Cultural Center." *Neworld* 2, no. 3 (Spring 1976):IC 1–8.

Belcher, Fannin Saffore, Jr. "The Place of the Negro in the Evolution of the American Theatre." Ph.D. diss., Yale University, 1945.

Bond, Frederick W. "The Direct and Indirect Contribution Which the American Negro Has Made to Drama and the Legitimate Stage, With the Underlying Conditions Responsible." Ph.D. diss., New York University, 1939.

Buchanan, Singer Alfred. "A Study of the Attitudes of the Writers of the Negro Press Toward the Depiction of the Negro in Plays and Films: 1930–65." Ph.D. diss., University of Michigan, 1968.

Conway, Moncure D. "The Negro as Artist." *The Radical: A Monthly Magazine Devoted to Religion* (September 1866):39–42.

Cowhig, Ruth. "Actors Black and Tawny in the Role of Othello—and Their Critics." *Theatre Research International* 4, no. 2 (1979):133–46.

Curtis, Mina. "Some American Negroes in Russia in the Nineteenth Century." *Massachusetts Review* 9, no. 2 (Spring 1968):268–96.

Edmonds, Randolph S. "Black Drama in the American Theatre, 1700–1970." *The American Theatre: A Sum of Its Parts*. New York: Samuel French, 1971.

Flanagan, Hallie. *Arena: The History of the Federal Theatre*. New York: Duell, Sloan, and Pearce, 1940.

Foreman, Ellen. "Two Macbeths." *Black American*, June 16–25, 1977, p. 8.

France, Richard. *The Theatre of Orson Welles*. Lewisburg, Pa.: Bucknell University Press, 1977.

Furness, Horace Edward. *A New Variorum Edition of Shakespare*. Vol. 6, *Othello*. Philadelphia: J. B. Lippincott Co., 1866.

Gaffney, Floyd. "The Black Actor in Central Park." *Negro Digest* 16, no. 6 (April 1967):28–34.

———. "In the Dark: *King Henry V." Negro Digest* 18, no. 6 (April 1969):36–41.

Gayle, Addison, Jr., ed. *The Black Aesthetic.* New York: Doubleday, 1971.

———. *Black Expression: Essays by and about Black Americans in the Creative Arts.* New York: Weybright and Talley, 1969.

Grebanier, Bernard. *Then Came Each Actor.* New York: David McKay Co., Inc., 1975.

Green, Michelle. "The Struggle to Be James Earl Jones." *Saturday Review,* February 1982, pp. 22–27.

Gregory, Montgomery. "The Drama of Negro Life." In *The New Negro,* edited by Alain Locke, pp. 153–60. 1925. Reprint. New York: Atheneum, 1968.

Hamilton, Virginia. *Paul Robeson: The Life and Times of a Free Black Man.* New York: Harper and Row, 1974.

Harrison, Paul Carter. *The Drama of Nommo.* New York: Grove Press, Inc., 1972.

Henderson, Mary. *The City and the Theatre.* Clifton, N.J.: James T. White and Company, 1973.

Hill, Errol, ed. *The Theater of Black Americans.* 2 Vols. Englewood Cliffs, N.J.: Prentice-Hall, Inc., 1980.

Houseman, John. *Run Through: A Memoir.* New York: Simon and Schuster, 1972.

Hoyt, Edwin P. *Paul Robeson: The American Othello.* Cleveland, Ohio: World Publishing Co., 1967.

Hughes, Langston, and Milton Meltzer. *Black Magic: A Pictorial History of the Negro in American Entertainment.* Englewood Cliffs, N.J.: Prentice-Hall, Inc., 1967.

Hutchens, John K. "Paul Robeson." *Theatre Arts,* October 1944, pp. 579–85.

Hutton, Laurence. *Curiosities of the American Stage.* New York: Harper and Bros., 1891.

Isaacs, Edith J. *The Negro in the American Theatre.* New York: Theatre Arts, 1947.

Johnson, James W. *Black Manhattan.* New York: Knopf, 1930

Jones, Eldred D. *The Elizabethan Image of Africa.* Washington, D.C.: Folger Shakespeare Library, 1971.

Kauffmann, Stanley. "Enroute to the Future." *New York Times,* July 31, 1966, sec. 2, p. 1.

Kelly, Kevin. "Bard in the Berkshires, A Midsummer's Dream." *Boston Globe,* August 9, 1981, p. A24.

Locke, Alain. "Broadway and the Negro Drama." *Theatre Arts,* October 1941, pp. 745–50.

———. "Max Reinhardt Reads the Negro's Dramatic Horoscope." *Opportunity,* May 1924, pp. 145–46.

———. "The Negro and the American Stage." *Theatre Arts,* February 1926, pp. 112–20.

———. "Steps Toward the Negro Theatre." *Crisis* 25 (December 1922):66–68.

Loney, Glenn, and Patricia MacKay. *The Shakespeare Complex: A Guide to Summer Festivals and Year-Round Repertory in North America.* New York: Drama Book Specialists, 1975.

Lovell, John, Jr. "Shakespeare's American Play." *Theatre Arts,* June 1944, pp. 363–70.

Mapp, Edward. *Directory of Blacks in the Performing Arts.* Metuchen, N.J.: Scarecrow Press, Inc., 1978.

Marshall, Herbert, and Mildred Stock. *Ira Aldridge: The Negro Tragedian.* Carbondale: Southern Illinois University Press, 1968.

Mitchell, Loften. *Black Drama: The Story of the American Negro in the Theater*. New York: Hawthorn Books, 1967.

Mullet, Mary B. "Where Do I Go From Here?" *American Magazine*, June 1921, pp. 54–55.

Notable Names in the American Theatre. Clifton, N.J.: James T. White and Company, 1976.

Nouryeh, Andrea J. "When the Lord Was a Black Man: A Fresh Look at the Life of Richard Berry Harrison." *Black American Literature Forum* 16, no. 4 (Winter 1982):142–46.

Novick, Julius. *Beyond Broadway: The Quest for Permanent Theatres*. New York: Hill and Wang, 1968.

Odell, George C. D. *Annals of the New York Stage*. 15 vols. New York: Columbia University Press, 1927–49.

Patterson, Lindsay. *Anthology of the American Negro in the Theatre*. New York: Publishers Company, 1967.

Peterson, Bernard L., Jr. "The Legendary Owen Dodson of Howard University: His Contributions to the American Theatre." *Crisis* 86 (November 1979):373–78.

Rosenberg, Marvin. *The Masks of Othello: The Search for the Identity of Othello, Iago, and Desdemona by Three Centuries of Actors and Critics*. Berkeley: University of California Press, 1961.

Rowland, Mabel. *Bert Williams: Son of Laughter*. New York: Negro University Press, 1923.

Sakamoto, Ed. "Inner City at 12: Stepping Forward, Looking Inward." *Los Angeles Times*, Calendar, February 19, 1978.

Salgado, Gamini. *Eyewitnesses of Shakespeare: First Hand Accounts of Performances, 1590–1890*. New York: Barnes and Noble, 1975.

Scott, Esther Fulks. "Negroes as Actors in Serious Plays." *Opportunity*, April 1923, pp. 20–23.

Shafer, Yvonne. "Black Actors in the Nineteenth Century American Theatre." *CLA Journal* 20, no. 3 (1977):387–400.

Shattuck, Charles H. *Shakespeare on the American Stage: From the Hallams to Edwin Booth*. Washington, D.C.: Folger Shakespeare Library, 1976.

Simmons, William J. "J. A. Arneaux, Esq." Chap. 65 in *Men of Mark: Eminent, Progressive and Rising*. 1887. Reprint. New York: Arno Press and New York Times, 1968.

"Theatre Goes Public: New York Shakespeare Festival." *Players* 45, no. 2 (December 1969–January 1970):56–61, 86–87.

Tobson, Elliot Harvey. "The Popular Image of the Black Man in English Drama, 1550–1699." Ph.D. diss., Columbia University, 1970.

Trewin, J. C. *Shakespeare on the English Stage, 1900–1964*. London: Barrie and Rockliff, 1964.

Vallillo, Stephen M. "The Shakespeare Productions of the Federal Theatre Project." *Theatre History Studies* 3 (1983):28–53.

Index

Photo Credits

Acme Photo: 90
Andrews, Bert: 186, 188
Atlanta University: 84, 85
Author's Collection: 93, 141
Bakrushin State Central Theatrical Museum, Moscow: 18, 26
Beloit College Alumni Records: 60
Black American: 162
Brown, Walter R., Jr.: 132
Colored American: 66
Colored American Magazine: 83
Daily Worker: 102
Forbes, Earle: 136
Fried, Geoffrey: 140
Friedman-Abeles: 138, 146, 148, 149, 152, 154, 159, 160, 173
Grafton Publishing Co., Los Angeles: 74
Harvard Theatre Collection: frontispiece, 21, 22
Library of Congress Federal Theatre Project Collection at George Mason University
    Libraries, Fairfax, Virginia: 104, 105, 106, 107, 113, 117
Men of Mark: 46
New York Age: 94
New York Dramatic News: 56
Odell, George C. D. *Annals of the New York Stage* (vol 3): 13
Performing Arts Research Center, New York Public Library: 115, 125, 127
Pinchot, Ben: 91
Reid, Bill: 166
Shakespeare and Company, Lenox, Mass.: 184
Stage Photo Company: 122, 123
Sterling, Philip: 87
Swope, Martha: 151, 168, 175
Tyne and Wear Museums Service: 28
Victoria and Albert Museum: 32

Library of Congress Cataloging in Publication Data
Hill, Errol.
Shakespeare in sable.
Bibliography: p.
Includes index.
1. Shakespeare, William, 1564–1616—Stage history.
2. Actors, Black—Biography. 3. Afro-American actors—
Biography. I. Title. II. Title: Black Shakespearean
actors.
PR3112.H5   1984   792.9'5   83–18106
ISBN 0–87023–426–9